ACE
Spelling
Dictionary

find words quickly
and improve your spelling

ACE
Spelling
Dictionary

David Moseley

Acknowledgements

The author would like to thank all those who took part in the field trials in England, Northern Ireland, Scotland and Wales. Special thanks are due to Ronald Beresford for his expert phonetic advice and to Bess Moseley for the animal drawings. Thanks also to Gwyn Singleton for editorial assistance, especially proofreading, and to George Macbride for helping me to meet the needs of Scottish users.

ACE Spelling Dictionary
LL 00425
ISBN 1 85503 214 7
First edition © David Moseley and Catherine Nicol
Second edition © David Moseley 1995

First published 1986
Reprinted 1986, 1987, 1988, 1989, 1990

Second edition 1995
Reprinted 1996, 1997, 1998, 1999, 2000, 2001, 2002, 2004, 2005

Printed in Great Britain by Goodmanbaylis

CONTENTS

INTRODUCTION

The main concern of any writer, whatever her/his age, is communication. All too often difficulty with spelling gets in the way of expression. The urge to convey something is blocked by the mechanics of the writing process, and many a writer becomes frustrated to the point of giving up.

The *ACE Spelling Dictionary* is designed for writers of all ages who need help with spelling, and is entirely suitable for both school and home use. Because it is quick and easy to use, it takes away the frustration of uncertainty about spelling. After just a little practice the user will be able to find any word in a few seconds.

The problem with English spelling is that it does not obey simple rules. There are many patterns of words and many exceptions to those patterns. The vowel sounds are the biggest source of difficulty; there are more than two hundred vowel spellings associated with the eighteen basic sounds. That leads to uncertainty and delay when looking up words in a standard dictionary.

The *ACE Spelling Dictionary* is the Aurally Coded English dictionary – it confronts the multitude of vowel sounds by classifying words according to the first one in each. To use the dictionary successfully, there are a few stages that need to be thoroughly understood. After this introduction there are two alternative sections to explain those: **How to Use the Spelling Dictionary by Yourself** and **How to Use the Spelling Dictionary with a Helper**. The latter includes three lessons that are suitable for use by individuals with adult help or for group work with a teacher.

The user will soon learn that the index is the key to the different sections of the dictionary. Once s/he has understood how to use it, s/he should never again have to ask someone else how to spell a word. Eventually, s/he will be able to save time by going straight to words without using the index at all.

The *ACE Spelling Dictionary* consists of three main parts, each including five or six sections. All the words in a section have the same or nearly the same vowel sound. Vowel sounds are made with the voice, with the mouth open.

The first five sections of 'short' vowel sounds are printed on pale blue paper. These sounds, as a rule, are the ones taught at school:

PART 1	a	as in cat		
	e	as in elephant		
	i	as in pig		
	o	as in dog		
	u	as in duck	& oo	as in woodpecker

The 'alphabet-name' vowel sounds are printed on darker blue paper. These are 'long' vowel sounds:

PART 2	ae	as in snail		
	ee	as in eagle		
	ie	as in lion		
	oe	as in goat		
	ue	as in newt	& oo	as in smooth

The last six sections include spellings with the letter 'r' and two double sounds. These are printed on pale blue paper and are also 'long' vowel sounds:

PART 3	ar	as in shark
	air	as in bear
	er	as in worm
	or	as in horse
	oi	as in oyster
	ou	as in owl

As this is a spelling dictionary, word meanings are given only if two or more words sound the same or nearly the same. However, using the *ACE Spelling Dictionary* to look up spellings will make it easier to use other dictionaries for looking up meanings. It should also improve spelling. The user will think of long words as made up of smaller parts, often corresponding to spoken syllables. As s/he becomes more aware of the common patterns, unusual spellings will stand out from the others and hold her/his attention. It is a good idea for her/him to write down unusual spellings in a personal spelling book, noting the 'tricky' part or parts and using the 'look–cover–write–check' routine.

At the end of the book there are some spelling activities. These focus on words that often cause difficulty and offer some strategies for getting them right.

HOW TO USE THE SPELLING DICTIONARY BY YOURSELF

To find a word you have to do two things:

1   Pick out the first strong or the first clear vowel sound.
2   Decide on what you think the first letter in the word is.

That will take you to the right page. Then you need to look down the right column. Each column has at the top one or more stars to show how many syllables each word in it has. Find out how many syllables there are in a word by saying it slowly and tapping at the same time. Try this rhyme if you need help:

> One tap for 'fun'
> And two for 'begun';
> Three taps for 'stadium'
> And four for 'gymnasium'.

If you want to find the word 'skyscraper' on page 190, for example, look in the column of three-syllable words. Words containing four or more syllables are on the right-hand side of each page. You will notice that every syllable contains a vowel sound.

Here is the basic routine

TO LOOK UP rhinoceros

First:

SAY 'rhi ...' >	SAY 'ie' >	GO TO INDEX >
Say the first syllable – really slowly.	Say the vowel sound on its own.	It is on pages xx to xxi.

Second:

FIND 'ie' (as in lion) >	FIND 'r' >	IT IS ON PAGE 189 >
Find the picture and the vowel sound.	Find the first letter.	

Third:

FIND page 189 >	OPEN BOOK in Part 2 >	LOOK AT PAGE 189 >
Page 189 is in Part 2.	Find the darker blue pages.	

Fourth:

TAP OUT
rhi-no-ce-ros ⟩

LOOK at the
**** column ⟩

YOU'VE GOT IT! ⟩

Neutral vowel sounds

If you find it hard to tell which is the first strong vowel sound in a word, take the first one you can hear clearly, as long as it is in the first or second syllable. Suppose you want to look up 'supposed'. The strong vowel sound is the 'oe' sound in the second syllable, and the word is under 'S' on page 207. However, if you pick out the 'u' sound, you will find the word on page 132, in the 'neutral vowel' box below the words in columns. So, if you cannot see a word where you think it should be, see if it is in a neutral vowel box. You will soon notice that the neutral vowels sound much the same as each other, rather like a quiet grunt.

Listen to the way you pronounce 'balloon', for example:

SAY 'ba ...' ⟩

SAY 'a' ⟩

A NEUTRAL SOUND! ⟩

Start to say the word,
at a normal speed.

You can hardly hear
this sound in the word.

It's not like the
'a' sound in 'cat'.

To find 'balloon' in the dictionary, listen for the strong vowel sound (in the second syllable):

SAY 'balloo ...' ⟩

SAY 'oo' ⟩

GO TO INDEX ⟩

In all the following words the strong vowel sound is in the second syllable. You will probably succeed in finding the words if you try to identify the letters used for the neutral vowel sound. However, it is easier to go by the strong vowel.

above	SHORT u	laboratory	SHORT o
advertisement	LONG er	magician	SHORT i
appearance	LONG ee	manoeuvre	LONG oo
approach	LONG oe	observer	LONG er
because	SHORT o	particular	SHORT i
before	LONG or	performer	LONG or
circumference	SHORT u	potatoes	LONG ae
collision	SHORT i	production	SHORT u
conductor	SHORT u	remain	LONG ae
confetti	SHORT e	remarkable	LONG ar
despair	LONG air	request	SHORT e
destroy	LONG oi	reverse	LONG er
discuss	SHORT u	surrender	SHORT e
emotional	LONG oe	surroundings	LONG ou
enough	SHORT u	survivor	LONG ie
exhaust	LONG or	towards	LONG or
guitar	LONG ar	trapeze	LONG ee
infectious	SHORT e	vocabulary	SHORT a

HOW TO USE THE SPELLING DICTIONARY WITH A HELPER

Counting syllables

Aim: The student should be able to say how many syllables there are in any spoken word (up to 4 syllables).

In one-to-one work a parent or friend should read out the words and say whether the responses are correct. A teacher can work with a group or whole class, asking for individual or group responses. The following three stages should be followed.

1   The helper (**H**) says a word slowly and taps out the syllables at the same time. The student repeats the word and taps out the syllables. **H** asks, 'How many taps?' This should be done with the following words.

play-ground	win-dow	ba-na-na	mud	un-for-tu-nate
TAP-TAP	TAP-TAP	TAP-TAP-TAP	TAP	TAP-TAP-TAP-TAP

Repeat more slowly if necessary, with the words in a different order.

2   **H** says a word without tapping and asks the student to repeat the word and tap it out. Each time **H** asks, 'How many taps?' This is done with words from the following list until ten words are tapped out correctly.

***	newspaper	**	picture	*	paint	****	television
**	spider	*	mice	**	monster	***	dinosaur
**	postman	**	burglar	***	acrobat	****	politician
**	pancake	***	margarine	****	supermarket	**	kitchen
*	crash	****	helicopter	**	rocket	***	motorbike

3   **H** says a word and simply asks, 'How many syllables?' This is done, taking words at random from the list below, until a success rate of 19/20 is obtained.

**	money	*	shop	**	birthday	**	present
**	bedroom	*	door	***	wallpaper	*	stairs
***	holidays	*	weeks	***	underground	****	underwater
***	crocodile	****	alligator	*	shark	**	danger
****	caterpillar	*	moth	***	butterfly	*	eggs
**	rabbit	****	invisible	*	hat	**	magic
*	win	***	manager	**	football	****	competition
****	everybody	**	children	**	mother	***	grandfather
*	clock	**	morning	***	afternoon	***	yesterday
****	mysterious	***	horrible	***	beautiful	***	exciting

LESSON 1

Aims: The student should be able to
    a)   identify long vowel sounds in a selection of words
    b)   use the long vowel sounds part of the index to find the page numbers for a selection of words
    c)   look up words in the darker blue part of the dictionary.

1   Begin with listening and speaking activities, starting with the long vowel animal names: **snail, eagle, lion, goat** and **newt**.

Ask the student if s/he can hear certain vowel sounds in each of these animal names. Use correct and incorrect vowel sounds, for example, 'Can you hear (**ae**) in **snail**?' 'Can you hear (**ee**) in **snail**?'

Make the vowel sounds longer and louder if you need to. Continue until responses are confident and correct and then move on to identifying long vowel sounds in other words. For example, 'Can you hear (**ee**) in **fine**?' 'Can you hear (**ae**) in **baby**?'

Again continue until all responses are confident and correct.

Selecting a long vowel sound, ask the student if s/he can hear the sound in a variety of words. For example, 'Can you hear (**ae**) in **pail, sail, tail, tile**?'

Finally, ask the student to give you the vowel sound s/he can hear in the long vowel animal names, giving a choice of three. For example, 'What is the vowel sound in **snail**: (**ae**), (**ee**) or (**ie**)?' Continue with different animals and three choices until the sounds in all the long vowel animal names are correctly identified.

2   Practise using the index to find page numbers. If working in a group each student should have a copy of the long vowel part in the middle of the index (see pages xx to xxi). Teachers may like to make an OHP for class tuition.

Beginning with the animal picture words, ask the student first to point to the snail picture next to the letters 'ae' which stand for the sound (**ae**). Ask which letter **snail** begins with and get her/him to find the letter, in the alphabet across the top of the page. Then, show her/him how to move one finger along the line of page numbers and the other finger down, until they meet at a page number. **Snail** is on page 149!

Repeat this exercise with **eagle, lion, goat** and **newt**. You may need to prompt the student with the vowel sound initially, but continue the exercise until the page numbers can be found by the student without any help.

Once the student can readily achieve this, ask her/him to find the page numbers for the following animal words: **ape, beaver, bison, mule, poodle, reindeer, sheep, snake, tiger, whale**.

This time s/he will need to identify the spelling picture for the vowel sound first. For example, what is the first vowel sound in **tiger**? It is (**ie**), which is the same as in **lion**.

Use these topic lists until the student has mastered using the index to find page numbers.

---

bacon, cake, cereal, cheese, doughnut, mousse, pie, steak, trifle, tuna

beans, beetroot, coleslaw, cucumber, leeks, maize, peanuts, peas, seaweed, swede

apricot, coconut, dates, grapefruit, lime, peach, pineapple, prunes, raisins, rhubarb

basin, bowl, knife, ladle, microwave, plate, scales, soap, teapot, toast

---

3   Practise looking up words from one or more of the above lists in the darker blue part of the dictionary. After turning to the page, say the word in distinct syllables and ask the student to say, tap and count the syllables. Make sure s/he looks in the correct column and, if there is a homonym, that s/he checks the meaning. Where the word is not given in plural form (e.g. prune), an 's' should be added. Note that in one case (swede) the target word is in a section which goes on for three pages.

LESSON 2

Aims: The student should be able to
  a) identify short vowel sounds in a selection of words
  b) use the short vowel sound part of the index to find the page numbers for a selection of words
  c) look up words in the first two parts of the dictionary.

  1   Begin with listening and speaking activities, starting with the short vowel animal names: **cat, elephant, pig, dog, duck** and **woodpecker.**

Ask the student if s/he can hear certain vowel sounds in each of these animal names, for example, 'Can you hear (**a**) in **cat**?' 'Can you hear (**e**) in **pig**?'

Make the vowel sounds longer and louder if you need to. Continue until responses are confident and correct and then move on to identifying short vowel sounds in other words. For example, 'Can you hear (**a**) in **active**?' 'Can you hear (**i**) in **big**?'

Again continue until responses are confident and correct.

Selecting a short vowel sound, ask the student if s/he can hear the sound in a variety of words. For example, 'Can you hear (**a**) in **pat, fat, mat, pet**?'

Finally, ask the student to give you the vowel sound in the short vowel animal names, giving a choice of three. For example, 'What is the vowel sound in **cat**: (**ae**), (**a**) or (**e**)?' Continue with the different animals and three choices until the sounds in all the short vowel animal names are correctly identified.

  2   Practise using the index to find page numbers first for short and then for both short and long vowel words. If working in a group, each student should have a copy of the first two parts of the index (see pages xx to xxi). Teachers may like to make an OHP for class tuition.

Beginning with the animal picture words, ask the student first to point to the cat picture next to the letter 'a', which stands for the sound (**a**). Ask which letter **cat** begins with and get her/him to find the letter, in the alphabet across the top of the page. Then, show her/him how to move one finger along the line of page numbers and the other finger down, until they meet at a page number. **Cat** is on page 7!

Repeat this exercise with **duck, pair, watchful** and **woodpecker.**

You may need to prompt the student with the vowel sound initially, but continue the exercise until the page numbers can be found by the student without any help.

Once the student can readily achieve this, ask her/him to find the page numbers for the following animal words: **camel, donkey, frog, hedgehog, kangaroo, leopard, monkey, pigeon, rabbit, rook.**

This time s/he will need to identify the spelling picture for the vowel sound first. For example, what is the first vowel sound in **rabbit**? It is (a), which is the same as in **cat**.

Use these topic lists until the student has mastered using the short vowel part of the index.

---

biscuit, bread, butter, chicken, chocolate, crisps, haddock, jam, popcorn, pudding
broccoli, cabbage, cauliflower, celery, lettuce, mushroom, onion, pepper,
   pumpkin, spinach
apple, blackberry, cherry, damson, fig, lemon, melon, orange, plum, tangerine
bottle, brush, clock, fridge, matches, mirror, rack, scissors, sieve, whisk

---

After working with the short vowel part of the index, ask the student to find the page numbers for both short and long vowel words from the following lists. If there is any confusion between short and long vowels, ask, for example, 'Is it short (a) as in **cat**, or long (ae) as in **snail**?' as appropriate.

---

black, blue, buff, crimson, gold, green, indigo, red, ruby, white
apron, boots, collar, dress, jeans, nightdress, shoes, sweater, tie, vest
bicycle, boat, glider, helicopter, motorcycle, scooter, submarine, train, van, yacht
bus, coach, cycle, ferry, hovercraft, liner, lorry, rocket, tricycle, truck
chewing, cooking, drinking, eating, helping, listening, nodding, sleeping,
   watching, writing
baker, bricklayer, cook, miner, optician, sailor, scientist, secretary, soldier, teacher

---

3   Practise looking up words from one or more of the above lists in the dictionary. After turning to the page, say the word in distinct syllables and ask the student to say, tap and count the syllables. Make sure s/he looks in the correct column and, if there is a homonym, that s/he checks the meaning. Note that in some cases (apple, biscuit, bus, butter, crimson, drinking, fridge, indigo, matches, optician, orange, spinach, sweater) the target word is in a section which goes on for two or more pages.

LESSON 3

Aims: The student should be able to
a) identify long vowel sounds, in the third part of the dictionary, in a selection of words
b) use the index to find the page numbers for a selection of words
c) look up words in all three parts of the dictionary.

1 Begin with listening and speaking activities, starting with the animal names from the third part of the dictionary: **shark, bear, bird, horse, oyster** and **owl.**

Ask the student if s/he can hear certain vowel sounds in each of these animal names, for example, 'Can you hear (**ar**) in **shark**?' 'Can you hear (**or**) in **owl**?'

Make the vowel sounds longer and louder if you need to. Continue until responses are confident and correct and then move on to identifying these long vowel sounds in other words. For example, 'Can you hear (**ar**) in **harmless**?' 'Can you hear (**oi**) in **early**?'

Again continue until the responses are confident and correct.

Selecting one of these long vowel sounds, ask the student if s/he can hear the sound in a variety of words. For example, 'Can you hear (**ar**) in **car, fir, jar, tar**?'

Finally, ask the student to give you the vowel sound s/he can hear in the third group of vowel animal names, giving a choice of three. For example, 'What is the vowel sound in **shark**: (**ar**), (**ae**) or (**or**)?'

Continue with the different animals and three choices until the sounds in all the animal names with long vowels in the third part of the dictionary are correctly identified.

2 Practise using the index to find page numbers for words containing the sounds (**ar**), (**air**), (**er**), (**or**), (**oi**) and (**ou**). If working in a group, each student should have a copy of the whole index (see pages xx to xxi). Teachers may like to make an OHP for class tuition.

Beginning with the animal picture words, ask the student first to point to the shark picture next to the letters 'ar', which stand for the sound (**ar**). Ask which letter **shark** begins with and ask her/him to point to the letter, in the alphabet across the top of the page.

Then, show her/him how to move one finger along the line of page numbers and the other finger down, until they meet at a page number. **Shark** is on page 234!

Repeat this exercise with **rare, worm, warlike, noisy** and **sound.**

You may need to prompt the student with the vowel sound initially, but continue the exercise until the page numbers can be found by the student without any help.

Once the student can readily achieve this, ask her/him to find the page numbers for the following animal words: **armadillo, cow, earthworm, hound, mouse, oyster, partridge, sardine, starfish, tortoise.**

This time s/he will need to identify the spelling picture for the vowel sound first.

For example, what is the first vowel sound in **partridge**? It is (**ar**), which is the same as in **shark**.

If more practice is needed with the five sounds of the third part of the index, use the following lists.

---

burger, cornflakes, flour, lard, marmalade, oil, pork, prawn, sardine, trout

garlic, herbs, parsley, parsnips, pear, soya, sprouts, strawberry, turnip, walnut

boiler, carton, door, fork, jar, larder, margarine, starch, torch, towel

---

After working with the third part of the index, ask the student to find the page numbers for words from any of the three parts, using the following lists. If there is any confusion between any pair of patterns, ask, for example, 'Is it (**a**) or (**ow**)?' 'Is it (**o**) or (**ar**)?' as appropriate.

---

aquamarine, brown, cream, ginger, grey, lilac, orange, pink, purple, rose, scarlet, silver, turquoise, violet, yellow

blouse, braces, coat, jacket, jumper, overalls, pullover, sandals, scarf, shorts, skirt, slippers, socks, tights, trousers

brushing, counting, cutting, ironing, learning, marking, painting, reading, serving, sewing, shaving, shopping, sweeping, swimming, working

actress, artist, dentist, doctor, fisherman, hairdresser, joiner, journalist, musician, nurse, plumber, porter, priest, tailor, typist

---

3   Practise looking up words from one or more of the above lists in the dictionary. Note that in some cases (aquamarine, cutting, slippers, sweeping, swimming) the target word is in a section which goes on for two or more pages.

GETTING THE MOST
OUT OF THE DICTIONARY

Looking up words in order to spell them correctly is only one way of using the *ACE Spelling Dictionary*. Other ways of using it can be just as valuable and can help to increase your speed of word recognition as well as your knowledge about words. You can do this by timing yourself as you look for words of a certain type. You might like to work with someone and take turns in looking up words. The words can be chosen by topic, by use, by length, by stress pattern, by sound, by features of spelling or by grammatical function. It can also be fun to think of combinations of these – for example, to find as many long words as possible that can be used to express enjoyment of food, picking out only those where the stress is (greedily) placed on the first syllable.

Some of the activities at the end of this book demonstrate specific ways of using the dictionary. Many more ideas for actively exploring it will be thought of by those who use it. What is provided here is a detailed account of some of the rules that have been followed, especially those that relate to alphabetical order and to the inclusion of different forms of the same word. You do not need to understand all of these before you start to use the dictionary, but you may need to refer to them at times and they may suggest some useful activities.

Alphabetical grouping of words

Within each section, words are grouped by initial letter, taken in alphabetical order. A letter is omitted if there are no words beginning with it in that section.

Within each column of words, there are smaller sets, each beginning with the same two letters. This makes the columns easier to scan, and cuts down word search time. It does not take long to learn that 'sc' is near the top of a column of words beginning with S, that 'sm' is about halfway down and that 'sw' is near the bottom.

Some words are entered in more than one place. This happens when the first sound in the word does not uniquely determine what the first letter is. For example, words beginning with a silent letter (like 'knife' and 'gnome') are entered according to initial sound as well as spelling. Words like 'ceiling' and 'chassis' are entered under both S and C. Words like 'kangaroo' and 'karate' are entered under C and under K. Lighter print is used for double-entered words when they begin with a different letter from the rest of the words in a column.

In certain cases, cross-reference pointers are used instead of double or multiple entries. A cross-reference is always provided from K to C within the same section, instead of repeating a long list of C words under K. Dropped Hs, confusion between initial E and I and between F and TH as well as uncertainty about the spelling of words beginning with QU are also taken care of by the use of cross-reference pointers.

Meanings

In cases where two words sound the same (or nearly the same) but have different meanings, you need to check that you have found the right word. All such words have an asterisk (*) against them and their meanings are given alongside. These words are called homonyms (words with the same sound but with different meanings). Some of them are also homographs (words with the same spelling but with different meanings).

If the meaning or meanings do not fit the word you are looking for, all you have to do is to try another similar-sounding word with an asterisk against it. That will be in the section you are looking at.

Plurals

If the plural form of a noun is not shown, it is safe to assume that you simply add an 's'. So, if you find 'journey', you will be able to spell 'journeys'.

All 'es' and '-ies' plurals are shown, for example 'box es' and 'baby -ies'. Where, as in 'baby -ies', there is a dash before the ending, part of the word has to be removed before the plural ending is added. The most common pattern is for a final 'y' to be removed before adding '-ies'. Irregular forms such as 'calves' are treated in a similar way: 'calf -ves'.

Present participles

These are given for the more common words and in all cases where a final consonant is doubled before 'ing' is added (for example, 'swim' and 'swimming').

When the present participle form (ending in 'ing') is not given, you can be sure that the spelling falls into one of two patterns:

    a)   for words not ending in 'e', add 'ing'
    b)   for words ending in 'e', remove the 'e' before adding 'ing'.

Past tenses

The past tense form is given for the more common words and whenever a final consonant is doubled before 'ed' is added (for example, 'skid' and 'skidded').

In all words where the final 'ed' has the sound 't' (as in 'ticked') the ending is given alongside: tick ed.

All irregular past tense forms are given in full. They are entered in the appropriate sections, but are also included, enclosed in square brackets, immediately below the corresponding present tense form. Two examples are the following:

bring   **buy**
[brought]   [bought]

Comparatives and superlatives

These are given in full for the more common words and whenever a final consonant is doubled (as in 'bigger' and 'biggest'). Where a final 'y' is changed to '-ier' or to '-iest' this is also always shown (for example, 'saucy -ier, -iest').

If you cannot find a particular word with the ending 'er' or 'est', you can be sure that the spelling falls into one of the two following patterns:

   a)   for words not ending in 'e', add 'er' or 'est'
   b)   for words ending in 'e', remove the 'e' before adding 'er' or 'est'.

DIALECTS

The vowel sound sections are based on BBC pronunciation, but regional differences have been taken into account. Particular care has been taken to make the dictionary suitable for use in Scotland. Trials have taken place throughout the British Isles, and wherever systematic shifts in the pronunciation of vowels have been noted, words have been entered in more than one section. Wherever a dash appears in front of a word it means that for some speakers the word is pronounced with the same vowel sound as the other words in the section.

In the 'a' section words pronounced in a BBC accent with an 'ar' sound have a dash in front of them. These words are pronounced with an 'a' in Scotland, and in most cases in the north of England. In the 'o' section the words with a dash in front of them belong there only for Scottish speakers. In the short vowel 'u' and 'oo' section, two BBC sounds have been put together, with a dash before the 'oo' sound words. In the north of England there may be no difference in pronunciation between the two groups. In the section containing words with the long 'oo' sound, the words with a dash before them belong there only for Scottish speakers. In parts of the Midlands the sounds 'air' and 'er' are pronounced in the same way. The 'air' words are therefore entered in the 'er' section as well, a feature which also makes sense for some of the words as pronounced in Scotland.

A major feature of Scottish speech is the rolled 'r' following a vowel. This has important implications for Scottish users of the dictionary, since the BBC 'ar', 'air', 'er' and 'or' sounds are pronounced differently in Scotland. Cross-reference pointers are given in the appropriate sections, but these will not be needed if users learn to refer to the third part of the book for words with vowels followed by an 'r'. This applies for all of the short vowels, and for the long vowels 'ae' or 'oe'. It does not, however, apply for the long vowels 'ee', 'ie' and 'ue'.

The following table is provided for the benefit of Scottish users:

Words with	Section	Examples
SHORT a followed by 'r'	ar	shark, article
SHORT e followed by 'r'	er	early, nervous
SHORT i followed by 'r'	er	bird, firmly
SHORT o followed by 'r'	or	horse, warning
SHORT u followed by 'r'	er	hurt, worm
LONG ae followed by 'r'	air	rare, airport
LONG ee followed by 'r'	ee	clear, steer
LONG ie followed by 'r'	ie	wire, tyre
LONG oe followed by 'r'	or	hoarse, bored
LONG ue/oo followed by 'r'	ue/oo	pure, poor

HOW THE WORDS
WERE CHOSEN

Both British and American sources have been used in compiling the *ACE Spelling Dictionary*. Also, words have been added as the result of field trials in which users kept records of words they needed but were unable to find.

When work started in 1967 on the first edition, the two main sources of vocabulary were *Words Your Children Use* by Edwards and Gibbon and Schonell's *The Essential Spelling List*. Later, words were added from the Thornike–Lorge list and from the adult reading vocabulary list of Kucera and Francis. However, the most recent and comprehensive source is the *American Heritage Word Frequency Book*. This contains no fewer than 86,741 word types (words and word forms) from books used in schools by children in the age-range 8 to 14. The complete range of school subjects is covered.

Unless they were judged to be unfamiliar to British users, all words (but not all word forms) in the first 23,000 word types of the American Heritage list are included in the *ACE Spelling Dictionary*. This is equivalent to excluding words only if they are used less than once in every 2,000,000 words of text. As explained above, plurals, present participles, past tense forms, comparatives and superlatives have not always been included if they are straightforward to spell.

In order to meet the needs of British students, lists supplied by subject teachers for all areas of the curriculum have also been included. Particular care has been taken to cover scientific, technical and mathematical vocabulary. The *Evans Technical Dictionary* and a list of mathematical terms published by the Scottish Examination Board are among the sources used.

A list of the publications from which words have been taken is given below:

Carroll, J. B., Davies, P. and Richman, B. (1971) *The American Heritage Word Frequency Book*. Boston, Houghton Mifflin.

Edwards, R. P. A. and Gibbon, V. (1964) *Words Your Children Use*. London, Burke.

Evans Technical Dictionary. (1982) London, Evans.

Hancock, R. (1992) An Appraisal of the *Aurally Coded English Spelling Dictionary*. BEd. project, University of Sunderland.

Kucera, H. and Francis, W. N. (1967) *Computational Analysis of Present-day American English*. Providence, Brown University Press.

Moseley, D. V. (1989) Utilisation d'un dictionnaire à codage oral pour l'orthographe et la reconnaissance des mots: une étude en milieu scolaire. *Glossa*, 14, 14–19.

Moseley, D. V. (1994) From Theory to Practice: Errors and Trials. In Brown, G. D. A. and Ellis, N. C. (eds.) *Handbook of Spelling: Theory, Process and Intervention*. London, Wiley.

Moseley, D. V. and Singleton, G. V. (1993) *ACE Spelling Activities*. Wisbech, LDA.

Schonell, F. J. and Wise, P. (1993) *Essentials in Teaching and Testing Spelling*. 2nd edition, Windsor, NFER-Nelson.

Scottish Examination Board (1984). Scottish Certificate of Education, Standard Grade.

Arrangements in Mathematics for Foundation, General and Credit Levels in and after 1986.

ACTION RESEARCH
WITH ACE

A survey of research on ways of improving spelling (Moseley, 1994) suggests that those which combine a variety of powerful features are the most successful. It is also important to see spelling as an integral part of writing. Work by the author in which a weekly piece of creative writing was produced with the help of the *ACE Spelling Dictionary* at home showed that dyslexic learners could make very rapid progress in only five weeks, when provided with individual targets and feedback. A similar approach was taken by Hancock (1992), working with a mixed-ability group of Year 6 children. The children used ACE for checking their work and also chose six words to learn per week. Hancock reported an improvement in the overall quality of written work (as judged 'blind' by an independent evaluator), a 50% reduction in spelling error rate and an improvement in written vocabulary. One boy with a spelling problem and with a negative attitude towards spelling 'was extremely enthusiastic to succeed ... and ... his small and frequent achievements ... did much to boost his confidence and self-esteem'.

In another classroom study (Moseley, 1989) it was those with weak spelling and reading who made the most progress. The pupils used the *ACE Spelling Dictionary* to proofread all written work, while the teacher was able to use one-to-one conferencing time for discussion of the content and structure of the writing. Spelling improved at an average rate of 1.7 months per month, while the seven poorest spellers progressed at more than twice this speed. These gains were accompanied by significant improvements in the quantity and quality of writing.

ACE Spelling Activities (Moseley and Singleton, 1993) grew out of earlier work with dyslexics in which learning activities were linked with ACE. There is now clear evidence that the differentiated use of spelling lists for the daily learning at home of four to six words is to be recommended (Moseley, 1994). In classroom trials in which the learning strategies included at the end of the dictionary were used, sixty-five pupils improved in their spelling by nineteen months in only five months. Both verbal and visual strategies proved effective, but two very important components were a) pronouncing the words in a different way, according to the spelling; and b) saying the letter names before writing each letter string.

One teacher has made imaginative use of dictation passages, followed by an ACE checking activity limited to ten words. Each of her pupils wrote to the author with evident confidence and enjoyment, saying that 'over thirty children have bought their own dictionaries'. One reassured the author about the use of the 'smooth newt' sound clue by saying, 'My friend and I found a newt we brought it bake and built an aquarium for the newt, its a female. At the moment its hibernating.'

It is hoped that the *ACE Spelling Dictionary* will continue to encourage teachers to devise new ways of using it to suit all pupils, with individual strengths and weaknesses and with different learning styles.

INDEX

			A	B	C	D	E	F	G	H	I	J	K	L	M
	SHORT VOWEL	a	1	5	7	10	11	12	14	16	17	18	18	19	20
	SHORT VOWEL	e	31	32	33	34	36	39	39	40	41	42	42	43	44
	SHORT VOWEL	i	56	57	59	61	65	68	70	71	72	77	78	79	80
	SHORT VOWEL	o	94	95	96	99	99	100	101	102	102	103	103	104	105
	SHORT VOWELS	u oo	116	116	118	120	120	121	122	123	123	124	124	125	126

			A	B	C	D	E	F	G	H	I	J	K	L	M
	LONG VOWEL	ae	137	138	139	140	141	142	143	144	144	145	145	145	146
	LONG VOWEL	ee	153	154	155	156	157	158	159	160	161	162	162	163	164
	LONG VOWEL	ie	176	177	178	178	180	181	182	182	183	184	184	185	186
	LONG VOWEL	oe	195	195	196	197	197	198	199	200	200	201	201	201	202
	LONG VOWELS	ue oo	210	211	212	213	213	214	214	215	215	216	216	216	217

			A	B	C	D	E	F	G	H	I	J	K	L	M
	LONG VOWEL	ar	225	226	227	228	228	229	229	230	230	230	231	231	232
	LONG VOWEL	air	236	236	236	237	237	238	238	238	239	—	—	239	239
	LONG VOWEL	er	242	243	244	245	245	246	246	247	247	248	248	248	249
	LONG VOWEL	or	256	257	258	259	259	260	261	261	262	262	262	263	263
	LONG VOWEL	oi	270	270	270	271	271	271	272	272	—	272	—	273	273
	LONG VOWEL	ou	276	276	277	278	278	279	279	279	—	280	—	280	280

xx

xxi

A

*	**	***	**** **
act	aback	abacus es	abnormally
	abbess es	abandon ed	aboriginal
add	abbey	abattoir	aborigine
*adds does add	abbot	abdomen	absolutely
*adze tool	abscess es	abnormal ly	
	absence	absentee	academic ally
-aft	absent	absolute	academy -ies
	abstract	abstraction	accentuate
-alms			accessory -ies
Alps	accent	accident ally	accidental ly
	access es	accurate	accuracy
am	accessed	acetate	accurately
	acid	acquiesce d	accusation
an	acne	acrobat	acquiescence
and	acrid	activate	acquisition
*ant insect	acted	actively	acrobatic ally
	acting	actual ly	activity -ies
apt	action	actuate	actuality -ies
	active		actually
as	actor	adamant	acupuncture
ash es	actress es	adapter / adaptor	
-ask ed	actual ly	additive	adaptable
ass es		addressee	adaptation
	adapt	adenoids	adequacy
at	added	adequate	adjectival ly
	addend	adjective	admirable
*-aunt relative	adder	admirable	admiration
	addict	admiral	adolescence
axe d	adding	adulthood	adolescent
	adult	-advancement	advantageous
	-advance d	-advancing	adverbial ly
	advent	-advantaged	adversary -ies
	adverb	adversary -ies	advocacy
	adverse	advertised	
		advocate	affirmation
	affix es		Afghanistan
	Afghan	affluence	
	-after	affluent	aggravation
		Africa	agitation
	-aghast	African	agoraphobia
	agile	-afternoon	agoraphobic
		-afterwards	agricultural ly
	alas		agriculture
	album	aggravate	
	alcove	aggregate	alabaster
	algae	agitate	alacrity
	Allah	agonise d	alcoholic
	alley	ze	alcoholism
	alloy ed	agony -ies	algebraic ally
	ally -ies		Algeria
	allied	Alaska	alimentary
	-almond	albatross es	☞
	alpha	*albumen white of egg	
	Alpine / alpine	*albumin protein	
	alto	☞	
	☞		

for H . . .
see page 16 ▷

for Scots: a-r
is on page 225 ▷

In these words you can hear the vowel sound **a** as in **cat**

1

A

**

amass es
amassed
amber
amble d
ambling
ambush es
ambushed
ampere
ample
amply

anchor
anger ed
angle d
*angler person who
fishes with hook and
line
angling
angry -ier, -iest
anguish ed
ankle
annexe d
annual ly
anode
-answer ed
anthill
anthrax
*antics strange
behaviour
antique
*antiques very old
objects
antlers
anvil
anxious

aphid / aphis
apple

Arab
arid
arrow ed

ashtray
-asking
aspect
asphalt
aspirin
asset
aster
asthma
☛

for H . . .
see page 16 ▷

***

alchemy
alcohol
algebra
alibi
alkali
alkaline
allegory -ies
allergy -ies
alphabet
Alsatian
altitude

amalgam
amateur
ambition
ambitious
ambulance
amethyst
amino
ammeter
ampersand
amplify -ies
amplified
amplitude
amputate
amylase

anagram
analogue
analyse d
      ze
anarchy
ancestor
ancestral
ancestry -ies
anchorage
andante
Anglican
angora
angrier
angriest
angrily
*angular with sharp
corners
animal
animate
aniseed
annual ly
anodise d
      ze
anorak
-answering
antarctic
anteater
antelope
antenna [antennae]
☛

**** ***

allegation
allegorically
allegory -ies
allegretto
alligator
alphabetical ly
alphanumeric
altimeter
aluminium

amalgamate
ambassador
ambidextrous
ambiguous
ammunition
amphibian
amphibious
amphitheatre
amplification
amplifier

anachronism
anaerobic
anaesthesia /
anesthesia
anaesthetic /
anesthetic
analogy -ies
analysis [analyses]
analytic ally
anatomical ly
anatomy -ies
angiosperm
Anglo-Saxon
animation
anniversary -ies
annually
anonymity
antagonise d
      ze
antagonism
antagonistic ally
Antarctica
antecedent
anterior
anthology -ies
anthropologist
anthropology
antibiotic
antibody -ies
☛

for Scots: a-r
is on page 225 ▷

In these words you can hear the vowel sound a as in cat

A

**

athlete
atlas *es*
atoll
atom
attach *es*
attached
attack *ed*
attic
attract

-Auntie / Aunty

average *d*

*axes more than one
axe or axis
*axis fixed or
imaginary line
axle

azure

impasse

***

anthracite
anthropoid
antidote
antifreeze
antonym
anxiously

apathy
aperture
apparent
appetite
applicant
appliqué
apprehend
aptitude

aquatic
aqueduct
aqueous

Arabic
arable
arrogance
arrogant
arrowhead

asbestos
aspirin
assassin
assonance
asterisk
asteroid
astronaut
asymptote

athletic *ally*
Atlantic
atmosphere
attaché
attachment
attacker
attitude
attracted
attraction
attractive
attributes

avalanche
avant-garde
avarice
avenue
average *d*

axial *ly*
axiom

**** ***

anticipate
anticipation
anticyclone
antimony
antipathy *-ies*
antiquated
antiquity *-ies*
antiseptic *ally*
antisocial
antitoxin
anxiety *-ies*

apostolic *ally*
apparatus
apparently
apparition
appetising
applicable
application
apposition
apprehension

aquamarine

aristocracy *-ies*
aristocrat
aristocratic *ally*
arithmetically

asparagus
aspiration
assassinate
assassination
astronomical *ally*
astrophysics

athletically
atmospheric *ally*

avaricious
avocado

axiomatic *ally*

for H . . .
see page 16 ▷

for Scots: a-r
is on page 225 ▷

In these words you can hear the vowel sound **a** as in cat

A

In these words the first letter 'a' is a neutral vowel.

AMAZING WORDS

abate
abbreviation
abeyance
abide
[abode]
ability -ies
ablaze
aboard
abode
abolish es
abolished
abominable
abominate
abortion
abound
about
above
abrasive
abreast
abroad
abrupt
abscond
absorb ed
absorber
absorption
abstain ed
absurd
abundance
abundant
abuse d
abysmal ly
abyss es
accelerate
acceleration
accelerator
accept able
acceptance
accepting
accessible
accessory -ies
acclaim ed
accommodate
accommodation
accompaniment
accompany -ies
accompanied
accomplice
accomplish es
accomplished
accomplishment
accord ance
according ly
accordion
account ant
accountancy
accrue d
accumulate
accumulation
accumulator
accusative
accuse d
accustom ed
acetylene
achieve d
achievement
acknowledge d
acknowledgement/
acknowledgment

acknowledging
acoustic ally
acquaint ance
acquire d
acquit ted
acquittal
acquitting
acropolis [acropoles]
across
acrylic
acute
addicted
addiction
addictive
additional ly
address es
addressed
adhere d
adhesive
adieu
adjacent
adjoining
adjourn ed
adjudicate
adjudication
adjudicator
adjust er
adjustment
administer ed
administrate
administration
administrator
admire d
admission
admit ted
admittance
admitting
adopt ion
adorable
adore d
adorn ed
adrift
adsorption
adultery
adventure
adventurous
adverbial ly
adversity -ies
advertisement
advice
advisable
advise d
adviser
advisory
Aegean
aesthetic ally
afar
affair
affect ed
affection
affectionate ly
affiliate
affirm ed
affirmative ly
affix es
affixed
afflict ion

afford
affront
afloat
afoot
afraid
again
against
agenda
aggression
aggressive
aggressor
agility
ago
agog
agree d
agreeable
agreement
ahead
ahoy!
ajar
alarm ed
alert
alight
align ed
alignment
alike
alive
allegiance
allegro
allergic
alliance
alliteration
allot ted
allotment
allotting
allow ed
allowable
allowance
allusion
alluvial
alluvium
aloft
alone
along side
aloof
aloud
amaze d
amazing
amenable
amend ment
America n
amid st
amino
amiss
ammonia
ammonium
amoeba
among st
amount
amuse d
amusement
anaemia / anemia
anaemic / anemic
anaesthetist /
anesthetist
anemone
anneal ed
annihilate

announce d
announcement
announcer
annoy ed
annoyance
anoint
anon ymous
another
apart
apartheid
apartment
apologetic ally
apologise d
apology -ies
apostle
apostrophe
appal led
appalling
appeal ed
appear ance
append
appendicitis
appendix -ices
applaud
applause
appliance
applicable
apply -ies
applied
appoint ment
appreciate
apprentice d
apprenticeship
approach es
approached
approaching
appropriate
approval
approve d
approximate ly
approximation
aquarium
Arabia
arena
arise
[arose]
[arisen]
arithmetic
aroma
arose
around
arouse d
arrange d
arrangement
array ed
arrest
arrival
arrive d
ascend ing
ascension
ascent
ascribe d
ashamed
ashore
aside
asleep
aspire d
assail ed

assailant
assault
assemble d
assembly -ies
assent
assert ion
assertive
assess es
assessed
assessment
assign ed
assignment
assimilate
assimilation
assist ance
assistant s
associate
association
associative
assorted
assortment
assume d
assumption
assurance
assure d
astern
astigmatism
astonish es
astonished
astonishment
astound ed
astounding
astray
astrology
astronomer
astronomy
asylum
atone d
atonement
atrocious
attain ed
attainment
attempt ed
attend ed
attendance
attendant s
attention
attentive
attorney
attribute
aurora
Australia
avail ed
availability
available
avenge d
avert
avoid ed
await
awake d
[awoke]
awaken ed
award
aware
away
awhile
awoke n
awry

B

*

back ed
*bad not good
*bade did bid
badge
bag ged
ban ned
*band strip of
material / stripe /
group
*bands more than one
band
bang ed
bank ed
*banned forbidden
*banns announcement
in church of plan to
marry
bash es
bashed
bat ted
batch es
-bath ed

black ed
blank ed
-blast

-bra
brad
brag ged
bran
-branch es
-branched
brand
-brass es
brat

**

babble d
babbling
backbone
background
backhand
backlash es
backlog
backpack ed
backstage
backstroke
backup
backwards
backyard
badger ed
badly
baffle d
baffling
baggage
bagging
baggy -ier, -iest
bagpipes
balance d
ballad
ballast
*ballet dance
*ballot ed voting
-balmy
bamboo
-banal
bandage d
bandit
bandy -ies
bandied
banger
bangle
banish es
banished
banjo es / s
banker
bankrupt
banner
banning
banquet
bantam
baptise d
      ze
Baptist
*baron lord
barrack ed
barracks
barrage d
barrel led
*barren not fertile
barrow ed
☞

***

bachelor
badminton
-Bahamas
balcony -ies
balloted
bamboozle d
-banana
bandwagon
Bangladesh
banishment
banister
baptism
baritone
barrelling
barricade
barrier
barrister
-basketball
bathysphere
battalion
battery -ies
battlefield
battleship

blackberry -ies
blanketed

bonanza

*-brassier more showy
*brassière bra
-bravado

****

bacteria
ballerina

beatitude

botanical

for Scots: a-r
is on page 226 ▷

In these words you can hear the vowel sound **a** as in cat

5

**

basalt
-basket
-bastard
-bathroom
batik
*baton short stick
*batted did bat
*batten board
batter
*battered did batter
batting
battery -ies
battle d
battling

began
-behalf

blackbird
blackboard
blacken ed
blackhead
blackmail ed
blackness
blackout
blacksmith
bladder
blanket ed
-blast-off

bracken
bracket
bradawl
braggart
bragging
bramble
-branches
brandish es
brandished
brandy -ies
brassière
-brassy -ier, -ies

for Scots: a-r
is on page 226 ▷

In these words the first letter 'a' is a neutral vowel. It sounds like the 'a' in 'astonish'.

baboon
balloon ed
barometer
bazaar

bazooka
blancmange
Brazil

In these words you can hear the vowel sound **a** as in cat

C

*

cab
cadge d
-calf
-calve d produce
  a calf
-calm ed
camp ed
can ned
*cant insincere talk /
  sloping edge / tilt
*-can't cannot
cap ped
cash es
  cashed
-cask
*-cast throw / mould /
  decide parts in a
  play / squint
  -[cast]
*-caste social class
cat
catch es
  [caught]

champ ed
*-chance lucky event /
  risk
-chanced
-chant
*-chants does chant /
  more than one chant
chap
chapped
chat ted

clad
clam med
clamp ed
clan
clang ed
clank ed
clap ped
clash es
  clashed
-clasp ed
-class es
-classed
☞

for Qu . . .
see page 24 ▷

**

cabbage
cabin
cackle d
cackling
cactus es / -i
*caddie person paid
  to carry golf clubs
*caddy -ies caddie /
  box to hold tea
  caddied
cadging
cafe / café
caffeine
*callous hard
*callus es hard growth
camber ed
camel
camera
campaign ed
camper
*campers people in
  a camp
campfire
camphor
camping
*campus es college
  or university grounds
camshaft
canal
cancel led
cancer
*candid frank
*candied sugar-coated
candle
candy
canning
*cannon gun / stroke
  in billiards
cannoned
cannot
canny -ier, -iest
*canon musical round /
  rank in church / laws /
  list of works
canteen
canter ed
*canvas cloth
*canvass ed seek
  opinions and/or
  support
*canyon deep and
  narrow valley
☞

***

cabinet
cadmium
calcium
calculate
calendar
calibrate
calibre
calico
callipers
calorie
camembert
camera
camouflage
Canada .
cancelling
candidate
candlelight
candlestick
canister
cannabis
cannibal
canopy -ies
capital
caramel
caravan
caribou
carolling
carrier
carrion
carrycot
carrying
casserole d
castanets
-castaway
casually
casualty -ies
catalogue d
catalyst
catapult
cataract
category -ies
*catholic wide-ranging
*Catholic belonging
  to the Roman Catholic
  church
cavalier
cavalry
cavity -ies

ceramic
☞

**** ***

cafeteria
calamity -ies
calculation
calculator
Cambodia
cantilever ed
capacitor
capacity -ies
capitalise d
      ze
Caribbean
caricature d
casually
casualty -ies
catamaran
catastrophe
catastrophic ally
category -ies
caterpillar

championship
chandelier
characterise d
      ze
characteristic ally
charioteer
charitable
chrysanthemum

classically
classification

collaborate
collaboration
collapsible
comparative
comparatively
comparison
compassionate
compatible
congratulate
congratulations
constabulary -ies
contaminate
contamination

for Scots: a-r ▷
is on page 227

C

*

crab
crack ed
-craft
crag
cram med
cramp ed
crank ed
crash es
crashed

for Qu . . .
see page 24 ▷

**

capping
capstan
capsule
captain ed
captive
captor
capture d
carafe
*carat measure of
purity of gold
carol led
carriage
*carrot vegetable
carry -ies
carried
cascade
cashew
cashier ed
*caster / castor caster
sugar / swivelling
wheel
-casting
-castle
*-castor castor oil
casual ly
catching
cathode
*catholic wide-ranging
*Catholic belonging to
the Roman Catholic
church
catkin
cattle
catty -ier, -iest
cavern

chaffinch es
chalet
challenge d
champagne
-chandler
channel led
chapel
chapter
-charade
chasm
chassis
*chatted had a chat
chatter
*chattered talked
quickly and too much /
rattled
chatty -ier, -iest
*chorale hymn tune
☞

***

champion ed
-chancellor
channelling
-chapati
character
chariot
charity -ies
chatterbox es

clarify -ies
clarified
clarinet
clarity
classical ly
classify -ies
classified

combatted
combatting
-commander
-commandment
companion
compassion
contraction
contractor
contralto s
contraption

kangaroo
-karate

-koala

for Scots: a-r
is on page 227 ▷

In these words you can hear the vowel sound a as in cat

C

* *

cladding
clamber ed
clamming
clammy -ier, -iest
clamour ed
clanger
clanking
clapper
clapping
claret
classic ally
-classmate
-classroom
clatter ed

collapse d
combat ted
-command
compact
contract
-contrast
*-**corral** enclosure for
cattle and horses

cracker
crackle d
crackling
-craftsman
craggy -ier, -iest
cramming
crankshaft
cranny -ies
crevasse

-khaki

-Koran / Qur'an

for Qu . . .
see page 24 ▷

for Scots: a-r
is on page 227 ▷

In these words the first letter 'a' is a neutral vowel. It sounds like the 'a' in 'astonish'.		
cacao	capillary -ies	catarrh
cadet	capricious	cathedral
Canadian	career ed	chameleon
canary -ies	caress es	charisma
canoe d	caressed	

In these words you can hear the vowel sound **a** as in cat

D

*

dab bed
dad
-daft
*dam water-barrier /
mother of animal
dammed
*damn swear word /
condemn
damned
damp ed
-dance d
dank
dash es
dashed

drab
*-draft rough plan /
selected group
drag ged
drank
*-draught current of
air / depth of ship
in water / piece in
game
-draughts

**

dabbing
dabble d
dabbling
dachsund
daddy -ies
dagger
dally -ies
dallied
damage d
dampness
damsel
damson
-dancer
-dancing
dandruff
dandy -ies
dangle d
dangling
dapple d
dashboard
dazzle d
dazzling

decamp ed
-demand
*despatch es send off
despatched
detach es
detached
detract

*dispatch es despatch /
message
dispatched
distract
divan

dragging
dragon
-drama
drastic ally
-draughty -ier, -iest

***

daffodil
dalmatian
damaging
damnation

-demanded
detachment

-disaster
-disastrous
dismantled
dismantling
distraction
distractor

dragonfly -ies
dramatically
dramatise d
ze
drastically

**** *

daddy-longlegs
dandelion

decapitate
declarative
defamatory

dilapidated
dissatisfy -ies
dissatisfied

dramatically
drastically

*for Scots: a-r
is on page 228* ▶

In these words you can hear the vowel sound a as in cat

E

*	**	***	**** *
	elapse d	ecstatic ally	ecstatically
	enact	elaborate	elaborate
	encamp ed	elastic ally	elaboration
	-enchant		elastically
	-entrance d	embankment	elasticity
		embarrass es	
	exact	embarrassed	emancipate
	expand	emphatic ally	embarrassing
	expanse		embarrassment
	extract	enamel led	emphatically
		enamour ed	
		-enchanting	enamelling
		entangle d	
		entangling	erratically
		-entrancing	
			establishment
		erratic ally	
			evacuate
		establish es	evacuation
		established	evacuee
			evaluate
		exactly	evaluation
		examine d	evangelism
		-example	evangelist
		expanded	evaporate
		expanding	evaporation
		expansion	
		expansive	exaggerate
		extraction	exaggeration
		extractor	examination
			examiner
			exasperate
			exasperation
			expandable
			explanatory
			extrapolate
			extravagance
			extravagant
			extravaganza

for H . . .
see page 16 ▷

for I . . .
see page 17 ▷

for Scots: a-r
is on page 228 ▷

In these words you can hear the vowel sound **a** as in **cat**

F

*	**	***	**** *
fact	fabric	fabulous	fabricated
fad	facet	factorise d	fabrication
fag ged	faction	ze	facsimile
fan ned	factor	factory -ies	factually
fangs	factory -ies	factual ly	fantastically
-fast	factual ly	faculty -ies	fascinating
fat ter, test	faddy	Fahrenheit	fascination
fax es	fagging	fallacy -ies	fashionable
faxed	faggots	family -ies	-father-in-law
	fallow	fanciful	
flag ged	famine	fantastic ally	financially
flan	famish es	fantasy -ies	
flange d	famished	fascinate	flabbergasted
flank ed	fanbelt	fascism	
flap ped	fancy -ies	-fastener	fractionally
flash es	fancied	fattening	frantically
flashed	fanning		
-flask	fascist	*-fiancé male engaged	philatelist
flat ted	fashion ed	to be married	
flax	-fasten ed	*-fiancée female	
	-faster	engaged to be married	
*franc French coin	-fastest	financial ly	
-France	*-father male parent		
*frank plain and	-fathered	flannelling	
honest	fathom ed		
franked	fatten ed	fractional ly	
	fattening	frantically	
	fatter		
	fattest		
	fatty -ier, -iest		
	finance d		
	flabby -ier, -iest		
	flagging		
	flagpole		
	flannel led		
	flapjack		
	flapper		
	flapping		
	flappy		
	flasher		
	flashing		
	*flatted made flat		
	flatten ed		
	flatter		
	*flattered did flatter		
	flattest		
	flatting		

for th . . .
see page 28

forbade
☞

for Scots: a-r
is on page 229

12   In these words you can hear the vowel sound **a** as in **cat**

**

fraction
fracture d
fragile
fragment
frantic ally

for th . . .
see page 28 ▷

for Scots: a-r
is on page 229 ▷

*-farther a greater
 distance

phantom

> **In these words the first letter 'a' is a neutral vowel. It sounds like the 'a' in 'astonish'.**
>
> facilitate   familiarity
> facility -ies   fatigue d
> fallacious   flamingo es / s
> familiar

In these words you can hear the vowel sound a as in cat

G

*

gag ged
gang
gap ped
gas es
gassed
gash es
gashed
-**gasp** ed

glad der, dest
-**glance** d
gland
-**glass** es

gnash es
gnashed
gnat

grab bed
gram / gramme
grand
-**grant**
-**graph** ed
-**grasp** ed
-**grass** es
-grassed

**

gabble d
gabbling
gadget
gagging
gaggle
gala
gallant
***galleon** ship
galley
***gallon** measure
gallop ed
gallows
gambit
***gamble** d risk
gambler
***gambling** taking risks
***gambol** led frisk
gamma
gammon
gander
gangling
gangplank
gangster
gangway
gannet
gantry -ies
gapping
garage d
garret
gasket
gassing
gastric
gasworks
gâteau
gather ed

-**Ghana**
-**ghastly** -ier, -iest

-**giraffe**

gladden ed
gladder
gladdest
gladly
glamour
-**glancing**
-**glasses**
-**glassy** -ier, -iest
☞

***

galaxy -ies
gallery -ies
galvanise d
          ze
***gambolling** frisking
garrison

-**Ghanaian**

glacier
glamorous
glandular

gradual ly
graduate
gramophone
grandchildren
granddaughter
grandfather
grandiose
grandmother
grandparent
granular
graphical ly
-**grasshopper**
gratitude
gravelling
gravity -ies

guarantee d

-**gymkhana**
gymnastics

****

gasometer

gelatinous

gladiator
gladiolus [gladioli]

gradually
graduation
graphically
gravitation

*for Scots: a-r
is on page 229* ▷

In these words you can hear the vowel sound **a** as in **cat**

G

* *

grabber
grabbing
gradual ly
grammar
grandad / **granddad**
grandchild
grandeur
grandma
grandpa
grandson
grandstand
granite
granny -ies
-**granted**
graphic ally
graphite
grapple d
grappling
-**grasping**
-**grassland**
-**grassy** -ier, -iest
-**gratis**
gravel led

for Scots: a-r
is on page 229 ▷

In these words the first letter 'a' is a neutral vowel. It sounds like the 'a' in 'astonish'.

galena   gazump ed
galore   gradation
galoshes   graffiti
gazelle

In these words you can hear the vowel sound a as in cat

H

*

hack ed
had
-half [halves]
-halve d
ham med
hand
hang
[hung]
hanged
has
hash es
hashed
hat
hatch es
hatched
hath
have
[had]

* *

habit
haddock
hadn't
haggard
haggle d
haggling
halal
hallo
hamlet
hammer ed
hamming
hammock
hamper ed
hamster
hamstring ed
[hamstrung]
handbag
handbrake d
handcuff ed
handed
handful
handgun
handle d
handler
handling
*hand-made made
by hand
*handmaid servant
handout / hand-out
handshake
*handsome good-
looking
handspring
*hangar building to
house planes
*hanger means of
hanging
hanging
hanky -ies
*hansom cab
happen ed
happy -ier, -iest
harass ed
harrow ed
hasn't
hassle d
hatchback
hatchet
hatching
hatter
haven't
having
havoc
hazard

hello

* * *

habitat
Halloween
hamburger
handicap ped
handicraft
handiwork
handkerchief s
handlebar
handwriting
handwritten
handyman
haphazard
happening
happier
happiest
happily
happiness
harassment
haricot
haversack
Hawaii
Hawaiian
hazardous

* * * *

habitation
handicapping

> **Here the first 'a' is spoken as a neutral sound.**
>
> habitual ly   hallucination

*for Scots: a-r
is on page 230* ▷

In these words you can hear the vowel sound a as in cat

I

*

**

impasse

intact

-Iran
-Iraq

-Islam

***

imagine d

inhabit ed

-Iraqi

Islamic

Italian
italic

**** *

imaginary
imagination
imaginative
immaculate
-impassable
implacable
impractical

inaccuracy -ies
inaccurate
inadequate
infatuate d
infatuation
inflammable
inflammatory
inhabitant
inhabited
inhabiting
insanitary
insanity
intractable
intransitive
invaluable

irrational ly

italicise d
ze

for E . . .
see page 11

In these words you can hear the vowel sound a as in cat

17

J

*
jab bed
jack ed
*jam fruit boiled with
sugar / crush / block
jammed
*jamb side post of
door or window
jazz es
jazzed

**
-giraffe

gymnast

jabber ed
jabbing
jackal
jackdaw
jacket
jack-knife d
jackpot
jagged
jamjar
jamming
jampot
jangle d
jangling
Japan
jasper

***
-gymkhana
gymnastics

jaguar
jamboree
Japanese
javelin

****
gelatinous

January

for dr . . .
see page 10

for Scots: a-r
is on page 230

In these words the first letter 'a' is a neutral
vowel. It sounds like the 'a' in 'astonish'.
Jacuzzi s   Jamaica   Jamaican

K

*
knack

**
-**khaki**

knapsack

-**Koran** / **Qur'an**

***
kangaroo
-**karate**

-**koala**

****
Karaoke

for C . . .
see page 7

for Qu . . .
see page 24

In these words the first letter 'a' is a neutral
vowel. It sounds like the 'a' in 'astonish'.
kaleidoscope   karate

18

In these words you can hear the vowel sound a as in cat

L

*

lack ed
*lacks does lack
lad
lag ged
lamb ed
lamp
-lance d
land
*lap thighs of seated
person / once round
a track / splash
gently / drink by
using tongue / be
placed together
or overlapping
*Lapp person from
Lapland
*Lapps more than
one Lapp
*lapse d slip / end
through disuse
lash es
lashed
lass es
-last
latch es
latched
-laugh ed
*lax slack

**

lacquer ed
ladder ed
lagging
lambing
lamp-post
lampshade
landed
landing
landlord
landmark
landscape
landslide
language
languid
languor
lanky -ier, -iest
lantern
Lapland
lapping
larynx
lasso ed
-lasted
-lather ed
Latin
latter
lattice d
-laughter
-lava
lavish es
lavished

-llama

***

Labrador
lacerate
laminate
Lancashire
landlady -ies
landowner
lariat
lasagne
lateral ly
latitude
lavatory -ies
lavender
laxative

****

lamentable
laminated
laryngitis
laterally
lavatory -ies

legality

for Scots: a-r
is on page 231

In these words the first letter 'a' is a neutral
vowel. It sounds like the 'a' in 'astonish'.

laboratory -ies   lament
laborious ly   lapel
laconic ally   lasagne
lagoon

In these words you can hear the vowel sound a as in cat

19

M

*	**	***	* * * * **
ma'am	mackerel	macabre	macaroni
mad der, dest	*madam English	mackerel	magically
mall	*madame French	mackintosh	magnesium
man [men]	madden ed	mademoiselle	magnetically
man ned	madder	madrigal	magnetism
Manx	maddest	magazine	magnificent
map ped	madness	magical ly	magnolia
mash ed	maggot	magistrate	maladjusted
-mask ed	magic ally	magnetic ally	malleable
mass es	magma	magnetise d	malnutrition
massed	*magnate wealthy	ze	mammalian
-mast	businessman	magnetite	manageable
*mat small rug	*magnet iron which	magnify -ies	manageress es
match es	attracts iron	magnified	manifesto
matched	magpie	magnitude	mannerism
*matt not shiny	malice	majesty -ies	manometer
	mallard	malleable	manually
	mallet	management	manufacture d
	mammal	manager	manufacturer
	mammoth	managing	manufacturing
	manage d	mandolin	marijuana
	mandrel	manganese	marionette
	mangle d	manicure d	masturbation
	mangling	manifest	mathematical ly
	mango es / s	manifold	mathematician
	manhood	*mannequin model	mathematics
	mankind	*mannikin dwarf	matrimony
	*manna food	manpower	maturation
	*manner way	manslaughter	
	mannered	mantelpiece	mechanical ly
	manning	manual ly	menagerie
	*manor large house	manuscript	metabolism
	with land	marathon	
	mansion	marigold	miraculous
	*mantel frame round	mariner	
	fire	maritime	morality
	*mantle cloak	mascara	
	manual ly	masculine	
	mapping	masquerade	
	marriage	massacre d	
	married	-masterpiece	
	marrow	-mastery	
	marry -ies	mastodon	
	married	masturbate	
	mascot	matador	
	massage d	matinée	
	masseur	maximum	
	masseuse		
	*massif highlands	meander ed	
	*massive huge	mechanic ally	
	-master ed	medallion	
	mastiff		
	☞	Mohammed	
		molasses	

for Scots: a-r
is on page 232 ▷

20

In these words you can hear the vowel sound **a** as in **cat**

M

**
matches
matching
*matted twisted in
a thick mass
matter
*mattered did matter
matting
mattress es
maxim

meringue

-mirage

-morale
-moustache d

for Scots: a-r
is on page 232 ▷

In these words the first letter 'a' is a neutral
vowel. It sounds like the 'a' in 'astonish'.

machine d	majority -ies	manipulation
machinery	malaria	manoeuvre d
machinist	Malaysia	manure d
magician	malicious	maroon ed
mahogany	malignant	material ly
majestic ally	mama	mature d
Majorca	manipulate	maturity

N

*
gnash es
gnashed
gnat

knack

nag ged
nap ped

**
knapsack

nagging
nana
nanny -ies
napkin
napping
nappy -ies
narrow ed
-nasty -ier, -iest

***
narrative
nasturtium
nationalist
nationally
naturalist
naturally
navigate

nomadic

**** **
nationalism
nationalistic
nationality -ies
nationally

naturalisation
   zation
naturalise d
   ze
naturalist
naturally
navigable
navigation
navigator

In these words the first letter 'a' is a neutral
vowel. It sounds like the 'a' in 'astonish'.

narrate	nasturtium
narrator	nativity

for Scots: a-r
is on page 232 ▷

In these words you can hear the vowel sound **a** as in **cat**

P

*

pack
*packed tightly filled
*pact agreement
pad ded
pal
-palm ed
pan ned
pang
pant
pants
-pass es
*-passed went by
*-past time that has
     passed / beyond
pat ted
patch es
patched
-path

plaid
plait
plan ned
plank ed
-plant
plaque

pram
-prance d
prank

-psalm

**

package d
packer
packet
packing
padded
padding
paddle d
paddling
paddock
paddy -ies
padlock ed
pageant
palace
*palate taste
*palette board for
     mixing colours
*pallet mattress / tool
pally -ier, -iest
pampas
pamper ed
pamphlet
pancake
*panda animal
*pander ed encourage
     by bad example or
     taste
panel led
panic
panicked
panning
pansy -ies
panther
panties
pantry -ies
parish -es
parrot
parry -ies
parried
passage
-passing
passion
passive
-passport
-password
pasta
*pastel crayon /
     soft colour
*pastille sweet
-pasture d
pasty -ies
☞

***

pacifist
-Pakistan
Palestine
pancreas
panelling
panicking
pantograph
pantomime
paprika
parable
parachute
paradise
paradox es
paraffin
paragraph ed
parakeet
parallel ed
paralyse d
        ze
paramount
paranoid
parapet
paraphrase
parasite
parasol
paratroop
parity
parody -ies
passageway
passenger
-passers-by
passionate
-Passover
pasteurise d
        ze
-pastoral ly
patio
patriot

patronage
patronise d
        ze

pianist
piano s
-piranha

planetary
-plantation
-plasterboard
plasticine
platinum
platitude
platypus es
☞

**** **

-Pakistani
palaeontologist /
paleontologist
palaeontology /
paleontology
panorama
papier-mâché
parabola
paracetamol
parallelogram
paralysis
[paralyses]
paralytic
paramecium
paraphernalia
parasitical ly
paratrooper
pastorally
pathological ly
patriotic ally
patriotism
patronising

philanthropist
philanthropy
philatelist
philately

pianoforte
-pistachio s

planetary

potassium

practicable
practically
preparatory

for Scots: a-r
is on page 233 ▷

22   In these words you can hear the vowel sound **a** as in **cat**

P

**

patchwork
patchy -ier, -iest
patent
*patted did pat
patter
*pattered did patter
pattern ed
patting
patty -ies

perhaps

phantom

pianist
piano s

placard
placid
planet
plankton
planner
planning
-**planted**
-**planter**
-**planting**
plasma
-**plaster** ed
plastic
plateau
platen
platform
platter
-**plaza**

*practice action
*practise d do or act /
repeat for
improvement

***

practical ly
practising
protractor

-**pyjamas**

for Scots: a-r
is on page 233 ▷

In these words the first letter 'a' is a neutral
vowel. It sounds like the 'a' in 'astonish'.

pagoda	pathology -ies
papa	patrol led
parade	patrolling
parenthesis -es	pavilion
pathetic ally	platoon

In these words you can hear the vowel sound **a** as in **cat**

Q

*

quack ed

**

quagmire
quango s
-Qur'an / Koran

***

quackery

****

R

*

rack ed
-raft
rag ged
ram med
ramp
ran
-ranch es
rang
rank ed
*rap knock / speech
music
*rapped knocked
*rapt entranced
rash es
-rasp ed
rat ted

*wrap cover by
winding or folding
*wrapped covered

**

rabbi
*rabbit animal
*racket racquet / din /
dishonest way of
making money
*racquet bat with
strings
radish es
raffle d
-rafter
ragged
ragging
rally -ies
rallied
ramble d
rambling
ramming
rampart
rancid
random
ransack ed
ransom ed
rapid
*rapping knocking
rapport
rapture
*rarebit cheese
on toast
-rascal ly
rasher
-raspberry -ies
ratchet
-rather
ration ed
ratted
ratting
rattle d
rattling
ratty -ier, -iest
ravage d
☞

***

rabbitted
rabbitting
radical ly
raffia
Ramadan
ramshackle
randomise d
                  ze
rapidly
-raspberry -ies
rationale
rational ly
rattlesnake
ravenous

reaction
reactor
refraction
regatta

romantic ally

**** *

radically
Rastafarian
ratification
rationalisation
                  zation
rationalised
                  ze
rationally
ravioli

reactionary -ies
reality -ies
retaliate
retaliation

romantically

*for Scots: a-r
is on page 233* ▷

In these words you can hear the vowel sound a as in cat

R

*

react
refract
relax es
relaxed

*for Scots: a-r
is on page 233* ▶

romance d

wrangle d
wrangling
wrapper
*wrapping covering

In these words the first letter 'a' is neutral.
raccoon / racoon
rapidity
ravine

S

*	**	***	**** **
-psalm	chalet	ceramic	chandelier
	champagne		
*sac pouch	-charade	**sabotage** d	**sacrificial** ly
*sack large bag /	chassis	**saccharin / saccharine**	**salivary**
plunder / dismiss		**sacrament**	**salmonella**
from a job	**sabbath**	**sacrifice** d	**salutary**
sack ed	**sadden** ed	-safari	**salutation**
sad der, dest	**sadder**	-Sahara	**sanatorium**
sag ged	**saddest**	-salami	**sanctuary** -ies
sand	**saddle** d	**salaried**	**sanitary**
sang	**sadly**	**salary** -ies	**sanitation**
sank	**sagging**	**salutary**	**satisfaction**
sash es	**salad**	**salvation**	**satisfactory**
sat	**salmon**	**sanctify** -ies	**saturated**
	salvage d	sanctified	**saturation**
scab	**samba**	**sanctity**	
scalp ed	-**sample** d	**sanctuary** -ies	**Scandinavian**
scamp	-**sampler**	**sandpaper**	-**scenario** s
scan	-**sampling**	**sandpiper**	
*scanned did scan	**sanction**	**sanitary**	-**Somalia**
*scant hardly enough	**sandal** led	**sanity**	
scrap ped	**sandbag**	**satellite**	**statically**
scratch es	**sandbank**	**satisfy** -ies	**statistician**
scratched	**sander**	satisfied	**statutory**
	sandstone	**saturate**	**strangulation**
shack	**sandwich** es	**Saturday**	
-**shaft**	sandwiched	**savanna**	**substantially**
shag	**sandy** -ier, -iest	**saveloy**	
shall	**sapling**	**saxophone**	**syllabically**
sham med	**sapphire**		**syllabification**
shank	**sapwood**	**scaffolding**	**syllabify** -ies
shrank	**satchel**	**scantiest**	syllabified
☛	**satin**		
	satire	-**soprano** s	*for Scots: a-r
is on page 234* ▶
	Saturn		
	savage d	**spatula**	
	Saxon	☛	
	☛		

In these words you can hear the vowel sound **a** as in **cat**

S

*

slab bed
slack ed
slam med
slang
-slant
slap ped
slash es
slashed

smack ed
smash es
smashed

snack
snap ped
snatch es
snatched

span ned
spank ed
spat
splash es
splashed
sprang
sprat

stab bed
stack ed
-staff ed
stag
stamp ed
-stance
stand
[stood]
stank
strand
strap ped

swag
swam
swank ed

**

scabbard
scabby -ier, -iest
scaffold
scallop ed
scalpel
scamper ed
scanner
scanning
scanty -ier, -iest
scatter ed
scavenge d
scrabble
scrabbling
scraggy -ier, -iest
scramble d
scrambling
scrapbook
scrapping
scrappy -ier, -iest
scrapyard
scratchy -ier, -iest

shabby -ier, -iest
shadow ed
shaggy -ier, -iest
shallow
shambles
shamming
shampoo ed
shamrock
shandy -ies
shanty -ies
shatter ed
shrapnel

slamming
slapping

smasher
smashing

snapping
snappy -ier, -iest
snapshot

Spaniard
spaniel
Spanish
spanner
spanning
sparrow
spasm
spastic
splashdown
☞

***

-staccato
stalactite
stalagmite
stamina
standardise d
　　　　ze
statically
statuesque
stratagem
strategy -ies
stratosphere

substantial ly
subtracting
subtraction
-sultana
-surpassing

syllabic ally

for Scots: a-r
is on page 234 ▶

In these words you can hear the vowel sound a as in cat

* *

stabbing
stagger ed
stagnant
stallion
stammer ed
stampede
standard
stand-by
standing
standpoint
standstill
stanza
static ally
statue
stature
statute
straggle d
straggling
stranded
strangle d
strangling
strapping
-**stratum** [strata]

subtract
-**surpass** es
-surpassed

for Scots: a-r
is on page 234 ▷

swagger ed

**In these words the first letter 'a' is a neutral
vowel. It sounds like the 'a' in 'astonish'.**

safari	salivary	spaghetti
Sahara	saloon	stability
salami	salute	statistical ly
salinity	samosa	statistics
saliva	satirical ly	strategic ally

T

*

tab
tack
*tacked did tack
*tacks more than
   one tack
*tact skill in putting
   things to people
tag ged
tan ned
tank
tap ped
-task
*tax es money taken
   by government
taxed

than
thank ed
that
thatch es
thatched
that's
*thrash es beat
thrashed
*thresh es beat corn
threshed

track
*track ed did track
*tract pamphlet
tram
tramp ed
-trance
trap ped
trash

twang ed

**

tabby -ies
tableau
tablet
tacit
tackle d
tackling
tacky -ier, -iest
tactful ly
tactics
tactile
tactless
tadpole
tagging
talcum
talent
tally -ies
tallied
tamper ed
tampon
tangent
tangle d
tangling
tango s
tangoed
tankard
tanker
tanner
tanning
tantrum
tappet
tapping
tariff
tarry -ies
tarried
tassel led
tattered
tattoo ed
tavern
taxi s

thankful ly
thank-you
that'd
that'll

timbre

tracksuit
traction
tractor
traffic
trafficked
tragic ally
trample d
trampling
☞

***

tabulate
tactfully
taffeta
tambourine
tangerine
tangible
tantalise d
      ze
tapestry -ies
taxation
taxpayer

thankfully

-tiara

tobacco s
-tomato es

trafficker
trafficking
tragedy -ies
tragically
trampoline d
tranquilly
transaction
transcendent
transcription
transferring
transformer
transfusion
transistor
transition
transitive
transitory
translation
translator
translucent
transmission
transmitted
transmitter
transmitting
transparent
transversal
transvestite
trapezoid
traveller
travelling

**** **

tabulation
tabulator
tachometer
Tanzania
tapioca
tarantula
Tasmania

theatrical ly

tobacconist

trafficator
tragically
trampolining
tranquilliser
      zer
tranquillity
transatlantic
transcendental
transferable
transformation
transistorised
      zed
transitional ly
transitory
transmutation
transparency -ies
transpiration
transportation
transubstantiation

tyrannical ly
tyrannosaurus es / -i

*for Scots: a-r
is on page 235* ▶

In these words you can hear the vowel sound **a** as in **cat**

T

* *

tranquil ly
***transact** make a deal
transcribe d
***transect** cut across
transept
transfer red
transfix es
transfixed
transform ed
transit
translate
transmit ted
transpire d
transplant
transport
transpose d
transverse
trapdoor
trapper
trapping
trappings
travel led
traverse d

for Scots: a-r is on page 235 ▶

In these words the first letter 'a' is neutral.

tattoo ed	traditional ly
trachea	trajectory -ies
tradition	trapeze

V

*	* *	* * *	* * * * *
valve d	**vaccine**	**vaccinate**	**vaccination**
van	**vacuum ed**	**vacillate**	**vacillation**
-vase	**valiant**	**vacuole**	**validation**
vast	**valid**	**vagabond**	**valuable**
	valley	**vaginal**	**valuation**
	valour	**valentine**	**vandalism**
	value d	**valiant**	
	vampire	**validate**	**vernacular**
	vandal	**valium**	
	vanish es	**valuable**	**vocabulary** -ies
	vanished	**vandalise** d	
	vanquish es	**ze**	**vulgarity** -ies
	vanquished	**vanity** -ies	
	-vantage	**vaseline**	
		Vatican	

veranda / verandah

for Scots: a-r is on page 235 ▶

-vibrato

Here the first letter 'a' is neutral.

vacate	validity
vacation	vanilla
vagina	variety -ies

In these words you can hear the vowel sound **a** as in **cat**

29

W

*

*rap knock / speech
 music
*rapped knocked

wag ged
wax ed

whack ed

*wrap cover
*wrapped covered
-wrath

**

wagging
waggle d
wagon
wagtail

wrangle d
wrangling
wrapper
*wrapping covering

***

****

Y

*

yank ed
yap ped

**

yapping

***

****

*for Scots: a-r
is on page 235*

Z

*

zapp ed

**

zapping

***

Zambia

-**Zimbabwe**

****

In these words you can hear the vowel sound **a** as in cat

*

**

abreast

***accept** take
something offered

address es
addressed

***affect** alter

again
against

ahead

amend

annexe d
any

arrest

ascend
***ascent** climb
***assent** agree
assess es
assessed

attempt
attend

avenge d

*effect alter

*except not including

***

acceptance
accepting

adventure

aesthetic ally

affected
affection

agenda
aggression
aggressive
aggressor

allegro
already

amendment

anyhow
anyone
anything
anyway
anywhere

appendix -ces
apprentice d

ascension
assemble d
assembly -ies
assessment

attempted
***attendance** those
present / rate of
attending
attendant
***attendants** servants
attended
attention
attentive

authentic ally

**** *

accelerate
acceleration
accelerator
acceptable
accessory -ies
acetylene

adrenalin
adventurous

aesthetically

affectionate
affectionately

America
American

anemone
anybody

appendicitis
apprenticeship

authentically

*for Scots: e-r
is on page 242* ▶

B

*

beck
bed ded
beg ged
*bell instrument
*belle beauty
belt
bench es
bend
[bent]
best
bet ted
[bet]

bled
blend
bless es
blessed
[blest]

*bread food
*breadth width
breast
*breath air passing
in and out of lungs
*bred produced
young / reared

**

beckon ed
bedding
bedrock
bedroom
bedside
bedtime
befell
befriend
beggar
begging
behead
beheld
Belgian
Belgium
bellow ed
belly -ies
bending
benzene
bereft

*beret flat, round cap
*berry -ies fruit
beset
[beset]
betted
better
betting
bevel led
beverage

blessed
blessing

breakfast
breastbone
breathless
brethren

*bury -ies place deep
down
buried

***

benefit ed
besetting
bevelling
beverage

breathalyse d
ze
breathtaking

burial

**** *

beneficial ly
benefited
benefiting
benevolent

breathalyser
zer

Here the first letter 'e' has a short 'i' sound.

B*E*NEVOLENT WORDS

became	believe d
because	belong ed
become	belonging
[became]	beloved
[become]	below
becoming	beneath
befall	bereave d
[befell]	beseech es
[befallen]	beseeched
before	[besought]
beforehand	beside
begin	besides
[began]	besiege d
[begun]	bestow ed
beginner	betray ed
beginning	betrayal
behalf	between
behave d	betwixt
behaviour	beware
behind	bewilder ed
behold	bewitch es
[beheld]	bewitched
belated	beyond
belief	

*for Scots: e-r
is on page 243* ▷

In these words you can hear the vowel sound **e** as in elephant

C

*

*cell unit
Celt
*cent money /
  hundred
*cents money

*check ed stop / test
chef
*cheque order to bank
chess
chest

cleanse d
clef
cleft
clench es
clenched

crêche
crêpe
crept
cress es
crest

kelp
kept
ketch es

*scent perfume / smell

*sell exchange for money
*sense understandable
  pattern
*sent made to go

for Qu . . .
see page 47 ▷

**

cadet
caress es
caressed
cassette

*cellar underground
  storage room
cello s
Celtic
cement
*censer pan for
  burning incense
*censor judge of what
  may not be published
*census official count
centaur
central ly
centre

checking
chemist
cherish es
cherished
cherry -ies
chestnut

cleansing
clever

collect
commence d
compel led
compress es
compressed
condemn ed
condense d
confess es
confessed
connect
consent
contempt
contend
content
contest
correct

credit ed
crescent
crevice

Kelvin / kelvin
kennel
kestrel
ketchup
kettle
☞

***

celandine
celebrate
celery
celestial
cellophane
cellular
celluloid
cellulose
Celsius
cemetery -ies
censorship
centigrade
centipede
centrally
century -ies
cerebral
cerebrum

chemical ly
chemistry

cleanliness

collecting
collection
collective
collector
compelling
complexion
compression
compressor
concentric
conception
concession
condenser
confession
confessor
confetti
conjecture d
connected
connecting
connection
connector
consensus
contestant
contention
convection
convector
convention
corrected
correction
correctly
☞

**** **

celebrated
celebration
celebrity -ies
celestial
centenary -ies
centimetre
centrifugal ly
centurion
cerebellum
ceremonial ly
ceremony -ies

chemically
cholesterol

commemorate
commemoration
competitive
competitor
confectioner
confectionery
confessional
congenital ly
consecutive
contemporary -ies
contemptible
contemptuous
conventional ly

crematorium

Czechoslovakia

kinetically

for Scots: e-r
is on page 244 ▷

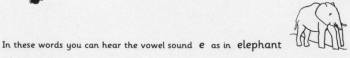

In these words you can hear the vowel sound **e** as in elephant

33

**

*seller person who sells
*senses means of gaining
information
*sensor detecting device

***

credential
credible
credited
creditor
crescendo s

*kinetic ally

for Qu . . .
see page 47 ▷

for Scots: e-r
is on page 244 ▷

> **Here the first letter 'e' has a short 'i' sound.**
> cremate   cremation   crevasse

D

*	**	***	**** **
dead	deaden ed	deafening	decimetre
deaf	deadline	debited	declaration
dealt	deadly -ier, -iest	December	decorated
death	deafen ed	deception	decoration
debt	deafer	deceptive	decorative
deck ed	deafest	decimal	decorator
den	debit ed	decorate	dedication
*dense closely packed /	debris	dedicate	defamation
stupid	debtor	defective	definitely
dent	debut / début	defector	definition
*dents more than one	*decade ten years	defendant	delegation
dent	deckchair	defender	delicacy -ies
depth	defect	defensive	deliquescent
desk	defence	deficit	delphinium
	defend	definite	democratic ally
dread ed	deflect	deflection	demonstration
dreamt	delta	delegate	dependable
dredge d	deluge d	delicate	dependency -ies
dregs	denim	democrat	deprivation
drench es	Denmark	demonstrate	derivation
drenched	dental	denigrate	designated
dress	dentist	density -ies	desolation
dressed	depend	*dependant person	desperation
	depot	who depends	despotism
dwell ed	depress es	*dependants people	destination
[dwelt]	depressed	who depend	detonator
	derrick	depended	detrimental
	descant	*dependence reliance	devastated
	descend	*dependent relying /	devastation
	*descent way down	hanging	developer
	desert	depression	developing
	desperate	depressive	development
	detect	deputy -ies	developmental ly
	detest	derelict	☞
	devil led	☞	
	dexterous / dextrous		

for Scots: e-r
is on page 245 ▷

In these words you can hear the vowel sound **e** as in elephant

D

**

digest
direct
dispense d
dissect
*dissent disagreement
distress es
distressed

dreaded
dreadful ly
dredger
dredging
dresser
dressing

dwelling

*decayed did decay

***

*descendant offspring
descended
*descendent moving
down
designate
desolate
desperate
dessicate
destiny -ies
destitute
detection
detective
detector
detention
*deterrence prevention
by causing fear
deterrent
*deterrents more than
one deterrent
detonate
detriment
devastate
develop ed

digestion
dilemma
dimension
directed
direction
directive
directly
director
discredit ed
discretion
dishevelled
dispelling
dispenser
displeasure
dissension
dissenter
distressing

domestic ally

dreadfully

dyslexic / dyslectic

**** **

digestible
directory -ies
discredited
discrepancy -ies

domestically
domesticate

dyslexia

Here the first letter 'e' has a short 'i' sound.

D**E**LIGHTFUL WORDS

debate	delirious	design ed
decamp ed	deliver ed	designer
decay ed	deliverance	desirable
decease d	delivery -ies	desire d
deceit	delusion	despair ed
deceive d	demand ed	despatch es
decide	demobbed	despatched
deciduous	democracy -ies	despise d
decipher ed	demolish es	despite
decision	demolished	despondency
decisive	demonstrative	despondent
declare d	denial	dessert
decline d	denomination	destroy ed
decree d	denominator	destroyer
decry -ies	denote	destruction
decried	denounce d	destructive
deduce d	deny -ies	detach es
deduct	denied	detached
deduction	depart	detain ed
deductive	department	deter red
defeated	departure	deterring
defer red	deport	detergent
deferring	deposit ed	deteriorate
defiance	depositing	deterioration
defiant	depreciate	determination
deficiency -ies	depreciation	determine d
deficient	deprive d	determiner
define d	derail ed	determining
deform ed	derailment	deterring
defy -ies	derivative	detract
defied	derive d	device
degree	derogatory	devise d
delay ed	describe d	devote d
delete	describing	devotion
deliberate ly	description	devour ed
delicious	descriptive	devout
delight ed	desert ed	
delightful ly	deserve d	

for Scots: e-r
is on page 245

E

*

ebb ed

edge d

egg ed

elf [elves]
elm
else

end

etch es
etched

**

*accept take something offered

*affect alter

any

echo ed

eddy -ies
eddied
edging
edit ed

*effect result / bring about
effort

eject

elbow ed
elder
eldest
elect
elsewhere

embed ded
ember
emblem
empire
empress es
empty -ies

ending
endless
engine
ensign
entail ed
enter ed
entrance
entrench es
entrenched
entry -ies
envy -ies
envied
enzyme

epic

erect
errand
error
☜

***

aesthetic ally

anyhow
anyone
anything
anyway
anywhere

ebony

eccentric ally
ecstasy -ies
ecstatic ally
Ecuador
eczema

edible
edifice
edited
editor
educate

effective
effervesce d
effigy -ies

ejection
ejector

elderly
election
electors
electric ally
electrode
electron
elegance
elegant
element
elephant
elevate
eleven th
eloquence
eloquent
☜

**** ***

aesthetically

anybody

eccentrically
economic
economical ly
economics
ecosystem
ecstatically
ecumenical ly

editorial ly
educated
education
educational ly
educator
Edwardian

effectively
effectiveness
effervescence
effervescent

electoral ly
electorate
electrical ly
electrician
electricity
electrocute
electrolyse d
    ze
electrolysis
electrolyte
electrolytic ally
electromagnetic ally
electronic ally
electrostatic ally
elementary
elevated
elevation
eligible
elocution
☜

See also E
-on page 65 ▷

for H . . .
see page 40 ▷

for I . . .
see page 41 ▷

for Scots: e-r
is on page 245 ▷

In these words you can hear the vowel sound **e** as in **elephant**

**

escort
esquire
essay
essence

etching
ethics
ethnic ally

event
ever
every

excel led
*except not including
*excerpt selected
passage
excess es
exempt
exhale d
exhort
exile d
exit
expect
expel led
expense
expert
exploit
export
express es
expressed
extend
extent
extra
extract

***

embargo es
embargoed
embedded
embellish es
embellished
embezzle d
embryo s
emerald
emery
*emigrant person who
goes abroad to live
*emigrate go abroad
to live
eminence
eminent
empathy
emperor
emphasis [emphases]
emphasise d
　　ze
emptiness

endeavour ed
endocrine
enemy -ies
energy -ies
engineer ed
entering
enterprise
entertain ed
envelope
envious

epilogue
episode
epitaph
epithet

equinox es

erection

escalate
escapade
Eskimo s
esplanade
essential ly
estimate
estuary -ies

ethical ly
ethnical ly
etiquette
☞

**** ***

embarkation
embryonic ally
*emigration going
abroad to live
emissary -ies
emphatically
empirical ly

energetic ally
engineering
entertainer
entertainment
enveloping
enviable

epicyclic ally
epidemic ally
epilepsy
epileptic ally

equatorial ly
equilibrium

escalator
especially
essentially
estimated
estimation

ethically
ethnically
etymological ly
etymology

eventually
everlasting
everybody
evidently

excavation
excellency -ies
exceptionally
exclamation
execution
executioner
executive
exemplary
exhibition
exhortation
☞

See also E
-on page 65 ▷

for H . . .
see page 40 ▷

for I . . .
see page 41 ▷

for Scots: e-r
is on page 245 ▷

In these words you can hear the vowel sound *e* as in elephant

E

Here the first letter 'e' has a short 'i' sound.

*E*XCITING WORDS

ecclesiastical ly	endurance	evasion
eclipse d	endure d	evasive
ecology	enfold	evict
edition	enforce d	evoke d
efficient	enforcement	evolve d
Egyptian	engage d	exact ly
elaborate	engagement	exaggerate
elaboration	engrave d	exaggeration
elastic ally	engraving	exalt ed
elasticity	engross es	examination
elate d	engrossed	examine d
elation	engulf ed	example
elicit ed	enjoy ed	exceed ingly
eliciting	enjoying	exchange d
eliminate	enjoyment	excite d
elimination	enlarge d	excitedly
Elizabethan	enlighten ed	excitement
ellipse	enlist	exciting
elliptical ly	enquire d	exclaim ed
elope d	enquiry -ies	exclamation
elude	enormous	exclude
elusive	enough	exclusion
emancipate	enrage d	exclusive ly
emancipation	enrich es	excrete
embankment	enriched	excretion
embargo es	enrol led	excuse d
embargoed	enrolment	excursion
embark ed	enslave d	exert ion
embarrass es	ensure d	exhaust ed
embarrassed	entangle d	exhaustion
embarrassing	enthusiasm	exhibit ed
embarrassment	enthusiast	exhibiting
embroider ed	enthusiastic ally	exist ed
embroidery	entire ly	existence
emerge d	entitle d	exotic ally
emergence	entrancing	expand ed
emergency -ies	entrust	expandable
emission	enumerate	expanding
emit ted	environment ally	expansion
emitter	envisage d	expansive
emitting	equality	experience d
emotional ly	equation	explain ed
emotive	equator	explanatory
emphatic ally	equip ped	explicit
empirical ly	equipment	explode
employ ed	equipping	explore d
employee	equivalence	explorer
employer	equivalent	exploring
employment	erase d	explosion
emulsion ed	eraser	explosive
enable d	erode	exponent
enabling	erosion	export
enact	erotic ally	expose d
enamel led	erratic ally	exposure
enamelling	erroneous ly	exquisite
enamour ed	erupt ed	exterior
encamp ed	eruption	exterminate
encase d	escape d	external ly
enchanting	escarpment	extinct ion
encircle d	establish es	extinguish ed
enclose d	established	extinguisher
enclosure	establishment	extract ion
encounter ed	estate	extractor
encourage d	estrange d	extraordinarily
encouragement	eternal ly	extraordinary
encroach es	evacuate	extrapolate
encroached	evacuation	extravagance
encyclopedia	evacuee	extravagant
endanger ed	evade	extravaganza
endear ed	evaluate	extreme ly
endearment	evaluation	extrusion
endorse d	evaporate	exuberance
endow ed	evaporation	exuberant

* * *

eventual	
evergreen	
everyday	
everyone	
everything	
everywhere	
evidence	
evident	
excavate	
excellence	
excellent	
excelling	
exception	
excessive	
exchequer	
execute	
exemption	
*exercise practice / use	
*exercise d take	
exercise / use	
*exorcise d cast out	
devil	
expectant	
expected	
expelling	
expensive	
exporter	
expressing	
expression	
expressive	
exquisite	
extended	
extending	
extension	
extensive	
external ly	
extravert / extrovert	

* * * *   * *

expectancy -ies	
expectantly	
expectation	
expedition	
expeditious	
expendable	
expenditure	
experiment	
experimenter	
experimental ly	
experimentation	
explanation	
exploitation	
exploration	
exponential ly	
exposition	
expressionism	
externally	
extraversion /	
extroversion	
extremity -ies	
exultation	

*-immigration coming
into a country to live
there

*-immigrant person who
comes to live in a country

*-immigrate come to live
in a country

See also E
-on page 65 ▷

for H . . .
see page 40 ▷

for I . .
see page 41 ▷

for Scots: e-r
is on page 245 ▷

In these words you can hear the vowel sound **e** as in *elephant*

F

*

fed
fell
*felled cut down
*felt did feel / type of
cloth
fence d
fend
fetch es
fetched
fête

fleck ed
fled
flesh ed
flex es
flexed

French
fresh
fret ted
friend

phlegm

**

feather
feldspar
fellow
ferment
ferret ed
ferry -ies
ferried
fester ed
festive
*feta cheese
*fetter ed chain

fledgeling / fledgling
Flemish

foretell
forget
forwent / forewent

freckles
Frenchman
[Frenchmen]
frenzy -ies
frenzied
fretful ly
fretsaw
fretted
fretting
friendly
friendship

pheasant

***

February
federal ly
fellowship
feminine
ferreted
ferreting
festival

fiesta

flexible
fluorescence
fluorescent

forensic
forever
forgetful ly
forgetting

Frenchwoman
[Frenchwomen]
frenetic ally
freshwater
fretfully
friendliness

phonetic ally

**** *****

February
federally
federation
festivity -ies

fidelity

flexibility
fluorescence
fluorescent

forgetfully
forget-me-not

frenetically

phonetically

for th . . .
see page 52

for Scots: e-r
is on page 246

Here the first letter 'e' has a short 'i' sound.	
ferocious	ferocity

G

*

gem
get
[got]

glen

guess
*guessed did guess
*guest person invited

jest
jet ted

In these words 'e' has a neutral sound.
geranium
guerilla / guerrilla

**

gazelle

general ly
generous
gentile
gentle
gently
gesture d
getting

ghetto es / s

jealous
jelly -ies
jellied
jemmy -ies
jester
jetted
jetty -ies

***

gelatine / gelatin
general ly
generalise d
    ze
generate
generous
genetic ally
gentleman
gentlemen
genuine
gestation
getaway

jealousy -ies
jellyfish
jettison ed

**** ******

generalisation
    zation
generalise d
    ze
generally
generation
generator
generosity
genetically
geriatric
gesticulate

for Scots: e-r
is on page 246

In these words you can hear the vowel sound *e* as in elephant

39

*	**	***	**** **
head	head-dress es	haematite / hematite	hectically
health	headed	haemorrhage /	helically
hedge d	heading	hemorrhage d	helicopter
held	headlamp		helter-skelter
hell	headland	headmaster	hereditary
helm	headlight	headmistress es	heredity
help ed	headline d	headquarters	heretical ly
hem med	headphones	headwaters	heroism
hemp	healthy -ier, -iest	healthier	hesitation
hen	heather	healthiest	heterosexual
hence	heaven	heavier	hexagonal ly
Herr [Herren]	heavy -ier, -iest	heaviest	
	heckle d	heavily	hysterically
	heckling	heaviness	
	hectare	heavyweight	
	hectic ally	hectically	
	hedgehog	helical ly	
	hedgerow	heliport	
	hedging	helmeted	
	hefty -ier, -iest	helpfully	
	heifer	hemisphere	
	hello	heraldry	
	helmet ed	heresy -ies	
	helper	heretic	
	helpful ly	heritage	
	helping	*heroin drug	
	helpless	*heroine female hero	
	hemming	hesitate	
	henceforth	hexagon	
	herald		
	*heron large bird	hysterics	
	*Herren German men		
	herring		
	herself		
	himself		

for Scots: e-r is on page 247 ▷

> **Here the first letter 'e' has a short 'i' sound.**
> heroic   heroically

In these words you can hear the vowel sound *e* as in elephant

I

* *

immense
impel led
impress es
impressed

incense d
indent
inept
infect
inject
inspect
instead
intend
*intense extreme
intent
*intents purposes
invent
invest

itself

* * *

impeller
impelling
impending
impregnate
impression
impressive

incentive
inception
incessant
indebted
indented
indenture d
infection
infectious
inflection
ingestion
inherent
inherit ed
injection
inspection
inspector
intensive
intention
intestine
invention
inventive
inventor
investment
investor

* * * * * *

illegible

immeasurable
immensity
impeccable
imperative
impregnable
impressionable
impressionism
impressionist

incredible
indefinitely
inedible
ineptitude
inevitable
inflexible
inheritance
inherited
inheriting
insecticide
insensitive
integrity
intelligence
intelligent
intelligible
intensify -ies
intensified
intensity -ies
intentional ly
interrogate
interrogation
investigate
investigation
investigator

irregular
irregularity -ies
irrelevance
irrelevant
irreparable

for E . . .
see page 36

for Scots: e-r
is on page 247

In these words you can hear the vowel sound **e** as in *elephant*

41

J

*	**	***	**** **
gem	generally	gelatine / gelatin	generalisation
	generous	generally	zation
jest	gentle	generalise d	generalise d
jet ted	gently	ze	ze
	gesture d	generate	generally
		generous	generation
	jealous	genetic ally	generator
	jelly -ies	gentleman	genetically
	jellied	gentlemen	gesticulate
	jemmy -ies	genuine	
	jester	gestation	
	jetted		
	jetty -ies	**jealousy** -ies	
		jellyfish	
		jeopardise d	
		ze	
		jettison ed	

for dr . . .
see page 34

for Scots: e-r
is on page 248

K

*	**	***	**** *
kelp	**Kelvin / kelvin**	**kinetic** ally	**kinetically**
kept	**kennel**		
ketch es	**kestrel**		
	ketchup		
knelt	**kettle**		

for C . . .
see page 33

for Scots: e-r
is on page 248

for Qu . . .
see page 47

In these words you can hear the vowel sound **e** as in elephant

L

*

*lead metal
*leant did lean
leaped / leapt
*led showed / shown
the way
ledge
left
leg ged
lend
*[lent] did lend
length
lens es
*Lent the 40 days
before Easter
less
let
[let]
let's

**

lament
lapel

leather ed
lectern
lecture d
ledger
legend
leggings
leisure d
lemon
lengthen ed
lengthy -ier, -iest
lentil
leopard
leper
*lessen ed make less
lesser
*lesson period of
instruction
letter ed
letting
lettuce
level led
levy -ies
levied

***

Lebanese
Lebanon
lecturer
legacy -ies
legendary
legislate
lemonade
leprechaun
leprosy
lesbian
lessening
lethargy
letterbox es
lettering
levelling
lexicon
lesbok
libretto [libretti]
lieutenant

****

legendary
legislation
legislative
legislator
legislature
levitation

*for Scots: e-r
is on page 248* ▷

Here the first letter 'e' has a short 'i' sound.

legality -ies   legitimate
legato   lethargic

In these words you can hear the vowel sound *e* as in elephant

M

*	**	***	**** **
meant	many	majestic ally	majestically
melt			
[molten]	meadow	measurement	mechanism
men	measure d	measuring	medically
mend	*medal award /	mechanise d	medication
mesh es	memento	ze	medieval
meshed	*meddle d interfere	meddlesome	meditation
mess es	*meddler person who	medical ly	Mediterranean
messed	interferes	medicine	melancholy
met	meddling	meditate	Melanesia
	medicine	megaphone	melanoma
	*medlar fruit	megaton	memorable
	medley	melody -ies	memorandum
	mellow ed	membership	meningitis
	melon	memento es / s	menopausal
	melted	memorable	menstruation
	melting	memorise d	mentality -ies
	member	ze	metabolic
	membrane	memory -ies	metabolism
	memo	meniscus es / -i	metallurgy
	memoirs	menopause	metamorphic
	menace d	menstruate d	metamorphosis -es
	mental ly	mentally	Methodism
	mention ed	merited	methylated
	menu	meriting	metrically
	merit ed	merrily	metrication
	merry -ier, -iest	merriment	metropolitan
	message	mesmerise d	
	Messieurs	ze	millennium
	messy -ier, -iest	messenger	[millennia]
	*metal mineral	metaphor	
	substance	Methodist	molecular
	metalled	metrical ly	
	method	metricate	
	metric ally	metronome	
	*mettle courage	Mexican	
		Mexico	
	misdealt		
	misled	momentum	
	misspell ed		
	[misspelt]		
	misspend		*for Scots: e-r is on page 249* ▷
	[misspent]		

Here the first letter 'e' has a short 'i' sound.

mechanic ally	meridian
melodic ally	methodical ly
melodious	meticulous
memorial	metropolis es
meniscus es / -i	mnemonic

In these words you can hear the vowel sound **e** as in elephant.

N

*	**	***	**** *
knelt	**necklace**	nebula	**necessarily**
	nectar	nebulous	**necessary**
neck ed	**neglect**	necessary	**necessity** -ies
nest	**nephew**	nectarine	**neglectfully**
net ted	**nestle** d	negative	**negligible**
next	**nestling**	**neglectful** ly	**nevertheless**
	netball	Netherlands	
	netted		
	netting	November	
	nettle d		
	network ed		*for Scots: e-r*
	never		*is on page 249*

Here the first letter 'e' has a short 'i' sound.

negation   negotiate   negotiation

O

*	**	***	**** *
	object	already	authentically
	obsess es		
	obsessed	authentically	**objectionable**
			obscenity -ies
	offence	**objection**	**obsessional** ly
	offend	**objective**	
		obscenity -ies	
	oppress es	**obsession**	
	oppressed	**obsessive**	
		offensive	
		oppression	
		oppressive	*for Scots: e-r*
		oppressor	*is on page 249*

In these words you can hear the vowel sound **e** as in elephant

P

*

peck ed
peg ged
pelt
pen ned
pence
pest
pet ted

phlegm

pledge d

press es
pressed

**

peasant
pebble
*pedal foot lever
pedalled
*peddle d carry and
try to sell
peddler
peddling
pegboard
pegging
pellet
pelvic
pelvis
penance
pencil led
pendant
penguin
pennant
penning
penny -ies
pension ed
pepper ed
perfect
peril
perish es
perished
perplex es
perplexed
pester ed
pestle
petal led
*petrel sea-bird
*petrol fuel
petting

pheasant

pleasant
pleasure
pledging
plenty

possess es
possessed
☛

***

pathetic ally

pedalling
pedalo s
pedestal
pedigree
pelican
penalty -ies
pendulum
penetrate
penniless
pensioner
pentagon
peppermint
percentage
perception
perceptive
perceptual ly
perfection
perilous
periscope
perpetual ly
perplexing
perspective
pessimist
pesticide
petrify -ies
petrified
petticoat

phonetic ally

plentiful ly

possession
possessive
potential ly

*precedence priority
precedent
*precedents previous
examples
precipice
predator
predatory
predicate
preferably
preference
pregnancy -ies
prejudice d
premature
premier
☛

**** **

parenthesis
[parentheses]
pathetically

pedestrian
penetration
penicillin
*peninsula land
almost surrounded
by water
*peninsular of or like
a peninsula
perceptually
perennial ly
perishable
peristalsis
perpetually
pessimistic ally

phonetically

pleasurable
plentifully

potentially

predatory
preferably
preferential ly
preparation
preposition
prepositional ly
presentable
presentation
preservation
presidential ly
professional ly
prophetically

pterodactyl

for Scots: e-r
is on page 250 ▷

In these words you can hear the vowel sound **e** as in **elephant**

P

**

precious
preface
preference
pregnant
prelude
premier
*presence being
present
present
*presents gifts
pressing
pressure d
prestige
presto
pretence
pretend
prevent
profess es
professed
progress es
progressed
project
propel led
prospect
protect
protest

***

presented
presenting
presently
president
pretended
pretentious
prevalent
prevention
preventive
procession
profession
professor
progression
progressive
projectile
projection
projector
propeller
prophetic ally
propelling
prospective
prospector
prospectus es
protected
protection
protective
protector

for Scots: e-r
is on page 250 ▷

The first letter 'e' in these words is a neutral short vowel. It is pronounced like the 'i' in 'pig'.

PH*E*NOMENAL WORDS

peculiar	petroleum	preceding	preliminary -ies	preserve d
peninsula	phenomenal ly	precipitate	prepare d	preside
peninsular	phenomenon	precipitation	preparing	presumably
perimeter	[phenomena]	predominant ly	prescribe d	presume d
peroxide	precaution	prefer red	prescription	presumptuous
petition ed	precede d	preferring	preservative	prevail ed

Q

*

quell ed
quench es
quenched
quest

**

quelling
question ed
quintet

***

*questioner person
who asks
*questionnaire set
of questions

****

questionable

R

*

read looked at
and understood
realm
red colour
rend
[rent]
rent
rest repose / ones
left over
retch es try to vomit
retched

wreck ed
wren
wrench ed
wrest seize
wretch unhappy
creature

**

ready -ier, -iest
rebel led
recess es
recessed
reckon ed
record
rector
rectum
redden ed
redder
reddest
reddish
redhead
redskin
redwood
reference
reflect
refresh es
refreshed
refuge
refuse
reggae
regret ted
reject
relent
relic
relish es
relished
remnant
render ed
renege d
rental
repel led
repent
reptile
request
rescue
resent feel angry at
resin
respect
respite
rested
restful
resting
restless
revel led
revenge d
reverence
reverend deserving
respect
Reverend title
reverent feeling or
showing reverence

rosette
☞

***

readier
readiest
readily
readiness
rebelling
rebellion
rebellious
reception
receptive
recession
recessive
recipe
recognise d
ze
recollect
recommend
reconcile d
rectangle
rectify -ies
rectified
rectory -ies
redemption
referee
reference d
reflected
reflection
reflector
reflexive
refreshment
refugee
regiment
register ed
registrar
registry -ies
regretful ly
regretted
regretting
regular
regulate
rejection
relative
relegate
relentless
relevance
relevant
remedy -ies
remedied
remember ed
remembrance
Renaissance
☞

**** **

receptacle
receptionist
recitation
recitative
recognisable
zable
recognising
zing
recognition
recollection
recommendation
reconciliation
recreation
rectangular
rectifier
referendum
reformation
regimental ly
registration
regretfully
regularity -ies
regularly
regulation
relatively
relativity
relegation
remembering
reminiscence
reminiscent
renovation
repetition
repetitive
representation
representative
represented
representing
reputable
reputation
resentfully
reservation
residential
resignation
resolution
respectable
respectfully
respectively
respiration
respiratory
restoration
resurrection
☞

*for Scots: e-r
is on page 251* ▷

48

In these words you can hear the vowel sound **e** as in **elephant**

R

**

wreckage
wrestle d
wrestler
wrestling
wretched

***

repartee
repellent
repelling
repentance
repertoire
repertory -ies
replica
represent
repression
repressive
requiem
resemblance
resemble d
resembling
resentful ly
resentment
reservoir
***residence** house
resident
***residents** occupiers
residue
resolute
resonance
resonant
respectful ly
respective
restaurant
résumé
retention
retentive
retina
retrograde
revelling
revelry -ies
revenue
reverence
***reverend** deserving
respect
***Reverend** title
***reverent** feeling or
showing reverence
reversal

rhetoric

**** **

revelation
revolution
revolutionary -ies

Here the first letter 'e' has a short 'i' sound.

R*E* FRESHING WORDS

rebound
rebuke d
recall ed
receding
receipt
receive d
receiver
receiving
reciprocal ly
reciprocate
recital
recite
reclaim ed
recline d
recoil ed
record ed
recorder
recording
recount
recourse
recover ed
recovery -ies
recruit
recur red
recurrence
recurrent
recurring
reduce d
reduction
redundancy -ies
redundant
refer red
referral
referring
refine d
refinery -ies
reform ed
refract ion
refractive
refrain ed
refrigerator
refund
refuse d
refusal
refute
regain ed
regard ed
regardless
regatta
rehearsal
rehearse d
rejoice d
rejoin ed
relate d

relation
relationship
relax es
relaxed
release d
reliable
reliability
reliance
relief
relieve d
religion
religious
reluctance
reluctant ly
rely -ies
relied
remain ed
remainder
remaining
remark ed
remarkable
remind ed
reminder
remote
removable /
removeable
removal
remove d
removing
renew ed
renewal
renown ed
repair ed
repay
[repaid]
repeal ed
repeat ed
repeating
replace d
replacement
reply -ies
replied
report ed
reporter
repose d
reprisal
reproach es
reproached
republic an
repudiate
repulsive
repute
require d
requirement

research es
researched
researcher
reserve d
resign ed
resist ance
resistor
resolve d
resort
resource d
resources
respire d
respond
response
responsibility -ies
responsible
responsive
restore d
restrain ed
restraint
restrict ion
result ed
resultant
resulting
resume d
resuscitate
resuscitation
retain ed
retard ed
retire d
retirement
retort
retreat
retrieve d
retriever
return ed
returnable
returning
reveal ed
reverberate
reverse d
reversal
reversible
review ed
revise d
revision
revival
revive d
revolt
revolve d
revolver
revue
revulsion
reward

for Scots: e-r
is on page 251 ▷

S

*

*cell unit
Celt
*cent money / hundred
*cents money

chef

said
says

*scent perfume / smell

sect
*sects religious groups
self
*sell exchange for
money
[sold]
send
[sent]
*sense understandable
pattern
sensed
*sent made to go
set
[set]
*sex es male / female
sexed

shed
[shed]
shelf [shelves]
shell ed
shelved
shred ded

sketch es
sketched

sledge d
slept

smell ed
[smelt]

speck
sped
spell ed
[spelt]
spend
[spent]
spread
[spread]
☞

**

*cellar underground
storage room
Celtic
cement
*censer pan for burning
incense
*censor judge of what
may not be published
*census es official count
centaur
central ly
centre d

sceptic
sceptre d
schedule d

second
section
sector
segment
seldom
select
selfish
*seller person who
sells
semblance
senate
sending
señor
*senses means of
gaining information
*sensor detecting
device
sensual ly
sentence d
sentry -ies
sepal
separate
session
setted
settee
setter
setting
settle d
settler
settling
seven th
sever ed
several
sexist
sextet
sexual ly
sexy -ier, -iest
☞

***

celandine
celebrate
celery
celestial
cellophane
celluloid
cellulose
Celsius
cemetery -ies
centigrade
centipede
centrally
century -ies
cerebral
cerebrum

sceptical ly

secateurs
secession
secondary -ies
second-hand
secretary -ies
secular
sedative
sediment
segregate
selected
selecting
selection
selective
selector
sellotape
semaphore
semibreve
seminar
senator
señora
sensation
sensible
sensitive
sensual ly
sensuous
sentiment
sentinel
separate
September
sepulchre
serenade
sesame
settlement
seventeen th
seventy -ies
several
severance
sexism
sexual ly
☞

**** ***

celebrated
celebration
celebrity -ies
celestial
centenary -ies
centimetre
centrifugal ly
centurion
ceremony -ies

scepticism

secondary -ies
secretarial
secretary -ies
sedimentary
segregation
self-reliant
self-sufficient
semicircle
semicircular
semicolon
semi-conductor
semi-detached
semifinal
semiquaver
semolina
señorita
sensational ly
sensitivity -ies
sentimental ly
separated
separately
separation
serenity
seventieth
severity -ies
sexuality -ies
sexually

sincerity

specialisation
    zation
speciality -ies
specification
spectacular
speculation
spherically
☞

*for Scots: e-r
is on page 252* ▷

In these words you can hear the vowel sound **e** as in elephant

S

*

squelch es
squelched

stealth
stem med
stench es
*step pace / stage
*steppe dry, treeless
plain
stepped
stet
strength
stress es
stressed
stretch es
stretched
sweat
swell
[swollen]
swept

**

shedding
shellfish
shelter ed
shepherd
sheriff
sherry -ies
shredded
shredding

sledging
slender

smelter

special ly
speckle d
spectre
spectrum [spectra]
speller
spelling
spending
splendid
splendour
spreading

steady -ies
steadied
stealthy -ier, -iest
stellar
stemming
stencil led
stepping
strengthen ed
stretcher
stretching

subject
subtend
success es
suggest
suppress es
suppressed
suspect
suspend
suspense

sweater
swelter

***

skeleton

spaghetti
specialise d
     ze
specialist
specially
specify -ies
specified
specimen
spectacle
spectacles
spectator
speculate
spherical ly

steadily
steadiness
stealthier
stealthiest
stencilling
stepbrother
stepdaughter
stepfather
stepmother
stepsister
stereo s
sterilise d
     ze
stethoscope
strenuous

subjection
subjective
successful ly
succession
successive
successor
suggested
suggesting
suggestion
suggestive
suppression
surrender ed
suspected
suspension

synthetic ally

****   *******

stegosaurus es / -i
stereophonic ally
stereoscopic ally
stereotype
stereotypical ly

successfully
suggestible
susceptible

symmetrical ly
synthetically

*for Scots: e-r
is on page 252* ▷

Here the first letter 'e' has a short 'i' sound.

scenario s	secretion	sequoia
seclude d	secure d	severe ly
secrete	security -ies	specific ally

T

*

tell
[told]
tempt
ten th
tend
*tense form of verb /
stretched tight
tensed
tenth
tent
*tents more than one
tent
test
text

theft
them
then
thence
thread ed
threat

tread
[trod]
[trodden]
trek ked
trench es
trend

twelfth
twelve

**

technique
teddy -ies
telling
temper ed
tempest
template
temple
tempo s
tenant
tender ed
tendon
tendril
*tenner ten pound
note
tennis
tenon ed
*tenor male voice
tension
tepid
terrace d
terrain
terror
tested
testing
testis [testes]
tether ed
textbook
textile
texture d

themselves
threadbare
threaded
threaten ed
threshold

treadle
treasure d
treble d
trebling
trekking
trellis ed
tremble d
trembling
tremor
trendy -ier, -iest
trestle

twenty -ies

***

technical ly
technician
telegraph ed
telephone d
telescope d
televise d
temperament
temperate
temperature
temporary
temptation
tendency -ies
tenderness
tenement
tentacle
tentative
tenuous
terrapin
terrible
terribly
terrier
terrify -ies
terrified
territory -ies
terrorise d
　　　ze
terrorist
tessellate
testament
testicle
testify -ies
testified
tetanus

therapy -ies

together
torrential ly

treacherous
treachery -ies
treasury -ies
tremendous

twentieth

**** ******

pterodactyl

technically
technological ly
technology -ies
telegraphy
telepathic ally
telepathy
telephonist
telephoto
television
temperamental ly
temperature
temporarily
temporary
terrarium
terrestrial ly
territorial ly
territory -ies
terrorism
tessellation
testimonial
testimony -ies
tetrahedron

therapeutic ally

torrentially

for Scots: e-r
is on page 253

> **Here the first letter 'e' has a short 'i' sound.**
> terrific ally　　　thesaurus es / -i

In these words you can hear the vowel sound **e** as in elephant

U

*

**

unless

***

****

V

*	**	***	**** *
Venn	**vector**	**vegetable**	**vasectomy** -ies
vent	**Velcro**	**venison**	
vest	**velvet**	**ventilate**	**vegetation**
vetted	**vending**	**ventricle**	**Venezuela**
vex es	**vendor**	**verify** -ies	**ventilation**
vexed	**vengeance**	verified	**ventilator**
	venom	**veteran**	**ventriloquist**
	venture d		**verification**
	very		**veterinary**
	vessel		
	vestry -ies		
	veteran		
	vetted		*for Scots: e-r*
	vetting		*is on page 254*

In these words the first 'e' is a neutral vowel.
velocity -ies   veranda / verandah

W

*

*rest repose / ones left
over
*retch es try to vomit
retched

wealth
web bed
wed ded
[wed]
wedge d
weft
*weld join metal by
heat
well
*welled gushed
Welsh
wench es
went
wept
west
*wet ted, ter, test
make wet / not dry
[wet]

whelk
whelp ed
when
whence
*whet ted sharpen

wreck ed
wren
wrench es
wrenched
*wrest seize
*wretch es unhappy
creature

**

waistcoat

wealthy -ier, -iest
weapon
*weather conditions
outside / survive
bad weather
weathered
webbing
wedded
wedding
wedging
Wednesday
welcome d
welfare
Welshman
[Welshmen]
western
westward
wetsuit
*wetted made wet
wetter
wettest
*wetting making wet

*whether if
*whetted sharpened
*whetting sharpening

wreckage
wrestle d
wrestler
wrestling
wretched

***

weathercock
weathering
weatherman
[weathermen]
weathervane
wellington
westerly

whenever

****

weatherwoman
[weatherwomen]

*for Scots: e-r
is on page 255*

X

*

**

X-ray

***

**** *

xenophobia
xenophobic

In these words you can hear the vowel sound **e** as in **elephant**

Y

*
yell ed
yelp ed
yen
yes
yet

* *
yelling
yellow

yourself
yourselves

* * *
yesterday

* * * *

for Scots: e-r
is on page 255 ▷

Z

*
Zen
zest

* *
zealot
zealous
zebra
zenith
zephyr

* * *

* * * * *
xenophobia
xenophobic

In these words you can hear the vowel sound *e* as in *elephant*

A

*	**	***	**** *
abyss es	**abysmal** ly	**ability** -ies
		abysmally
acquit ted	**acquittal**	
	acquitted	**additional** ly
admit ted	**acquitting**	**administer** ed
adrift	**acrylic**	**administrate**
		administration
affix es	**addicted**	**administrator**
affixed	**addiction**	
afflict	**addictive**	**affiliate**
	addition	
amid	**admission**	**alliteration**
amidst	**admittance**	
amiss	**admitted**	**applicable**
	admitting	
assist		**arithmetic**
	affliction	
		-assimilate
	agility	**assimilation**
		astigmatism
	ambition	
	ambitious	**auxiliary** -ies
	arisen	
	***assistance** help	
	assistant	
	***assistants** helpers	

*for Scots: i-r
is on page 242*

| | | **attribute** | |

In these words you can hear the vowel sound i as in pig

B

*

*__been__ past form of 'be'

__bib__
__bid__
[bade]
[bid]
[bidden]
__big__
__bill__
*__billed__ did bill
*__bin__ container
__binge__
__bit__
__bitch__ es
bitched

__blink__ ed
__bliss__

__brick__ ed
__bridge__ d
__brim__ med
__bring__
[brought]
__brink__
__brisk__

*__build__ construct
[built]

**

*-__bazaar__ Eastern market

__became__
__because__
__become__
[became]
[become]
__befall__
[befell]
[befallen]
__before__
__befriend__
__begin__
[began]
[begun]
__behalf__
__behave__ d
__behead__
__beheld__
__behind__
__behold__
[beheld]
__belief__
__believe__ d
__belong__ ed
__beloved__
__below__
__beneath__
__bereave__ d
[bereft]
__beseech__ es
beseeched
[besought]
__beset__
[beset]
__beside__
__besides__
__besiege__ d
__besought__
__bestow__ ed
__betray__ ed
__between__
__betwixt__
__beware__
__bewitch__ es
bewitched
__beyond__
☞

***

__becoming__
__befallen__
__beforehand__
__beginner__
__beginning__
__behaviour__
__belonging__
__beloved__
__besetting__
__bewilder__ ed

__biblical__
__bickering__
__bikini__
__bishopric__

__blissfully__
bitch
__bricklayer__
__brigadier__

__busier__
__busiest__
__busily__
__businessman__
[businessmen]
__businesswoman__
[businesswomen]

**** *

__beatitude__
__belligerent__
__benevolent__
__bewilderment__

__bibliography__ -ies
__binocular__
__binoculars__

__Bolivia__

for Scots: i-r
is on page 243 ▷

In these words you can hear the vowel sound i as in pig

* *

bicker ed
bidden
bidding
bigger
biggest
bilious
billiards
billion
billow ed
biscuit
bishop
***bitten** past form of
'bite'
bitter
***bittern** bird
***bizarre** peculiar

blinkered
blinkers
blissful ly
blister ed
blizzard

Brazil
breeches
bridging
brigade
brilliance
brilliant
brimming
bringing
bristle d
bristling
***Britain** country
British
***Briton** British person
brittle

builder
building
business
busy -ies
busied
busy -ier, -iest

*for Scots: i-r
is on page 243* ▷

In these words you can hear the vowel sound **i** as in **pig**

C

*	**	***	**** *
chick	cement	capricious	calligraphy
chid			capillary -ies
chill ed	chicken ed	celestial	
chimp	chidden	ceramic	celebrity -ies
chin	chiffchaff		celestial
chink	chiffon	charisma	certificate
chintz	chilblain	chickenpox	
chip ped	children	chicory	Christianity
	*Chile country	chimpanzee	chrysanthemum
cinch es	*chilli hot spice	chiselling	
	*chilly -ier, -iest cold	chivalrous	ciliary
click ed	chimney	chivalry	citizenship
cliff	chipboard	christening	civilisation
cling	chipmunk	chrysalis	zation
[clung]	chipping		
clink ed	chisel led	cigarette	clinically
clip ped	christen ed	*cilia more than one	
	christening	cilium	commissioner
crib bed	Christian	ciliary	conditional ly
cringe d	Christmas	cilium [cilia]	conditioner
crisp		cinema	configuration
crypt	cigar	cinnamon	coniferous
	cinder	citizen	considerable
cyst	cirrus	civilian	considerate
	cistern	civilise d	consideration
kick ed	citrus	ze	consistency -ies
kid ded	city -ies	civilly	conspicuous
kids	civic		conspiracy -ies
kill ed	civil ly		conspirator
kiln		clinical ly	constituency -ies
kilt	clinic ally	clitoris	constituent
king	clipper		contingency -ies
kink ed	clipping	collision	continual ly
kiss ed		commission ed	continuance
kit ted		commitment	continuation
	commit ted	committed	continuous
	conflict	committee	continuum
	conscript	committing	contributed
	consist	condition ed	
	convict	conscription	criminally
	convince d	consider ed	critically
		consistent	criticism
	create	consisting	
	cremate	constriction	curriculum [curricula]
	cribbing	continual ly	
	cricket	continue d	cylindrical
	crimson	contribute	cynically
	crinkle d	conviction	cynicism
	crinkly	☞	
	cripple d		kilometre
	crippling		kindergarten
	crisscross ed		
	critic ally		
	crystal		
	☞		

for Qu . . .
see page 83 ▷

for Scots: i-r
is on page 244 ▷

In these words you can hear the vowel sound i as in pig   **59**

C

**

*cygnet young swan
*cymbals discs to
clash
cystic

kidded
kidding
kidnap ped
kidney
killer
killing
kindle d
kindling
kingdom
kinky -ier, -iest
kipper
kissing
kitchen
kitted
kitten
kitting

*signet seal / ring

*symbols signs

***

created
creating
creation
creative
cremation
crescendo s
criminal ly
crinoline
critical ly
criticise d
        ze
crystalline
crystallise d
        ze

cylinder
cynical ly
Cypriot
cystitis

kidnapper
kidnapping
kilogram
kimono s

for Qu . . .
see page 83 ▷

for Scots: i-r
is on page 244 ▷

In these words you can hear the vowel sound i as in pig

D

*	**	***	**** **
did	debate	deceitful ly	decapitate
dig ged	decamp ed	December	deceitfully
[dug]	decay ed	deception	deciduous
dim med	*decayed did decay	deceptive	deficiency -ies
din	decease d	decipher ed	deliberate
ding	deceit	decision	deliberately
dip ped	deceive d	decisive	delightfully
disc / disk	decide	deduction	delinquency
dish es	declare d	deductive	delirious
dished	decline d	defeated	deliverance
ditch es	decrease d	defective	delivery -ies
ditched	decree d	defector	democracy -ies
	decry -ies	defendant	demonstrative
drift	decried	defender	demoralise d
drill ed	deduce d	defensive	ze
drink	defeat	defiance	denomination
[drank]	defect	defiant	denominator
[drunk]	defence	deficient	dependable
drip ped	defend	deflection	dependency -ies
	define d	deletion	deposited
	deflect	deliberate	depositing
	deform ed	delicious	depreciate
	defy -ies	delighted	depreciation
	defied	delightful ly	derivative
	degree	deliver ed	desirable
	delay ed	delusion	despicable
	delete	demanded	deteriorate
	delight	demeanour	deterioration
	demean ed	demolish es	determination
	demand	demolished	determining
	demobbed	denial	developer
	denote	department	developing
	denounce d	departure	development
	deny -ies		
	denied	*dependant person	dictatorial ly
	depart	who depends	dictionary -ies
	depend	*dependants people	differential
	deport	who depend	differently
	depress es	depended	difficulty -ies
	depressed	*dependence	digestible
	deprive d	reliance	digitally
	derail ed	*dependent relying /	dilapidated
	derive d	hanging	diphtheria
	descend	deposit ed	diplodocus
	*descent way down	depression	diplomacy
	describe d	depressive	diplomatic ally
	*desert leave	descendant	directory -ies
	deserve d	descended	☛
	design ed	describing	
	desire d	description	
	despair ed	descriptive	
	*despatch es send off	deserted	
	despatched	designer	
	despise d	destroyer	
	despite	destruction	*for Scots: i-r*
	*dessert sweet dish	destructive	*is on page 245*
	destroy ed	☛	
	☛		

In these words you can hear the vowel sound **i** as in pig

61

D

**

detach es
detached
detain ed
detect
deter red
detest
detract
*device gadget / plan
*devise d invent /
work out
devote
devour ed

dictate
diction
didn't
differ ed
difference
different
diffuse d
digest
digger
digging
digit
dimmer
dimming
dimple d
*dinghy -ies small boat
*dingy -ier, -iest dull
dinner
diphthong
dipper
dipping
dipstick
direct
disarm ed
discard
discern ed
discharge d
disclose d
disco s
discount
*discreet careful not
to embarrass
*discrete separate
*discus es heavy disc
to throw in games
*discuss es debate
*discussed debated
disdain ed
disease d
disgrace d
disguise d
*disgust strong dislike
☞

***

detachment
detection
detective
detector
detention
detergent
determine d
*deterrence prevention
by causing fear
deterrent
*deterrents more than
one deterrent
deterring
develop ed
devoted
devotion

dictation
dictator
dictionary -ies
difference
different
differently
difficult
diffusion
digestion
digital ly
dignify -ies
dignified
dignity -ies
dilemma
dimension
diminish es
diminished
diploma
diplomat
directed
direction
directive
directly
director
disable d
disabling
disagree d
disappear ed
disappoint
disapprove d
disaster
disastrous
disbelief
☞

**** **

disability -ies
disablement
disadvantage d
disagreeable
disagreement
disappearance
disappointment
disapproval
disarmament
disciplinarian
discovery -ies
discredited
discrepancy -ies
discriminate
discrimination
disgracefully
disinfectant
disintegrate
disloyally
disloyalty
disobedience
disobedient
disorganise d
        ze
disposition
disproportion
disqualify -ies
disqualified
dissatisfaction
dissatisfy -ies
dissatisfied
dissimilar
distinguishable
distribution
distributive
distributor
diversity
divinity -ies
divisibility
divisible

dysentery
dyslexia

*for Scots: i-r
is on page 245* ▷

In these words you can hear the vowel sound **i** as in **pig**

D

** **

dishcloth
dishes
diskette
dislike d
dislodge d
disloyal ly
dismal ly
dismay ed
dismiss ed
dismount
disown ed
dispatch es despatch /
message
dispatched
dispel led
dispense d
disperse d
displace d
display ed
displease d
dispose d
disprove d
[disproven]
dispute
disrupt
dissect
*dissent disagreement
dissolve d
distance d
distant
distil led
distinct
distort
distract
distress es
distressed
district
distrust
disturb ed
disused
dither ed
ditto
divan
diverge d
diverse
divert
divide
divine d
divorce d
dizzy -ier, -iest
☛

*** ***

disciple
discipline d
discomfort
discontent
discordant
discothèque
discourage d
discover ed
discredit ed
discretion
discussing
discussion
disgraceful ly
disgusting
dishearten ed
dishevelled
dishonest
dishwasher
disinfect
dislodging
disloyally
disloyalty
dismally
dismantle d
dismissal
dismissing
dispelling
dispenser
displacement
displeasure
disobey ed
disorder ed
disposal
disproven
disregard
disruption
disruptive
dissension
dissenter
distilling
distinction
distinctive
distinguish es
distinguished
distortion
distraction
distractor
distressing
distribute
disturbance
divided
dividend
dividers
dividing
division
divisor
divorcee
☛

for Scots: i-r
is on page 245 ▷

In these words you can hear the vowel sound **i** as in pig

D

** ――

dribble d
dribbling
drifted
driftwood
drinker
drinking
dripping
driven
drizzle d
drizzling

dwindle d
dwindling

dick

*-decade ten years

***

dynasty -ies
dysentery
dyslexic / dyslectic
dystrophy -ies

*for Scots: i-r
is on page 245* ▷

In these words you can hear the vowel sound i as in pig

E

*

*accept take something
offered

*affect alter

éclair
eclipse d

*effect result / bring
about

eject

elect
élite
ellipse
elope d
elude

embark ed
embed ded
embrace d
embroil ed
emerge d
emit ted
employ ed

enact
encamp ed
encase d
enchant
enclose d
encroach es
encroached
endear ed
endorse d
endow ed
endure d
enfold
enforce d
engage d
England
English
engrave d
engross es
engrossed
engulf ed
enjoy ed
enlarge d
enlist
enough
enquire / inquire d
enrage d
enrich es
enriched
enrol led
☛

for H . . .
see page 71 ▷

for I . . .
see page 72 ▷

* *

eccentric ally

edition

effective
efficient

Egyptian

ejection
ejector

elaborate
elastic ally
election
electors
electric ally
electrode
electron
eleven th
*elicit ed draw out
élitist
*elusive hard to find

embankment
embargo es
embargoed
embarrass es
embarrassed
embedded
embedding
embellish es
embellished
embezzle d
embody -ies
embodied
embroider ed
emergence
emission
emitted
emitter
emitting
emotion
emotive
emphatic ally
employee
employer
employment
emulsion ed
☛

* * *

eccentrically
ecclesiastical ly
ecology
economy -ies

effectively
effectiveness
efficiency
efficiently

elaborate
elaboration
elastically
elasticity
electoral ly
electorate
electrical ly
electrician
electricity
electrocute
electrolysis
electrolyse d
    ze
electrolyte
electrolytic ally
electromagnetic ally
electronic ally
elicited
eliciting
eliminate
elimination
élitism
Elizabethan
elliptical ly

emancipate
emancipation
embarrassing
embarrassment
embroidery
emergency -ies
emotional ly
emphatically
empirical ly
☛

* * * *   * * * *

In these words you can hear the vowel sound i as in pig

E

**

enslave d
*ensure d make certain
entail ed
entire
entrance d
entrench es
entrenched
entrust / intrust

equate
equip ped

erase d
erect
erode
erupt

escape d
escort
estate
esteem ed
estrange d

evade
event
evict
evoke d
evolve d

exact
exalt
exceed
excel led
*except not including
excess es
exchange d
excite
exclaim ed
exclude
excrete
excuse d
exempt
exert
exhaust
exhort
exist
☞

***

enable d
enabling
enamel led
enamour ed
enchanting
encircle d
enclosure
encounter ed
encourage d
endanger ed
endearment
endeavour ed
endurance
enforcement
engagement
Englishman
engraving
enigma
enjoying
enjoyment
enlighten ed
enormous
enquiry / inquiry -ies
enrolling
enrolment
entangle d
entirely
entitle d
entrancing
enveloping
envisage d

equation
equator
equipment
equipping

eraser
erection
erosion
erotic ally
erratic ally
erupted
eruption
☞

**** ****

enamelling
encouragement
encyclopedia
Englishwoman
[Englishwomen]
enthusiasm
enthusiast
enthusiastic ally
enumerate
environment
environmental ly

equality
equivalence
equivalent

erotically
erratically
erroneous ly

especially
essentially
establishment

eternally

evacuate
evacuation
evacuee
evaluate
evaluation
evangelism
evangelist
evaporate
evaporation
eventually

exaggerate
exaggeration
examination
exceedingly
exceptionally
excitedly
exclamation
exclusively
excruciating
☞

for H . . .
see page 71 ▷

for I . . .
see page 72 ▷

In these words you can hear the vowel sound i as in pig

E

* *

expand
expanse
expect
expel led
expense
explain ed
explode
exploit
explore d
export
expose d
express es
expressed
extend
extent
extinct
extract
extreme
exult

*insure d protect against
loss

* * *

escarpment
essential ly
establish es
established

eternal ly

evasion
eventual ly

exactly
exalted
examine d
example
excellent
excelling
exception
excessive
exchequer
excited
excitement
exciting
exclusion
exclusive
excretion
excursion
exemption
exertion
exhausted
exhaustion
exhibit ed
existed
existence
exotic ally
expanded
expanding
expansion
expansive
expectant
expected
expelling
expensive
explaining
explicit
explorer
exploring
explosion
explosive
exponent
exposure
expressing
expression
expressive
exquisite
☛

* * * *   * * *

executive
exemplary
exhibited
exhibiting
exhilarating
exotically
expandable
expectantly
expediency
expedient
expenditure
experience d
experiment
experimental ly
explanatory
exploratory
exterior
exterminate
externally
extinguisher
extraordinarily
extraordinary
extrapolate
extravagance
extravagant
extravaganza
exuberance
exuberant

for H . . .
see page 71 ▷

for I . . .
see page 72 ▷

In these words you can hear the vowel sound i as in pig

E

* * *

extended
extending
extension
extensive
external ly
extinction
extinguish es
extinguished
extraction
extractor
extremely
extremist
extrusion

*illicit illegal
*illusive deceptive

for H . . .
see page 71 ▷

for I . . .
see page 72 ▷

F

*	*** ***	*** * ***	*** * * ***
fib bed	**fibbing**	**familiar**	**facilitate**
fifth	**fiction**		**facility** -ies
fig	**fiddle** d	**ferocious**	**familiarity**
fill ed	**fiddler**		
film ed	**fiddling**	*fiancé man engaged	**ferocity**
filth	**fiddly**	to be married	**fertility**
fin ned	**fidget** ed	*fiancée woman	
finch es	**fifteen** th	engaged to be married	**fidelity**
Finn	**fifty** -ies	**fictional**	**figurative**
fiord / fjord	**figure** d	**fictitious**	**financially**
fish es	**filler**	**fidgeted**	**financier**
fished	**fillet**	**fidgeting**	
fist	**filling**	**fidgety**	**frenetically**
fit ted	**filly** -ies	**fiesta**	
fix es	**filter** ed	**fiftieth**	phenomena
fixed	**filthy** -ier, -iest	**filament**	phenomenally
fizz es	**finale**	**filthiest**	phenomenon
fizzed	**finance** d	**filtration**	philatelist
	finger ed	**financial** ly	philosophically
flick ed	*finish es end	**fingernail**	philosophy-ies
flinch es	**finished**	**fingerprint**	physically
fling	**Finland**	**fingertip**	physiologically
[flung]	*Finnish language	**finicky** -ier, -iest	physiology
flint	spoken by Finns / of	**finishing**	
flip ped	or from Finland	**fisherman**	
flit ted	**fiord / fjord**		
☞	☞	**flamingo** es / -s	for Scots: i-r
is on page 246 ▷
		☞	

for th . . .
see page 90 ▷

In these words you can hear the vowel sound i as in pig

F

*

fridge
frill ed
fringe d
frisk ed

* *

fiscal
*fisher man who fishes
fishes
fishing
fission
*fissure d crack
fitness
fitted
fitting
fixture
fizzle d
fizzy -ier, -iest

flicker ed
flimsy -ies
flipper
flipping
flitted
flitting

forbid
[forbade]
[forbidden]
forgive
[forgave]
[forgiven]

friction
frigate
frigid
fritter ed
frizzy -ier, -iest

fulfil led

physics
physique

* * *

forbidden
forbidding
forgiven
forgiveness

frenetic ally
frivolous

fulfilling

physically
physician
physicist

for th . . .
see page 90 ▷

for Scots: i-r
is on page 246 ▷

In these words you can hear the vowel sound i as in pig

G

*

gift
gig
*gild paint with gold
*[gilt] gilded
gills
gin
gist
give
[gave]
[given]

glib
glimpse d
glint

grid
*grill ed cook by
direct heat /
bars for cooking /
food so cooked
*grille protecting set
of bars in door or
window
grim
grin ned
grip ped
grit ted

*guild association
*guilt responsibility
for doing wrong

gym

jib bed
jig ged
jilt
jinx es
jinxed

* *

giggle d
giggling
gilded
*gilder person who
gilds
gimlet
ginger ed
gingham
gipsy / gypsy -ies
giraffe
given
giver
giving

glimmer ed
glisten ed
glitter ed

grenade
griddle
grimace d
grinning
gripping
*grisly -ier, iest horrible
gristle
gritting
grizzle d
grizzling
*grizzly -ier, iest grey /
bear

*guilder Dutch coin
guilty -ier, -iest
*guinea twenty one
old shillings
*Guinea West African
country
guitar

gymnast
gymslip
gypsy / gipsy -ies

jibbing
jiffy
jigging
jigsaw
jingled
jingling

* * *

genetic ally

gibberish
Gibraltar
gingerbread

glycerine

*gorilla ape

*guerrilla / guerilla
agent of political
violence
guillemot
guillotine d

gymkhana
gymnastics
gymnosperm

* * * * * *

gelatinous
genetically
geographical ly
geography -ies
geological ly
geology
geometrical ly
geometry -ies
geranium

gymnasium

*for Scots: i-r
is on page 246* ▷

In these words you can hear the vowel sound i as in pig

H

*	**	***	**** **
hid	hiccup ped	habitual ly	habitually
hill	hidden		
hilt	hillside	heroic ally	hereditary
*him that male	hilltop		heredity
individual	himself	hiccupping	heroically
hinge d	hinder ed	hickory	
hint	hindrance	hideous	higgledy-piggledy
hip	Hindu	historic ally	hilarious
his	hissing	history -ies	Himalayas
hiss ed	hither	hitherto	Hinduism
hit	hitting		hippopotamus es / -i
[hit]		hypnosis	historian
hitch es	hymnal	hypnotic ally	historical ly
hitched		hypnotise d	
		ze	hypnotically
*hymn song with		hypocrite	hypnotism
verses sung in church		hysterics	hypocrisy
			hypocritical ly
			hysteria
			hysterical ly

I

*

if

ill

imp

*in not outside
inch es
inched
ink
*inn small hotel

is

it
itch es
itched
*its belonging to it
*it's it is

◁ for E . . .
see page 65

◁ for H . . .
see page 71

**

*ensure d make sure

igloo
ignite
ignore d

illness es

image d
immense
immerse d
immune
impact
impair ed
impart
impasse
impede d
impel led
implore d
imply -ies
implied
import
impose d
impress es
impressed
imprint
improve d
impulse
impure

incense d
incest
*incite encourage
strong feeling or
action
incline d
include
income
increase d
incur red
indeed
indent
index es
[indices]
indexed
indoors
induce d
indulge d
inept
inert

☞

***

*elicit ed draw out
*elusive hard to find

idiom
idiot

igneous
ignition
ignorance
ignorant

*ileum part of
intestine
*ilium [ilia] part of
hip-bone
illegal ly
*illicit illegal
*illusion false belief or
appearance
*illusive deceptive
illustrate

imagery
imagine d
imitate
immature
immediate
immersion
immigrant
immigrate
immobile
immortal ly
immunise d
ze
impartial ly
impatience
impatient
impeachment
impeller
impelling
imperfect
impetus es
implement
impolite
importance
important
impotence
impotent
impregnate
impression
impressive
imprison ed
☞

**** ***

idiomatic ally
idiotic ally

iguanodon

illegally
illegible
illiterate
illogical ly
illuminate
illumination
illustration
illustrative
illustrator
illustrious

imaginary
imagination
imaginative
imitation
immaculate
immeasurable
immediate
immediately
immensity
immigration
immortality
immortally
immovable
immunisation
zation
immunity
impartial ly
impassable
impeccable
imperative
imperial ly
imperialism
impermeable
impersonal
impersonate
impersonation
impertinent
impervious
implacable
implication
impossibility
impossible
☞

for Scots: i-r
is on page 247 ▷

In these words you can hear the vowel sound i as in pig

I

** | *** | **** ***

infant
infect
infer red
infirm
inflame d
inflate
inflict
inform ed
ingot
inhale d
inject
injure d
inland
in-law
inlet
inmate
innate
inner
innings
input
inquest
inquire / **enquire** d
insane
inscribe d
insect
insert
*****inshore** near the shore
inside
*****insight** understanding
insist
inspect
inspire d
instal led
*****instance** example
instant
*****instants** moments
instead
instinct
instruct
insult
*****insure** d protect against loss
intact
intake
intend
*****intense** very strong
intent
*****intents** purposes
interest
into
intrigue d
intrude
intrust / **entrust**
☞

impromptu s
improper
improvement
improving
improvise d
impudence
impudent
impulsive

incarnate
incentive
incessant
*****incidence** rate of happening
incident
*****incidents** events
incision
incisor
included
including
inclusion
inclusive
incoming
incomplete
incorrect
increasing
incurring
indebted
indented
indenture d
India
Indian
indicate
indifferent
indignant
indigo
indirect
indiscreet
indistinct
induction
inductive
indulgence
indulgent
industry -ies
inertia
infamous
infancy
infantile
infantry
infection
infectious
inference
inferring
☞

impractical
impregnable
impressionable
impressionism
impressionist
improvisation
impunity
impurity -ies

inability
inaccessible
inaccuracy -ies
inaccurate
inadequate
inappropriate
inattentive
inaudible
inaugural
inauguration
incapable
incidental ly
inclination
incognito
incompatible
incomprehensible
incongruity -ies
incongruous
inconsistent
inconvenience
inconvenient
incorporate d
increasingly
incredible
incubator
incubation
incurable
indecisive
indefinitely
independence
independent
indicated
indication
indicator
indifferent
indigestible
indigestion
indignation
indiscretion
indispensable
☞

for E . . .
see page 65

for H . . .
see page 71

for Scots: i-r
is on page 247 ▷

In these words you can hear the vowel sound **i** as in **pig**

**	***	**** ***
invade	infinite	individually
invent	inflation	individualism
inverse	inflection	individuality
invert	influenced	indivisible
invest	informally	Indonesia
invite	informant	industrially
invoiced	informer	industrialisation
involved	infra-red	zation
inward	infrequent	industrialised
	ingenious	ze
Iran	inhabited	industrialist
Iraq	inhaler	industrious
	inherent	inedible
Islam	inherited	ineffective
isn't	inhibit	ineffectually
Israel	inhuman	inefficiency
issued	initialled	inefficient
isthmus	injection	ineptitude
	injury -ies	inequality -ies
itself	injustice	inevitable
	innermost	inexpensive
	innkeeper	inexperienced
	*innocence freedom	infatuated
	from guilt	infatuation
	innocent	inferior
	*innocents people who	inferiority
	have done no wrong	infinitesimally
	inquiry / enquiry -ies	infinitive
	inscription	infinity
	insecure	infirmary -ies
	insertion	inflammable
	insider	inflammation
	insisted	inflammatory
	insolence	inflationary
	insolent	inflexible
	inspection	influentially
	inspector	influenza
	installing	informally
	instalment /	information
	installment	informative
	instantly	infuriate
	instinctive	ingenious
	institute	ingenuity
	instruction	ingredient
	instructive	inhabitant
	instructor	inhabited
	instrument	inhabiting
	insulate	inheritance
	insulin	inherited
	insulting	inheriting
	insurance	inhibition
	☞	inhospitable
		☞

for E . . .
see page 65

for H . . .
see page 71

for Scots: i-r
is on page 247 ▷

In these words you can hear the vowel sound i as in pig

I

***

integer
integral
integrate
intensive
intention
intercept
interchange
interested
interesting
interface
interfere d
interim
interlock ed
interlude
internal ly
interpret ed
interrupt
intersect
intersperse d
interval
intervene d
interview ed
intestine
intimate
intricate
intriguing
introduce d
introvert
intruder
intrusion
intrusive
invaded
invader
invalid
invasion
invention
inventive
inventor
inventory -ies
inversion
investment
investor
invited
involvement
involving
☞

for Scots: i-r
is on page 247 ▷

**** **

iniquity
initialling
initiate
initiative
injurious
innovation
innumerable
inoculate
inoculation
inorganic ally
inquisition
inquisitive
insanitary
insanity
inscrutable
insecticide
insensitive
insignificant
insoluble
insomnia
inspiration
installation
instantaneous
institution
instrumental ly
insufficient
insulation
insulator
insuperable
integration
integrity
intellectual ly
intelligence
intelligent
intensify -ies
intensified
intensity -ies
intentional ly
interaction
interception
interchangeable
interested
interesting
interference
interior
intermediate
interminable
intermission
intermittent
internally
international ly
interpolate
interpretation
interpreted
☞

for E . . .
see page 65

for H . . .
see page 71

In these words you can hear the vowel sound **i** as in **pig** **75**

I

* * *

Iraqi
irrigate
irritate

Islamic
Israel
Israeli

Italian
italic
Italy

* * * * * *

interpreter
interpreting
interrogate
interrogation
interrogative
interrupted
interruption
intersection
intervention
interwoven
intestinal ly
intimacy -ies
intimidate
intolerable
intolerance
intonation
intoxicate
intoxication
intransitive
intravenous
introduction
introductory
introversion
intuition
intuitive
invaluable
invariably
inventory -ies
invertebrate
investigate
investigation
investigator
invincible
invisible
invitation
involuntarily

Iranian
irrational ly
irregular
irregularity -ies
irrelevance
irrelevant
irreparable
irresistible
irresponsible
irrigation
irritability
irritable
irritation

italicise d
ze
itinerant
itinerary

for E . . .
see page 65

for H . . .
see page 71

for Scots: i-r
is on page 247

In these words you can hear the vowel sound i as in pig

J

*

gin
gist

.
gym

jib bed
jig ged
jilt
jinx es
jinxed

* *

ginger ed
gipsy / gypsy -ies
giraffe

gymnast
gymslip
gypsy / gipsy -ies

jibbing
jiffy
jigging
jigsaw
jingle d
jingling

* * *

genetic ally

gibberish
Gibraltar
gingerbread

gymnastics
gymnosperm

* * * * * *

gelatinous
genetically
geographically
geography -ies
geologically
geology
geometrically
geometry -ies
geranium

gymnasium

for dr . . .
see page 61

K

*	**	***	****
kick ed	kick-off	kidnapper	kilometre
kid ded	kidded	kidnapping	kindergarten
kids	kidding	kilogram	kinaesthetic ally
kill ed	kidnap ped	kimono s	
kiln	kidney	kinetic	knickerbocker
kilt	killer		
kin	killing		
king	kindle d		
kink ed	kindling		
kiss ed	kingdom		
kit ted	king-size		
kith	kinky -ier, -iest		
	kinship		
*knit ted loop together	kipper		
with needles	kissing		
[knit]	kitchen		
	kitted		
*nit egg of louse / nitwit	kitten		
	kitting		
	knickers		
	knitted		
	knitting		

◀ for C . . .
see page 59

for Scots: i-r
is on page 248 ▶

for Qu . . . ▶
see page 83

In these words you can hear the vowel sound i as in pig

L

*

lick ed
lid
lift
limb
limp ed
link ed
*links connections /
golf course
lip
lisp ed
list
lit
live d

lynch es
lynched
*lynx es animal

* *

liberal ly
lichen
licorice
lifted
lifting
lift-off
lily -ies
limit ed
limpet
linen
linger ed
linguist
linking
linseed
lintel
lipstick
liquid
liquor
liquorice
listed
listen ed
listless
litmus
litter ed
little
liver
livid
living
lizard

lyric ally

* * *

legato
lethargic

liberal ly
liberate
liberty -ies
libretto [libretti]
licorice
ligament
limited
limiting
linear
linguistic ally
liniment
liquefy -ies
liquefied
liquidate
liquorice
literal ly
literate
literature
lithium
liturgy -ies
liverish
livery -ies

lyrical ly

* * * * *

legitimate

liberally
liberation
limitation
linguistically
linoleum
listeria
literacy
literally
literary
literature

lyrically

*	**	***	**** **
midge	miaow	magician	manipulate
midst	mickey	malicious	manipulation
milk ed	midday	malignant	
mill ed	middle		mechanical ly
*mince cut into small	midget	meander ed	melodically
pieces	midnight	mechanic ally	melodious
minced	midpoint	medallion	memorial
mink	midway	melodic ally	menagerie
mint	midwife	melodious	meridian
*mints more than one	mildew ed	memento es / s	methodical ly
mint	milkman	meniscus es / -i	meticulous
Miss	[milkmen]		metropolis es
miss es	miller	midsummer	
*missed did miss	millet	militant	military
*mist thin fog	million	military	millennium
mitt	mimic ked	militia	[millennia]
mix es	mineral	milligram	millilitre
mixed	mingle d	milliner	millimetre
	mingling	millionaire	millionairess es
myth	minim	millipede	mineralogy
	minnow	mimicking	minestrone
	minstrel	mimicry	minority -ies
	minute	mineral	miraculous
	mirage	miniature	misbehaviour
	mirror ed	minimal ly	miscellaneous
	mischief	minimum	miserable
	misdeal	minister ed	missionary -ies
	[misdealt]	Minorca	misunderstand
	misjudge d	minuend	
	mislay	miracle	mysterious
	[mislaid]	mischievous	mysticism
	mislead	miserable	mythology -ies
	[misled]	misery -ies	myxomatosis
	missile	misfortune	
	missing	misgivings	
	mission	mishap	
	misspell ed	missionary -ies	
	[misspelt]	mistaken	
	misspend	mistletoe	
	[misspent]		
	mistake	mnemonic	
	[mistook]		
	[mistaken]	myriad	
	mistress es	mystery -ies	
	mistrust	mystical	
	misuse d	mystify -ies	
	mitten	mystified	
	mixture	mythical	

Monsieur [Messieurs]

Mr
Mrs

mystic al
mystique

for Scots: i-r
is on page 249 ▷

In these words you can hear the vowel sound i as in pig

N

*	**	***	**** *
*knit ted loop together with needles [knit]	knickers knitted knitting	mnemonic	knickerbocker
		negation **neglectful** ly	**nativity** -ies
nib **nil** **nip** ped *nit egg of louse / nitwit	**neglect**		**necessity** -ies **neglectfully** **negotiate** **negotiation**
	nibble d **nibbling** **nickel** **nickname** **nimble** **nipping** **nipple** **nitwit**		**Nicaragua**
nymph			

O

*	**	***	**** **
	omit ted	**official** ly	auxiliary -ies
		omission **omitted** **omitting**	**obliterate** **oblivion** **oblivious** **obsidian**
		opinion	**officially**
			original ly **originality** **originate**

In these words you can hear the vowel sound i as in pig

P

*

pick ed
pig ged
pill
pin ned
pinch es
pinched
pink ed
pip ped
pit ted
pitch es
pitched
pith

prick ed
*****prince** son of king
print
*****prints** more than
one print

**

permit ted
persist

physics
physique

pianist
piano s
picket
picking
pickle d
pickling
pickup
picnic
*****picture** painting,
drawing or
photograph
picture d
*****pidgin** mixture of
two languages
*****pigeon** bird
pigging
piglet
pigment
pigtail
pilchard
pilgrim
pillar
pillow ed
pimple d
pincers
ping-pong
pinion
pinning
pipping
*****pistil** part of flower
*****pistol** small handgun
piston
pitchblende
*****pitcher** container
for liquids
pitchfork
pitching
piteous
pitfall
pitting
pity -ies
pitied
pivot ed
pixie
pizza
☞

***

Pacific
pavilion

peculiar
permission
permitted
permitting
persistence
persistent
petition ed

physical ly
physician
physicist

pianist
piano s
piccolo s
picturesque
pilgrimage
pinafore
pincushion
pinnacle
piranha
piteous
pitiful ly
pivoted
pivoting

position ed

precaution
preceded
preceding
precisely
precision
precocious
prediction
preferring
preparing
prescription
presented
presenting
presumptuous
pretended
pretentious
prettier
prettiest
prevention
preventive
primitive
☞

**** ***

particular
particularly

peculiar
pedestrian
*****peninsula** land
almost surrounded
by water
*****peninsular** of / like
a peninsula
perimeter
peripheral
periphery -ies
permissible
petroleum

phenomena
phenomenal ly
phenomenon
[phenomena]
philatelist
philosophical ly
philosophy -ies
physically
physiological ly
physiology

pianoforte
pistachio s
pituitary

political ly

precipitate
precipitation
predictable
predominant ly
preliminary -ies
preoccupation
presentable
presumably
presumptuous
principally
proficiency
prohibited
prohibiting
prohibitive
proliferate
proliferation
prolifically
provisional ly
proximity

publicity

In these words you can hear the vowel sound i as in pig

P

**

precede
precise
predict
prefer red
prepare d
prescribe d
present
preserve d
preside
presume d
pretence
pretend
pretty -ier, -iest
prevail ed
prevent
prickle d
prickly
primrose
princess es
printed
printer
printing
prism
prison
prisoner
privet

pygmy -ies

***

*principal chief
principally
*principle rule for
action
principled
prisoner
privacy
privilege d
prodigious
proficient
prohibit ed
prolific ally
provincial
provision
provisions

pyjamas
pyramid
Pyrenees
pyrites

Q

*

quick
quid
quill
quilt
quin
quince
quip ped
quit ted
[quit]
quiz zed

**

quibble d
quibbling
quickly
quintet
quipping
quitted
quitting
quiver ed

***

quicksilver
quintuplet
quizmaster

*for Scots: i-r
is on page 251* ▷

In these words you can hear the vowel sound i as in pig

R

*

*real genuine

rib bed
rich es
rid ded
[rid]
ridge d
rift
rig ged
*rill small stream
rim med
*ring ed circle
*ring sound
[rang]
[rung]
ringed
rink
rinse d
rip ped
risk ed

*wring twist
[wrung]
wrist

**

react
really
rebel led
rebound
rebuke d
recall ed
receipt
receive d
recess es
recessed
recite
reclaim ed
recoil ed
record
*recount tell a story
recruit
recur red
reduce d
refer red
refine d
reflect
reform ed
refract
refrain ed
refresh es
refreshed
refund
refuse d
regain ed
regard
regret ted
rehearse d
reject
rejoice d
rejoin ed
relate
relax es
relaxed
release d
relent
relief
relieve d
rely -ies
relied
remain ed
remark ed
remind
remote
remove d
renege d
renew ed
renown ed
repaid
repair ed
repay
[repaid]
☞

***

reaction
reactor
reagent
realise d
ze
rebelling
rebellion
rebellious
receding
receiver
receiving
reception
receptive
recession
recessive
recital
recorded
recorder
recording
recover ed
recurrence
recurrent
recurring
redemption
reduction
redundant
referral
referring
reflected
reflection
reflector
reflexive
refraction
refreshment
refusal
regarded
regardless
regatta
regretful ly
regretted
regretting
rehearsal
rejection
related
relating
relation
relentless
reliance
religion
religious
reluctance
reluctant
remainder
remaining
remember ed
remembrance
☞

**** **

rapidity
reactionary -ies
realism
realistic ally
reality -ies
receptacle
receptionist
recipient
reciprocal ly
reciprocate
recovery -ies
redundancy -ies
refinery -ies
refrigerate
refrigeration
refrigerator
regretfully
relationship
reliability
reliable
reluctantly
remarkable
remembering
removable /
removeable
repetitive
republican
repudiate
resentfully
respectable
respectfully
respectively
responsibility -ies
responsible
resuscitate
resuscitation
retaliate
retaliation
returnable
reverberate
reversible

rhetorical ly
rhythmically

ridiculous
ritually

In these words you can hear the vowel sound i as in pig

R

**

repeal ed
repeat
repel led
repent
replace d
reply -ies
replied
report
repose d
reproach es
reproached
repute
request
require d
research es
researched
resent
reserve d
resign ed
resist
resolve d
resort
resource d
respect
respire d
respond
response
restore d
restrain ed
restraint
restrict
retrieve d
result
resume d
retain ed
retard
retire d
retort
retreat
return ed
reveal ed
revenge d
reverse d
review ed
revise d
revive d
revolt
revolve d
reward

rhythm
rhythmic ally
☞

***

reminded
reminder
remission
remittance
removal
removing
Renaissance
renewal
repeated
repeating
repellent
repelling
repentance
replacement
reported
reporter
repression
repressive
republic
repulsive
requirement
researcher
resemblance
resemble d
resembling
resentful ly
resentment
resistance
resistor
resources
respectful ly
respective
resplendent
responsive
restriction
resultant
resulted
resulting
retarded
retention
retentive
retirement
retriever
returning
reversal
revision
revival
revolver
revulsion
rewritten

rhythmical ly
☞

** * * **   * * * *

ribbing	**rickety**
ribbon	**ricochet** ted / ed
riddance	**ridicule** d
ridded	**rigorous**
ridden	**ringleader**
ridding	**ritual** ly
riddle d	**riveted** / **rivetted**
riddling	**riveting** / **rivetting**

*****rigger** person who rigs

rigging

rigid

*****rigor** rigid state

*****rigour** severe
conditions

rimming

ringing

ripping

ripple d

rippling

risen

ritual ly

river

rivet ed / ted

*-recount count again

wriggle d

wriggling

wrinkle d

wrinkling

written

In these words you can hear the vowel sound i as in pig

*	**	***	**** **
cinch es	cement	celestial	celestial
			certificate
cyst	chiffon	chiffon	
		chivalrous	citizenship
schist	cigar	chivalry	civilisation
scrimp	cirrus		zation
scrip	cistern	cigarette	
script	citrus	*cilia more than one	cylindrical
	city -ies	cilium	cynically
shift	civic	ciliary	cynicism
shin ned	civil ly	cilium [cilia]	
ship ped		cinema	**salinity**
shrill	*cygnet young swan	cinnamon	**satirical** ly
shrimp	*cymbals discs to clash	citizen	
shrink	cystic	civilian	**scenario**
[shrank]		civilise d	**schizophrenia**
[shrunk / shrunken]	*Scilly Isles	ze	**schizophrenic** ally
	scissors	civilly	
sick	scribble d		**security** -ies
sieve d	**scripture**	cylinder	**severity** -ies
sift		cynical ly	
sill	**seclude**	Cypriot	**significant**
silk	**secrete**	cystitis	**similarity** -ies
silt	**secure** d		**similarly**
sin ned	**select**	scriptural ly	**simplicity**
since	**settee**		**simplification**
sing	**severe**	**secession**	**simulation**
[sang]		**secluded**	**simultaneous**
[sung]	**shilling**	**secretion**	**sincerity**
sink	**shimmer** ed	**selected**	**sister-in-law**
[sank]	**shingle**	**selecting**	**situated**
[sunk / sunken]	**shipment**	**selection**	**situation**
sip ped	**shipping**	**selective**	
sit	**shipwreck** ed	**selector**	**solicitor**
[sat]	**shiver** ed	**sequoia**	**solidity**
six th	**shrinkage**	**severely**	**sophisticated**
	shrivel led		
skid ded		**shipbuilding**	**specifically**
skill ed	**sickness**	**shrivelling**	**spiritually**
skim med	**signal** led		
skimp ed	*signet seal / ring	**Sicily**	**stability**
skin ned	*silly -ier, -iest	**signalling**	**statistical** ly
skip ped	lacking sense	**signature**	**stimulation**
skit	silver ed	**signify** -ies	
	simmer ed	signified	**subsidiary** -ies
slick	**simple**	**silhouette**	**sufficiently**
slid	**simpler**	**silica**	☞
slim med	**simply**	**silicon**	
sling	**sincere**	*sillier more silly	
[slung]	**sinew**	**silliest**	
slink	**sinful** ly	**silverware**	
[slunk]	**singer**	**similar**	
slip ped	**singing**	**simile**	
slit	**single** d	**simplify** -ies	
[slit]	**singly**	simplified	for Scots: i-r
☞	**sinning**	**simulate**	is on page 252
	☞	☞	

In these words you can hear the vowel sound i as in pig

S

*

smith

sniff ed
snip ped

sphinx es
spill ed
[spilt]
spin
[span]
[spun]
spit
[spat]
[spit]
splint
split
[split]
sprig
spring
[sprang]
[sprung]

squib
squid
squint

stick
[stuck]
stiff
still ed
stilts
sting
[stung]
stink
[stank]
[stunk]
stint
stitch es
stitched
strict
string
[strung]
strip ped

swift
swill ed
swim
[swam]
[swum]
swing
[swung]
swish ed
Swiss
switch ed

**

sipping
sissy -ies
sister
sitter
sitting
sixpence
sixteen th
sixty -ies
sizzle d
sizzling

skidded
skidding
skilful ly
skillet
skimming
skinhead
skinning
skinny -ier, -iest
skipper
skipping
skittle

slimming
slipper ed
slippery
slipping
slipstone
slither ed
slitting

smitten

sniffle d
sniffling
snigger ed
snippet
snivel led

sphincter
spilling
spinach
spindle
spinning
spinster
spirit
spitting
splinter ed
splitting
springboard
springtime
sprinkle d
sprinkler
sprinkling
☞

***

sincerely
sinfully
Singapore
singular
sinister
sixtieth

skilfully

slippery

smithereens

snivelling

specific ally
spiritual ly

statistics
stimulant
stimulate
stimulus [stimuli]
stinginess

submission
submissive
submitted
submitting
subscription
subsistence
sufficient
suspicion
suspicious

Switzerland
swivelling

sycamore
syllabic ally
syllable
symbolic ally
symbolise d
    ze
symmetry -ies
sympathise d
    ze
sympathy -ies
symphonic ally
symphony -ies
☞

**** **

syllabically
syllabification
symbiosis
symbiotic ally
symbolically
symbolism
symmetrical ly
sympathetic ally
symphonically
symposium
[symposia]
synonymous
synthesiser
    izer
synthetically
systematic ally

*for Scots: i-r
is on page 252* ▷

In these words you can hear the vowel sound **i** as in pig

** **

*cymbals discs to
clash

squirrel

sticking
sticky -ier, -iest
stigma
stillness
stingy -ier, -iest
stipple d
stippling
stirrup
stitches
stitching
stricken
stridden
stringent
stringy -ier, -iest
stripper
stripping
striptease
striven

submit ted
subsist

swiftly
swimmer
swimming
swimsuit
swindle d
swindling
swinging
swivel led

symbol
***symbols** signs
symptom
syntax
syringe d
syrup
system

*** ***

synagogue
synchromesh
synchronise d
          ze
syndicate
synonym
synoptic
synthesis [syntheses]
synthesise d
          ze
synthetic ally
Syria
syrupy -ier, -iest

*for Scots: i-r
is on page 252* ▷

In these words you can hear the vowel sound i as in pig

T

*

thick
thin ned
thing
think
[thought]
this
thrift
thrill ed

tick ed
till
tilt
tin ned
tint
tip ped
tit

trick ed
trim med
trip ped

twig ged
twin ned
twinge
twist
twit
twitch es
twitched

**

terrain

thicket
thickness
thimble
thinker
thinner
thinning
thistle
thither
thrifty -ier, -iest
thriven

ticket
tickle d
ticklish
tiller
timber
timid
tinder
tingle d
tingling
tinkle d
tinkling
tinning
tinsel
tipping
tiptoe d
tissue
titter ed

tribute
trickle d
trickling
tricky -ier, -iest
trigger ed
trillion
trimming
trimmings
trinket
triple d
triplet
tripling
tripping

twiddle d
twiddling
twigging
twinkle d
twinkling
twinning
twisted
twisting
twitter ed

***

terrific ally

tiara
tiddlywinks
timpani

tradition
tremendous
tributary -ies
trickery
trilogy -ies
Trinidad
Trinity
trivial

typical ly
tyrannise d
      ze
tyranny -ies

**** **

telegraphy
telepathy
telephonist
terrestrial ly
terrifically

theatrical ly
theodolite
theological ly
theology -ies
theoretical ly

traditional ly
tribulation
tributary -ies
trigonometric
trigonometry
triviality -ies

typically
tyrannical ly
tyrannosaurus es / -i

*for Scots: i-r
is on page 253* ▶

In these words you can hear the vowel sound **i** as in **pig**

U

*   **   ***   ****

until

V

*   **   ***   **** **

vicar	vanilla	validity
vicious		
victim	vermilion	velocity -ies
victor		
victual	vibrato	vicinity
vigil	vicarage	victimisation
vigour	victimise d	zation
villa	ze	Victorian
village	victory -ies	victorious
*villain wicked person	video	Vietnamese
*villein free villager in	Vietnam	vigilante
medieval times	vigilance	visibility
villus [villi]	vigilant	visualise d
vineyard	vigorous	ze
virile	villager	visualisation
visage	vinegar	zation
viscose	viola	visually
vision	visible	
visit ed	visited	
visual ly	visiting	
vivid	visitor	
vixen	visual ly	
	visualise d	
	ze	
	vitamin	
	vitreous	*for Scots: i-r*
	vivacious	*is on page 254* ▷

In these words you can hear the vowel sound i as in pig

91

W

*

*ring ed circle
*ring sound

whelk
*which that /
which one
whiff ed
Whig
whim
whip ped
whisk ed
whist
*whit little bit
whiz zed

wick
width
wig ged
will ed
wilt
win
[won]
wince d
winch es
winched
wind
wing ed
wink ed
wish es
wished
wisp
*wit humour /
humorous person
*witch woman said
to use magic
with

*wring twist
[wrung]
wrist
writ

* *

whimper ed
whinny -ies
whinnied
whippet
whipping
whisker ed
whiskey
whisky -ies
whisper ed
whistle d
whistling
*whither to which
place
Whitsun
whittle d
whittling
whizzing

wicked
wicker
wicket
widow ed
wigging
wiggle d
wiggling
wigwam
willing
willow
windmill
window
windpipe
windscreen
windsurf ed
windward
windy -ier, -iest
wingspan
winkle d
winkling
winner
winning
winter ed
wintry
wisdom
wishing
wistful ly

* * *

whichever

wilderness es
windowpane
window-sill
windsurfer
wintertime
wishfully
wistfully
withdrawal

* * * *

witticism

*for Scots: i-r
is on page 255*

In these words you can hear the vowel sound i as in pig

W

* *

witchcraft
withdraw
[withdrew]
withdrawal
withdrawn
*wither ed become
dry and shrivelled
withhold
[withheld]
within
without
withstand
[withstood]
witness ed
witty -ier,-iest
wizard
wizened

women

wriggle d
wriggling
wrinkle d
wrinkling
written

*for Scots: i-r
is on page 255* ▷

Z

*

zinc
zip ped

* *

zigzag ged
zipper
zipping
zither

* * *

zigzagging
Zimbabwe

* * * *

   93

*	**	***	**** ****

*-all every one
-alms

*-awe fear and wonder
*-awed made to feel awe
*-awl boring tool

*-odd unusual

*-or -marks choice

-ought

-abroad
abscond

across

adopt

agog

allotted
almost
aloft
along
-alright
-also
*-altar holy table
*-alter ed change
-although
-always

anon

-appal led
-applaud
-applause

assault

-auburn
-auction ed
*-auger tool
*-augur suggest for the future
-August month
-august impressive
-aural ly
-austere
-author
-autumn

-awesome / awsome
-awful ly
-awkward
-awning

abolish es
abolished

acknowledge d

adoption

allotment
allotted
allotting
-almighty
alongside
-already
-alternate

apostle
-appalling

astonish es
astonished

-audible
-audience
-auditory
-aurally
-aurora
-Austria
-authentic ally
-authoress es
-authorise d
    ze
-autocrat
-autograph ed

-awfully

abdominal
abominable
abominate

accommodate
accommodation
acknowledgement /
acknowledgment
acknowledging
acropolis
[acropoles]

-alternating
-alternative
-alternator
-altogether

anonymous

apologetic ally
apologise d
    ze
apology -ies
apostrophe
approximate
approximately
approximation

astonishment
astrology
astronomer
astronomy

-auditory
Australia
-authentically
-authority -ies
-autobiographical ly
-autobiography -ies
-autocracy -ies
-autocratic
-automatic ally
-automation
-automobile
-autonomic
-autonomous
-auxiliary -ies

for H . . .
see page 102 ▷

for Scots: o-r
is on page 256 ▷

In these words you can hear the vowel sound o as in dog

B

*

*-**bald** lacking hair
-**balk**/**baulk** ed
*-**ball** round object /
  dance
*-**balled** made into a
  ball
*-**balm** ointment
-**baulk**/**balk** ed
*-**bawl** yell
*-**bawled** did yell

blob
block ed
*-**blond** man with
  fair hair
*-**blonde** woman with
  fair hair
blot ted

bob bed
bog ged
*-**bomb** explosive
  device
bombed
bond
boss es
bossed
botch es
botched
-**bought**
box es
boxed

-**brawl** ed
-**broad**
bronze d
broth
-**brought**

**

-**ballpoint**
-**ballroom**
-**balmy** -ier, -iest
-**balsa**
balsam
-**Baltic**
-**basalt**
-**bauxite**

because
-**befall**
[befell]
-[befallen]
belong ed
beyond

blancmange
blockade
blockboard
blossom ed
blotted
blotter
blotting

bobbing
bodice
body -ies
bodied
boggy -ier, -iest
bombard
bomber
bombshell
bondage
bonfire
bonnet
bonny -ier, -iest
borrow ed
bossy -ier, -iest
botching
bother ed
bottle d
bottling
bottom ed
boxer
boxing

-**broadcast**
-[broadcast]
-**broadside**
bronchial
bronco

***

-**befallen**
belonging

bodily
borrowing
botanist
botany
bottleneck

-**broadcasting**
broccoli
bronchitis
brontosaur

****

barometer

binocular
binoculars

Bolivia

brontosaurus es / -i

In these words the first letter 'o' is a neutral
vowel. It sounds like the 'o' in 'occurring'.

Bolivia   botanical
bonanza   brocade

---

for Scots: o-r
is on page 257 ▷

In these words you can hear the vowel sound o as in dog

C

*

*-**call** ed   shout / name
-**calm** ed
*-**caught**   got / trapped
-**caulk** ed
-**cause** d
-**caw** ed
*-**cawed**   did caw

-**chalk** ed
chop ped

*-**clause**   words in
sentence / part of
written agreement
-**claw** ed
*-**claws**   curved nails
or limbs
clock ed
clod
clot ted
cloth

cob
cock ed
*-**cod**   fish
*-**col**   gap between
mountains
cop ped
*-**cops**   the police
*-**copse**   small wood
cost
[cost]
*-**cot**   baby's bed
cough ed

-**crawl** ed
crock ed
croft
crop ped
cross es
crossed

for Qu . . .
see page 109 ▷

* *

-**calling**
-**cauldron**
-**causing**
-**caustic** ally
-**caution** ed
-**cautious**

chocolate
chopper
chopping
choppy -ier, -iest
chopsticks
chronic ally

clockwise
clotted
clotting

cobbler
cobweb bed
cocker
cockerel
cockle
Cockney
cockpit
cockroach es
cocksure
cocktail
codfish
coffee
coffin
*-**collage**   picture made
by sticking items to
a board
collar ed
colleague
collect
*-**college**   educational
establishment
collie
collier
column ed
combat ted
combine
comet
comic
comma
comment
commerce
common
commune
☞

* * *

cauliflower
-**caustically**

chloroform ed
chlorophyll
cholera
chorister
chronically
chronicle d

cochlea
cockatoo
cockerel
colliery -ies
colonise d
ze
colonist
colony -ies
colossal ly
combatted
combatting
comedy -ies
comical ly
commentary -ies
commonplace
commonwealth
communal ly
communist
compensate
competence
competent
*-**complement**
something that
completes
complicate
*-**compliment**
expression of praise
or politeness
composite
comprehend
compromise
concentrate
concentric
concoction
conference
confidence
confident
confiscate
confluence
congregate
congruence
congruent
conical
conifer
conjugate
connoisseur
☞

* * * * *

-**caustically**

choreographer
choreography
chronically
chronological ly
chronology

colonisation
zation
colossally
combination
comically
commentator
commodity -ies
communally
communism
commutative
commutator
comparable
compensation
competition
*-**complementary**
making up a whole
complication
*-**complimentary**
expressing praise
composition
compositor
comprehension
comprehensive
computation
concentration
concertina
condemnation
condensation
confidential ly
confirmation
confrontation
conglomerate
conglomeration
congregation
connotation
conquistador

☞

for Scots: o-r
is on page 258 ▷

In these words you can hear the vowel sound **o** as in dog

C

* *

compact
complex es
compound
comrade
concave
concept
concert
concoct
concord
concourse
concrete
condom
conduct
conflict
congress
*conker horse
chestnut
conic
*conquer ed defeat
conquest
conscience
conscious
conscript
console
constant
contact
content
contents
contest
context
contour ed
contract
contrast
convent
converse
convert
convex
convict
convoy
copper
copping
copy -ies
copied
*coral substance
formed from bones
of sea creatures
*corral enclosure for
horses and cattle
cosmic ally
costly -ier, -iest
costume d
cottage
cotter ed
cotton ed
☞

* * *

conqueror
consciousness
consecrate
consequence
consequent
consonant
constitute
consulate
contemplate
continent
contraband
contradict
contrary
convalesce d
copulate
correspond
corridor
cosmetic ally
cosmically
cosmonaut
cottoning

crockery
crocodile

* * * * *

conscientious
consecration
consequently
conservation
consolation
constellation
constipated
constipation
constitution
continental ly
continuity -ies
contraception
contraceptive
contradiction
contribution
controversial ly
controversy -ies
conversation
copulation
coronation
correlation
*correspondence
exchange of letters /
similarity
correspondent
*correspondents those
sending letters or
reports
corresponding
corrugated
cosmetically
cosmically

kilometre

for Qu . . .
see page 109 ▷

for Scots: o-r
is on page 258 ▷

In these words you can hear the vowel sound **o** as in dog

* *

-crawling
cropping
crossbar
crossing
crossroads
crosswise
crossword
crotchet

for Qu . . .
see page 109 ▷

for Scots: o-r
is on page 258 ▷

In these words the first letter 'o' is a neutral vowel.

CORRECT WORDS

cholesterol	commuter	conclude	connector	contention
chorale	companion	conclusion	conscription	contest ant
cocoon ed	compare d	conclusive	consecutive	contingency -ies
collapse d	comparing	concurrent	consensus	continual ly
collapsible	comparison	concuss es	consent	continuation
collect ing	compartment	concussed	conservatory -ies	continue d
collection	compassion ate	concussing	conservatism	continuous
collective	compatible	concussion	conservative	continuum
collector	compel led	condemn ed	conserve d	contract
collide	compelling	condense d	consider ed	contraction
collision	compete	condenser	considerable	contractor
colloquial ly	competitive	condition ed	considerate	contralto s
cologne	competitor	conditional ly	consideration	contraption
colonial ly	compile d	conducive	consist ing	contrary
colonialism	complacency	conduct	consistency -ies	contrast
combat ted	complacent	conduction	consistent	contribute d
combatting	complain ed	conductor	console d	control led
combine d	complaint	confectioner	conspicuous	controller
combining	complete ly	confectionery	conspiracy -ies	controlling
combustible	completion	confer red	conspire d	convection
combustion	complexion	conferring	constabulary -ies	convector
comedian	component	confess es	constituency -ies	convenience
comedienne	compose d	confessed	constituent	convenient
command er	composer	confession al	constrain ed	convention
commandment	composure	confessor	constraint	conventional ly
commemorate	compress es	confetti	construct ed	converge d
commemoration	compressed	confide	construction al	convergent
commence d	compression	confine d	constructive	converse d
commercial ly	compressor	confirm ed	consult	conversion
commission ed	comprise d	conflict	consultancy -ies	convert ible
commissioner	comprising	conform ed	consultant	convey ed
commit ted	compulsion	conformist	consume d	conveyor /
commitment	compulsive	conformity	consumer	conveyer
committee	compulsory	confront	consumption	convict ion
committing	compute	confuse d	contagious	convince d
commodity -ies	computer	confusion	contain ed	convulse d
commotion	computerise d	congenital ly	container	convulsion
communal ly	conceal ed	congratulate	contaminate	convulsive
commune d	conceit ed	congratulations	contamination	correct ed
communicate	conceive d	coniferous	contemporary -ies	correction
communication	concentric	conjecture d	contempt	correctly
communion	conception	conjunction	contemptible	corrode
community -ies	concern ed	connect ed	contemptuous	corrosion
commutative	concerning	connecting	contend	corrosive
commute	concession	connection	content	corrupt ion

In these words you can hear the vowel sound **o** as in **dog**

D

*

-**daub** ed
-**dawn** ed

dock ed
dodge d
dog ged
doll ed
don ned
dong ed
dot ted

*-**draw** pull / sketch
  [drew]
  -[drawn]
*-**drawer** sliding
  container
-**drawl** ed
  drop ped

* *

-**daughter**
-**dawdle**
-**dawdling**

demobbed

dislodge d
dissolve d

doctor ed
doctrine
dodgem
dodger
dodging
dodgy -ier, -iest
dogging
doghouse
doldrums
dollar
dollop
dolphin
donkey
donning
dotted
dotting

-**drawbridge**
-**drawing**
droplet
dropout
dropping

* * *

demolish es
demolished
deposit ed
despondent

dishonest
dislodging

doctrinal ly
document
doggedly
dominant
dominance
dominate
domino es

* * * * *

democracy -ies
demonstrative
denomination
denominator
deposited
depositing
derogatory
despondency
dishonorable

disqualify -ies
disqualified

doctrinally
dolphinarium
domination

dromedary -ies

> In these words the first letter 'o' is a neutral
> vowel. It sounds like the 'o' in 'occurring'.
>
> domain   domestic ally   domesticate

for Scots: o-r
is on page 259 ▷

E

*

* *

encore d

evolve d

exalt
-**exhaust**

* * *

embody ies
embodied

envelope

erotic ally

exalted
-**exhausted**
-**exhaustion**
exotic ally

* * * *

ecology
economy -ies

entrepreneur

equality

erotically

exotically

for 1 . . .
see page 102 ▷

for Scots: o-r
is on page 259 ▷

In these words you can hear the vowel sound O as in dog

F

*

-**fall**
 [fell]
 -[fallen]
 false
 -**fault**
 *-**faun** goat-god
 *-**fawn** young deer /
  colour / try to win
  favour
 -**fawned**

 -**flaunt**
 -**flaw** ed
 flock ed
 flog ged
 flop ped

 fog
 fond
 font
 -**fought**
 fox,es
 foxed

 -**fraud**
 frock
 frog
 from
 frond
 frost
 froth ed

for th . . .
see page 133 ▷

* *

-**falcon**
-**fallen**
-**falling**
-**fallout**
 falter ed
-**faulty** -ier, -iest

flogging
flopping
floppy -ier, -iest
floral
florist

fodder
foggy -ier, -iest
foghorn
follow ed
folly -ies
fondle d
fondling
forage d
forehead
foreign
forest
forgone / foregone
forgot
fossil
foster ed
foxglove
foxy -ier, -iest

frogman [frogmen]
frolic ked
frostbite
frosty -ier, -iest
frothy -ier, -iest

phosphate

* * *

foggiest
follower
following
foreigner
forestry
forgotten
fossilise d
 ze

frolicking
frostbitten

phosphorus

* * * * *

ferocity

phenomena
phenomenally
phenomenon
[phenomena]
philosophy -ies
photographer
photography

for Scots: o-r
is on page 260 ▷

In these words the first letter 'o' is a neutral vowel. It sounds like the 'o' in 'occurring'.

forensic   forever   forget-me-not

In these words you can hear the vowel sound **o** as in **dog**

G

*

-gaunt
-gauze

genre

gloss es
glossed

-gnaw ed
*-gnawed did gnaw

god
God
golf ed
gone
gong
gosh
got

*nod move the head
down and up

* *

-gaudy -ier, -iest

genre

globule
glossy -ies

gobble d
*gobbling greedily
eating
goblet
*goblin evil spirit
goddess es
goggles
golly
gosling
gospel
gossip ed
Gothic

grotto es / s
grotty -ier, -iest
grovel led
grovelling

* * *

galoshes

geography

Gibraltar

globular
glockenspiel
glossary -ies

godparents
golliwog
gossiping

grovelling

*guerilla / guerrilla
agent of political
violence

* * * *

geography
geology
geometry -ies

for Scots: o-r
is on page 261

> In this word the letter 'o' is a neutral vowel.
>
> gorilla

In these words you can hear the vowel sound o as in dog

H

*

*-**hall** large room /
   passage
halt
*-**haul** drag /
   amount gained
-**hauled**
-**haunch** es
-**haunt**
*-**hawk** bird / carry
   and try to sell / clear
   the throat noisily
-**hawked**

hob
*-**hock** leg joint / wine /
   pawn
hog ged
honk ed
hop ped
hot

**

-**halter**
-**haughty** -ier, -iest
-**haunches**
-**hawthorn**

hobble d
hobbling
hobby -ies
hockey
hogging
Holland
holler ed
hollow ed
holly
homage
honest
Hong Kong
honour ed
hopper
hopping
hopscotch
horrid
horror
hospice
hostage
*-**hostel** place to stay in
*-**hostile** unfriendly
hotch-potch
hotter
hottest
hovel
hover ed

***

-**haughtily**

historic ally

holiday
hollyhock
holocaust
hologram
holograph
homograph
homonym
honestly
honesty
honourable
horoscope
horrible
horrify -ies
horrified
hospital
hovercraft

hypnotic ally

**** *

historical ly

holography
*-**homogeneous** of the
   same kind throughout
*-**homogenous** of the
   same genetic origin
honorary
honourable
horizontal ly
horrifying
hospitable
hospitalise d
                  ze
hospitality
hostility -ies

hypocrisy
hypnotically

In this word the 'o' is neutral.

horizon

---

*for Scots: o-r
is on page 261* ▷

I

*

**

-**instal** led
involve d

***

impromptu s
improper

-**installing**
-**instalment** /
   installment
involvement

**** **

illogically

impossibility
impossible

-**inaugural**
-**inauguration**
incongruous
inoculate
inoculation
insoluble
insomnia
intolerable
intolerance
intoxicate
intoxication
involuntary

◁ *for E . . .
see page 99*

*for Scots: o-r
is on page 262* ▷

In these words you can hear the vowel sound O as in dog

J

*	**	***	****
-**jaunt**	-**jaunty** -ier, -iest	-Gibraltar	geography
-**jaw** ed			geology
	jobbing	**jocular**	geometry
job bed	**jockey** ed		
jog ged	**jockstrap**		
jolt	**jodhpurs**		
jot ted	**jogger**		
	jogging		
	jolly -ies		
	jollied		
	jostle d		
	jostling		
	jotted		

◁ for dr . . .
see page 99

jotter
jotting

for Scots: o-r
is on page 262 ▷

K

*	**	***	****
knob	**knocker**		**kilometre**
knock ed	**knockout**		
***knot** ted tied	**knotted**		**knowledgeable**
fastening / hard part	**knotting**		
of wood / sea mile	***knotty** -ier, -iest full		
[per hour]	of knots		
	knowledge		
*-naught / nought zero			
	*naughty -ier, -iest badly		
*not used in denial,	behaved		
negation, refusal			
*-nought / naught zero			

> **In these words the letter 'o' is a neutral vowel.**
> Korea   Korean

◁ for C . . .
see page 96

for Scots: o-r
is on page 262 ▷

for Qu . . .
see page 109 ▷

L

*	**	***	**** **
-**launch** es	-**launcher**	**laconic** ally	**laboratory** -ies
-**launched**	-**launder** ed	-**launderette**	**laconically**
-**law**	-**laundry** -ies		
-**lawn**	**laurel**	**logical** ly	**logarithm**
	-**lawyer**	**lollipop**	**logically**
lob bed		**longitude**	**longitudinal** ly
***loch** Scottish word	**lobbing**	**lottery** -ies	
for 'lake'	**lobby** -ies		
***lock** fastening device	**lobbied**		
locked	**lobster**		
lodge d	**locker**		
loft	**locket**		
log ged	**locus** [loci]		
long ed	**lodger**		
lop ped	**lodging**		
loss es	**lofty** -ier, -iest		
lost	**logging**		
lot	**logic** ally		
	longer		
	longest		
	lopping		
	lorry -ies		
	lotto		
	lozenge		

for Scots: o-r
is on page 263 ▷

In these words you can hear the vowel sound o as in dog

M

*

*mall public walk /
walk lined with shops
malt
*-maul ed handle
roughly / heavy mallet
-mauve

mob bed
mock ed
mop ped
mosque
moss es
moth

**

Malta

mobbing
model led
modelling
moderate
modern
modest
module
mollusc
monarch
mongol
mongoose s
monsoon
monster
monstrous
mopping
*moral ly concerning
right and wrong
*morale confidence
morrow
mossy -ier, -iest
motley
mottled
motto es / s

***

melodic ally

mnemonic

moccasin
mockery -ies
modelling
moderate
modernise d
ze
modesty
modify -ies
modified
molecule
monastery -ies
monitor ed
monochrome
monotone
monoxide
monument
moralise d
ze
morally
Morocco
mosquito es

mnemonic

**** ***

mahogany
majority -ies

melodically
methodical ly
metropolis es

moderation
moderato
modernisation
zation
modification
modifier
modulation
molecular
monochromatic ally
monopolise d
ze
monopoly -ies
monotheism
monotonous
monumental ly

mythology -ies

*for Scots: o-r
is on page 263* ▷

In these words the letter 'o' is a neutral vowel.
Mohammed   molasses   momentum

N

*

*-gnaw ed did gnaw

knob
knock ed
*knot ted tied fastening /
hard part of wood /
sea mile [per hour]

*-naught / nought zero

*nod ded move head
down and up
*not used in denial,
negation, refusal
notch es
notched
*-nought / naught zero

**

knocker
knotted
knotting
*knotty -ier, -iest full of
knots
knowledge

*-naughty -ier, -iest
badly behaved

nodding
nodule
nonsense
nostril
novel
novice
nozzle
noxious

***

-naughtier
-naughtiest
-naughtiness
-nautical ly

neurotic ally

nocturnal ly
nominal ly
nominate
nominee
nostalgic ally
novelist
novelty -ies

**** *

knowledgeable

-nautically

neurotically

nocturnally
nominally
nomination
nonconformist
notwithstanding

*for Scots: o-r
is on page 263* ▷

In these words you can hear the vowel sound **o** as in dog

O

*   ******   *******   ****** ******

*-all every one
-alms

 awe
*-awed made to feel awe
*-awl boring tool

***odd** unusual

of
off

on

-**ought**

ox en

almost
-alright
-also
*-altar holy table
*-alter ed change
-although
-always

-auburn
-auction ed
*-auger tool
*-augur suggest for the
  future
-August
-august
-aural ly
-austere
-author
-autumn

-awesome / awsome
-awful ly
-awkward

honest
honour ed

object
oblique
oblong

o'clock
octane
octave

oddment

offer ed
offering
office
offset
offshore
offside
offspring
offstage
often

olive

omelette

onset
onslaught
onward
☞

-almighty
-already
-alternate

-audible
-audience
-auditory
-aurally
-aurora
-Austria
-authentic ally
-authoress es
-authorise d
     ze
-autograph ed

-awfully

honestly
honesty
honourable

obsolete
obstacle
obvious

occupant
occupy -ies
occupied
octagon
October
octopus es / -i
ocular
oculist

oddity -ies

offering
offertory -ies
officer

ominous
omnibus

oncoming
onlooker

opera
operate
ophthalmic
opossum
opposite
optical ly
optician
optimal ly
optimist
optional
☞

-alternating
-alternative
-alternator
-altogether

-auditory
 Australia
-authentically
-authority -ies
-autobiographical ly
-autobiography -ies
-automatic ally
-automation
-automobile
-autonomic
-autonomous
-auxiliary -ies

 honorary
 honourable

obligation
observation
obsidian
obviously

occupation
occupier
octagonal

offertory -ies

onomatopoeia

operated
operatic ally
operating
operation
operator
opportunity -ies
opposition
optically
optimally
optimistic ally

orientation
orienteering

oscillation
☞

◀ for H . . .
see page 102

for Scots: o-r
is on page 264 ▶

In these words you can hear the vowel sound o as in dog

O

**	***	**** **
opera	orangeade	oxidisation
optic ally	orator	zation
option	oratory	oxyacetylene
	origin	
orange		
	oscillate	
osprey	osmium	
ostrich es	osmosis	
	ossicle	
otter		
	oxidise d	

◁ *for H . . .* oxen ze *for Scots: o-r*
see page 102 oxide oxygen *is on page 264* ▷

In these words the first letter 'o' is a neutral vowel. It sounds like the 'o' in 'occurring'.

*O*RIGINAL WORDS

obedience	oblivious	obsessional ly	occurrence	oppose d
obedient	obscene	obsessive	occurring	oppress es
obey ed	obscenity -ies	obstruct	offence	oppressed
object	obscure d	obstruct ion	offend	oppression
objection	obscurity -ies	obstructive	offensive	oppressive
objectionable	observant	obtain ed	official ly	oppressor
objective	observatory -ies	obtuse	omission	original ly
oblige d	observe d	occasion	omit ted	originality
oblique	observer	occasion al	omitting	originate
obliterate	observing	occasionally	opinion	
oblivion	obsess ed	occur red	opponent	

In these words you can hear the vowel sound o *as in* dog **107**

P

*	**	***	**** **
-**palm** ed	-**palfrey**	**peroxide**	**pathology**
paunch es			
*-**pause** brief gap /	**phosphate**	**phosphorus**	**personification**
hesitate			**personify** -ies
-**paused**	**plotted**	**podgier**	personified
*-**paw** foot of animal	**plotting**	**podgiest**	
*-**pawed** examined by		**policy** -ies	**phenomena**
paw	**pocket**	**politics**	**phenomenal** ly
-**pawn** ed	**podded**	**pollinate**	**phenomenon**
*-**paws** feet of animal	**podding**	**pollution**	[phenomena]
	podgy -ier, -iest	**poltergeist**	**philosophy** -ies
plot ted	**polish** es	**polygon**	**photographer**
	polished	**polythene**	**photography**
*-**pod** ded form pods /	**polka**	**ponderous**	
casing	**pollen**	*-**populace** common	**politician**
pomp	**pompom**	people	**pollination**
pompous	**ponder** ed	**popular**	**polyester**
poncho s	**pontoon**	**populate**	**Polynesia**
pond	**popcorn**	*-**populous** full of	**polynomial**
pop ped	**poplar**	people	**polyphonic** ally
pot ted	**poplin**	**positive**	**polyphony**
pothole	**popping**	**possible**	**polystyrene**
	poppy -ies	**possibly**	**polytechnic**
-**prawn**	**porridge**	**postulate**	**polytheism**
prod ded	**possum**	**pottery** -ies	**polyurethane**
prompt	**posture** d	**poverty**	**pomegranate**
prong ed	**potted**		**popularity**
prop ped	**potting**	-**precaution**	**population**
		probable	**possibility** -ies
-**psalm**	**problem**	**probably**	
	prodded	**prodigal**	**predominant** ly
*-**poor** badly off	**prodding**	**prodigy** -ies	**probability** -ies
*-**pore** tiny hole / study	**produce**	**profited**	**proclamation**
closely	**product**	**profiting**	**profitable**
	*-**profit** ed gain	**progeny**	**promiscuity**
	project	**promenade**	**promontory** -ies
	prolong ed	**prominence**	**propaganda**
	promise d	**prominent**	**proposition**
	proper	**promising**	**prosecution**
	*-**prophet** inspired	**promontory** -ies	**prosecutor**
	religious leader	**propagate**	**prosperity**
	propping	**properly**	**prostitution**
	prospect	**property** -ies	**provocation**
	prosper ed	*-**prophecy** -ies statement	**provocative**
	prostate	about a future event	**proximity**
	prostrate	*-**prophesy** -ies make	
	proverb	a statement about	*for Scots: o-r*
	province	the future prophesied	*is on page 265*
		prosecute	
		prosperous	
		prostitute	
		Protestant	
		providence	
		provident	

for Scots: o-r is on page 265 ▷

In these words you can hear the vowel sound **o** as in **dog**

P

In these words the first letter 'o' is a neutral vowel. It sounds like the 'o' in 'occurring'.

PR**O**FOUND WORDS

phonetic ally	potatoes	professing	promote	protect ed
photographer	potential ly	professional ly	promotion	protection
photography	probation	professor	pronounce d	protective
police	procedure	proficiency	pronouncement	protector
policeman	proceed	proficient	pronouncing	protest
[policemen]	proceeding	profound	pronunciation	protractor
policewoman	procession	profuse	propel led	protrude
[policewomen]	proclaim ed	profusion	propeller	provide
polite ly	procure d	progression	propelling	provided
political ly	prodigious	progressive	proportional ly	providing
pollute	produce d	prohibit ed	proposal	provincial
pollution	producer	prohibiting	propose d	provision
polyphony	producing	prohibitive	proprietor	provisional ly
position ed	production	project	propulsion	provisions
possess es	productive	projectile	prospect	provocative
possessed	profane	projection	prospective	provoke d
possession	profess es	projector	prospector	
possessive	professed	prolific ally	prospectus es	

Q

*	**	***	**** *
	quadrant	**quadrangle**	**quadrilateral**
	quagmire	**quadratic**	**qualification**
	quarrel led	**quadruped**	**qualitative**
	quarry -ies	**quadruple** d	**quantitative**
	quarried	**quadruplet**	
		qualify -ies	
		qualified	
		quality -ies	
		quandary -ies	
		quantity -ies	
		quarantine	
		quarrelling	

In these words you can hear the vowel sound **o** as in **dog**

109

R

*	**	***	**** **
-raw	-recall ed	rendezvous	responsibility -ies
	resolve d	responsive	responsible
rob bed	respond	revolver	
rock ed	response		rhetorical ly
rod ded	revolt	robbery -ies	
romp ed	revolve d	rockery -ies	
rot ted		rollicking	
	rhombus		
wrath			
wrong ed	robber		
	robbing		
	robin		
	rocker		
	rocket		
	rocky -ier, -iest		
	rodded		
	rodding		
	*rollick act with enjoyment		
	*rollock / rowlock pivot for oar		
	rosin ed		
	roster		
	rotted		
	rotten		
	rotting		
	*rowlock / rollock pivot for oar		

for Scots: o-r is on page 266 ▷

> In these words the first letter 'o' is a neutral vowel. It sounds like the 'o' in 'occurring'.
>
> romance   romantic ally

In these words you can hear the vowel sound o as in dog

S

*

-psalm

salt
-sauce
*-saw looked at /
    cutting tool
*-sawed did saw
-[sawn]

-scald
scoff ed
scone
scotch ed
Scotch
-scrawl ed

-shawl
shock ed
shod
shone
shop ped
shot

slog ged
slop ped
slosh es
sloshed
slot ted

-small
smock ed
smog

snob

sob bed
sock ed
*sod turf
soft
solve d
song
-sought

-spawn ed
spot ted
-sprawl ed

squad
squash ed
squat ted
-squawk ed
☞

**

-salty -ier, -iest
-saucepan
-saucer
-saucy -ier, -iest
-saunter ed
sausage

scholar
scoffing
Scotland
Scottish

shoddy -ier, -iest
shoplift
shopper
shopping
shotgun

-slaughter ed
slogging
slopping
sloppy -ier, -iest
slotted
slotting

-smaller
-smallest
-smallpox
smocking

snobbish

sobbing
soccer
socket
sodden
soften ed
softer
softly
software
soggy -ier,-iest
solace
solder ed
solemn
solid
solvent
solving
sombre
sonic
sonnet
sorrow ed
sorry -ier, -iest
sovereign
☞

***

-saucily

scholarship

shopkeeper

soldering
solenoid
solitary
solitude
soluble
sombrero s
sovereignty -ies
soviet

sponsorship

stockbroker
-strawberry -ies
strontium

swastika

symbolic ally
symphonic ally
synoptic

**** *

solidarity
solubility

spontaneity
spontaneous

symbolically
symphonically
synonymous

*for Scots: o-r
is on page 267* ▷

S

*	**
*-**stalk** ed stem / follow prey quietly / stride stiffly	**sponsor** ed
-**stall** ed	**spotlight**
-**staunch** es	**spotted**
-staunched	**spotting**
*****stock** ed supply	**spotty** -ier, -iest
stodge	**sprocket**
stop ped	
-**straw**	**squabble** d
strong	**squabbling**
	squadron
	squalid
	squander ed
swab bed	**squatted**
swamp ed	**squatter**
swan	**squatting**
swap ped	
*****swat** slap with a flat object	-**stalling**
*****swot** study hard	-**stalwart**
	stockade
	stocking ed
*-**soar** fly high	**stodgy** -ier, -iest
*-**sore** painful	**stoppage**
	stopper
	stopping
	stopwatch es
	-**strawberry** -ies
	stronger
	strongest
	stronghold
	strongly
	swabbing
	swallow ed
	swapping
	*****swatted** -see 'swat'
	*****swatting** -see 'swat'
	*****swotted** -see 'swot'
	*****swotting** -see 'swot'

for Scots: o-r is on page 267 ▷

In these words the first letter 'o' is a neutral vowel. It sounds like the 'o' in 'occurring'.

society -ies	soliloquy -ies
solicitor	solution
solidified	Somalia
solidify -ies	sophisticated
solidity	soprano s

In these words you can hear the vowel sound o as in dog

T

*	**	***	****
-talk ed	-talking	-talkative	theodolite
-tall	-taller		thermometer
*-taught instructed	-tallest	-thoughtfully	
-taunt			tonsillitis / tonsilitis
*-taut tight	-thoughtful ly	toboggan	topography
	throbbing	tolerance	topology
-thaw ed	throttle d	tolerate	topsy-turvy
thongs		tomahawk	
-thought	toddle d	tommy-gun	tropically
throb bed	toffee	tomorrow	
throng ed	toggle	topical	
	tomboy		
tongs	tomcat	tropical ly	
top ped	tonic		
toss ed	tonsil		
	topic		
trod	topping		
trot ted	topple d		
trough ed	toppling		
	topsoil		
	torrent		
	toxic		
	toxin		
	trodden		
	trolley		
	trombone		
	tropic ally		
	trotted		
	trotting		

for Scots: o-r is on page 268 ▷

> In these words the first letter 'o' is a neutral
> vowel. It sounds like the 'o' in 'occurring'.
>
> | | |
> |---|---|
> | tobacco s | tomato es |
> | tobacconist | torrential ly |

U

*	**	***	****
	upon		

V

*	**	***	**** *
*vault gymnastic leap / underground room / arched roof	vodka	volatile	velocity -ies
	volley ed	volcano es / s	
	voltage	volcanic ally	volcanically
	volume	voluntary	
*volt unit of electrical force	vomit ed	volunteer ed	

> **In this word the letter 'o' is a neutral vowel.**
> vocabulary -ies

W

*	**	***	****
waft	wadding	-wallflower	-walkie-talkie
-walk ed	waddle d	-wallpaper ed	watercolour
-wall ed	waddling	warrior	
waltz es	waffle d	washable	
waltzed	waffling	watchfully	
wand	-walking	-waterfall	
want	wallet	-waterfowl	
was	-wallflower	-waterproof ed	
wash es	wallow ed	-watershed	
washed	-walnut	-watertight	
wasp	-walrus	-watery	
watch es	wander ed		
watched	wanted	whatever	
*watt unit of electric power	wanting		
*watts units of electric power	wanton	wrongdoing	
	warrant		
	warren		
	washer		
*what that or those which / which / how much / I do not understand	*washers people or machines that wash / insulating rings		
*what's what is	*washes cleans with water		
	washing		
wrath	wasn't		
wrong ed	watchdog		
-wrought	watchful ly		
	watching		
	watchman		
	watchword		
	-water ed		

for Scots: o-r is on page 269 ▶

wobble d
wobbling
wobbly
wonky -ier, -iest

114

In these words you can hear the vowel sound o as in dog

Y

*

yacht
-yawn ed

* *

yoghourt / yoghurt /
yogurt
yonder

* * *

* * * *

for Scots: o-r
is on page 269 ▷

Z

*

* *

zombi / zombie

* * *

* * * *

zoology

In these words you can hear the vowel sound o as in dog   **115**

A

*	**	***	**** *
	above	abundance	accompaniment
	abrupt	abundant	accompany -ies
			accompanied
	-adjourn ed	accomplice	accomplishment
	adjust	accomplish es	
	adult	accomplished	adultery
		accustom ed	
	affront		
	-afoot	adjuster	
		adjustment	
	among		
	amongst	another	
	-assure d	assumption	*for Scots: ur + ir*
		-assurance	*are on page 242* ▷
	-august		

B

*	**	***	****
blood	because	becoming	brother-in-law
bluff ed	become	beloved	
blunt	[became]		budgerigar
blush es	[become]	bloodthirsty	Bulgaria
blushed	begun		
	beloved	brotherhood	
-book ed			
	bloodshed	buccaneer ed	
-brook ed	bloodstream	bucketful	
brush es	bloody -ier,-iest	bucketing	
brushed	blubber ed	-Buddhism	
	blunder ed	budgerigar	
buck ed		budgeting	
bud ded	-bookcase	buffalo es	
budge d	-booklet	-bulldozer ed	
buff ed	-bookshelf	-bulletin	
bug ged	-[bookshelves]	bumblebee	
bulb	borough	bungalow	*for Scots: ur + ir*
bulge d	-bosom	buttercup	*are on page 243* ▷
bulk		butterfly -ies	
-bull	brother	buttermilk	
☞	Brussels	butterscotch	
	☞		

-or oo as in woodpecker

In these words you can hear the sound u as in duck

B

*

bump ed
bun
bunch es
bunched
bung ed
bunk ed
bus es
-bush es
-bushed
*bussed carried by bus
*bust upper part of
body / break / arrest
*but except / instead /
yet
*butt large cask /
person made fun of /
thick end of tool or
weapon / push with
head
buzz es
buzzed

* *

bubble d
bubbling
bucket ed
buckle d
buckling
-Buddha
-Buddhist
budding
buddy -ies
budget ed
budgie
budging
buffer ed
*buffet ed push roughly
*buffet self-service meal
buffing
bugging
buggy -ies
bulbous
bulky -ier, -iest
-bulldog
-bullet
-bullfrog
-bullock
-bullseye
-bully -ies
-bullied
-bulrush es
bumper
bundle d
bundling
bungle d
bungling
bunion
bunker ed
bunny -ies
Bunsen
burrow ed
-bushel
busker
bustle d
-butcher ed
butler
*butted pushed with
head
*butter ed spread with
butter
button ed
buttress es
buttressed
butty -ies
buzzard
buzzer

for Scots: ur + ir
are on page 243 ▷

-or **oo** as in **woodpecker**

In these words you can hear the sound **u** as in **duck**

C

*

chuck ed
chug ged
chum med
chump
chunk ed

club bed
cluck ed
clump ed
clung
clutch ed

come
[came]
[come]
-cook ed
-could

-crook
crumb
crunch es
crunched
crush es
crushed
crust
crutch es

cub
cuff ed
cup ped
-cure d
cut
[cut]

**

chuckle d
chuckling
chugging
chumming
chutney

clubhouse
clumsy -ier, -iest
cluster ed
clutter ed

-colonel
colour ed
comfort
coming
compass es
concuss es
concussed
conduct
confront
conjure d
construct
consult
convulse d
-cooker
-cooking
corrupt
-couldn't
country -ies
couple d
coupling
courage
cousin
cover ed

-crooked
crumble d
crumbling
crumpet
crumple d
crumpling
crutches
☞

***

colander / cullender
colourful ly
colourless
combustion
comfortable.
company -ies
compulsion
compulsive
concurrent
concussing
concussion
conduction
conductor
conjunction
conjurer / conjuror
constable
constructed
construction
constructive
consultant
consumption
convulsion
convulsive
-cookery
corruption
countryman
[countrymen]
countryside
covenant
coverage
covering

crustacean

cul-de-sac
culminate
cultivate
cultural ly
cumbersome
-curator
-curio
-curious
currency -ies
custody
customary
customer
cutlery

**** *

circumference

colourfully
combustible
comfortable
compulsory
constructional
consultancy -ies

crustacean

culmination
cultivation
culturally
-curiosity -ies
customary

*for Scots: ur + ir
are on page 244* ▷

In these words you can hear the sound **u** as in **duck**

-or **oo** as in **woodpecker**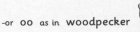

C

**

-cuckoo
cuddle d
cuddling
culprit
culture d
cunning
cupboard
cupful
cupping
-curate
*currant fruit
*current flowing
stream / present
curry -ies
curried
-cushion ed
custard
custom
customs
cutter
cutting

*for Scots: ur + ir
are on page 244* ▷

> **Here there are two neutral 'ou' vowel sounds.**
> courageous

-or **oo** as in woodpecker

In these words you can hear the sound **u** as in duck

D

*

does
done
*dost old form of 'do',
used with 'thou'
doth
dove

drug ged
drum med
drunk

duck
*ducked did duck
*duct tube or pipe
dug
dull ed
dumb
dump ed
dunce
dung
dusk
*dust particles of
earth or waste matter
Dutch

* *

*-discus es heavy disc
to throw in games

*discuss es debate
*discussed debated
*disgust strong
dislike
disrupt
distrust

doesn't
double d
doubling
dozen

drugging
drummer
drumming
drumstick
drunkard
drunken

duchess es
duckling
duffel / duffle
dugout
dummy -ies
dumpling
dungeon
-during
dustbin
duster
dusty -ier, -iest

* * *

deduction
deductive
destruction
destructive

discomfort
discourage d
discover ed
discussing
discussion
disgusting
disruption
disruptive

drunkenness

dungarees

* * * *

discovery -ies

*for Scots: ur + ir
are on page 245* ▷

E

*

* *

-endure d
engulf ed
enough
*-ensure d make certain
entrust

erupt

*for I . . .
see page 123* ▷

-Europe

*-insure d protect against
loss

* * *

emulsion ed

encourage d
-endurance

erupted
eruption

* * * *

encouragement

-European

*for Scots: ur + ir
are on page 245* ▷

-or oo as in **woodpecker**

F

*	**	***	**** *
flood	floodlight	fluctuate	fluctuation
fluff ed	floodlit	-fluorescence	-fluorescence
flung	flourish es	-fluorescent	-fluorescent
flush es	flourished		
flushed	fluffy -ier, -iest	frontier	functionally
flux es	-fluoride	frustrating	fundamental ly
	-fluorine	frustration	
-foot	flurry -ies		
	flurried	-fulfilling	
front	fluster ed	functional ly	
	flutter ed	funnelling	
fudge d		funnier	
-full	-football	funniest	
fun	-foothill	-furious	
fund	-foothold		
fuss es	-footnote		
fussed	-footpath		
	-footstep		
	-forsook		

frontier
frustrate

fudging
-fulcrum
-fulfil led
-fuller
-fullest
-fully
fumble d
fumbling
function ed
funfair
fungi
*fungous spongy or
in other ways like a
fungus
*fungus type of plant
funnel led
funny -ier, -iest
furrow ed
-fury -ies
fuzzy -ier, -iest

for th . . .
see page 133 ▷

for Scots: ur + ir
are on page 246 ▷

-or oo as in woodpecker

In these words you can hear the sound u as in duck

121

G

*	**	***	**** *
glove d	gazump ed	gluttony	governmental ly
glum			
glut	glutton	-gooseberry -ies	gutturally
		government	
-good	-goodbye	governor	
-goods	-goodness		
-gourd	-goodnight	gullible	
	-gooseberry -ies	gunpowder	
grub bed	govern ed	guttering	
grudge d		guttural ly	
gruff	grubbing		
grunt	grubby -ier, -iest		
	grudging		
gulf	grumble d		
gull ed	grumbling		
gulp ed	grumpy -ier, -iest		
gum med			
gun ned	gudgeon		
gush es	gullet		
gushed	gulley / gully -ies		
gust	gulling		
gut ted	gumboil		
guts	gumming		
	gunner		
	gunning		
	guppy -ies		
	-guru s		
	gusto		
	gusty -ier, -iest		
	gutter		
	gutting		
	guzzle d		
	guzzling		

*for Scots: ur + ir
are on page 246* ▷

-or oo as in woodpecker

In these words you can hear the sound u as in duck

H

*
-hood
-hook ed

hub
huff
hug ged
hulk
hull
hum med
hump ed
hunch es
hunched
hung
hunk
hunt
hush es
hushed
husk
hut
hutch es

* *
honey ed

hubbub
huddle d
huddling
hugging
hulky -ier, -iest
hullo
humble d
humbling
humming
hundred
hundredth
hunger ed
hungry -ier, -iest
hunted
hunter
hunting
-hurrah!
-hurray!
hurry -ies
hurried
husband
husky -ies
hustle d
hustling

* * *
honeybee
honeycomb
honeydew
honeymoon

hummingbird
Hungary
hungrier
hurricane
hurrying

* * * *
honeysuckle
hullabaloo
Hungarian

*for Scots: ur + ir
are on page 247* ▷

I

*

* *
*ensured make certain

indulge d
instruct
insult
*-insure d protect
  against loss
intrust / entrust

* * *
impulsive

induction
inductive
indulgence
indulgent
injunction
injustice
instruction
instructive
instructor
insulting
-insurance

* * * * * * *
illustrious

-impurity -ies

-incurable
industrial ly
industrialist
industrialisation
            zation
industrialise d
            ze
industrious
-infuriate
-injurious

◁ *for E . . .
see page 120*

*for Scots: ur + ir
are on page 247* ▷

-or oo as in woodpecker

In these words you can hear the sound u as in duck

J

*

judge d
jug ged
jump ed
junk
just
jut ted

◁ for dr . . .
see page 120

* *

judgement / judgment
judging
juggle d
juggler
juggling
jumble d
jumbling
jumper
jumping
junction
juncture
jungle
-juror
-jury -ies
justice
jutting

* * *

juggernaut
justify -ies
justified
juxtapose d

* * * * *

-jurisdiction
-jurisprudence
justifiable
justification
juxtaposition

K

*

◁ for C . . .
see page 118

* *

knuckle d
knuckling

* * *

* * * *

for Scots: ur + ir
are on page 248 ▷

-or oo as in woodpecker

In these words you can hear the sound u as in duck

L

*	**	***	****
-look ed	London	lovable	luxuriant
love d	-lookout	loveliest	luxurious
	lovely -ier, -iest		
luck	lover	luckier	
lug ged		luckiest	
lugs	lucky -ier, -iest	luckily	
lull ed	luggage	lullaby -ies	
lump ed	lugging	lumbago	
lunch es	*lumbar lower back	lumberjack	
lunched	*lumber junk / timber /	Luxembourg /	
lung	move awkwardly	Luxemburg	
lunge d	lumbered	luxury -ies	
-lure d	lumpy -ier, iest		
lush	luncheon ed		
lust	luscious		
	lustre		
	lusty -ier, -iest		

*for Scots: ur + ir
are on page 248* ▷

-or oo as in woodpecker

In these words you can hear the sound u as in duck

M

*

monk
month
-moor ed

much
muck ed
mud
muff ed
mug ged
mulch es
mum
mumps
munch es
munched
mung
mush
musk
must

**

-manure d
-mature d

misjudge d
-mistook
mistrust

Monday
money ed
mongrel
monkey ed
-mooring
-Moslem
mother ed

muddle d
muddling
muddy -ier, -iest
mudguard
*muffin teacake
*muffing missing a
shot or catch
muffle d
muffling
mugger
mugging
muggy -ier, -iest
mulberry -ies
mumble d
mumbling
mummy -ies
*muscat wine / grape
*muscle body tissue
muscled
muscling
mushroom ed
*musket gun
-Muslim
*muslin fine thin cotton
*mussel shellfish
mustang
*mustard plant with
hot-tasting seeds
muster
*mustered called
together
mustn't
musty -ier, -iest
mutter ed
mutton
muzzle d
*muzzling putting a
muzzle on

***

mulberry -ies
multiple
multiply -ies
multiplied
multitude
muscatel
muscular

**** **

-maturity

mother-in-law
mother-of-pearl

multicultural ly
multiplicand
multiplication
multiplicative
multiplicity
multiplier
musculature

> **Here the 'ou' is a neutral vowel.**
>
> moustache

---

for Scots: ur + ir
are on page 249
-or oo as in woodpecker

In these words you can hear the sound u as in duck

N

SHORT VOWEL **u** SHORT VOWEL **oo**

*	**	***	****
*none not any	knuckle d	nonetheless	-neurological ly
-nook	knuckling		-neurologist
		nullify -ies	-neurology
nudge d	-neuron / neurone	nutcracker	
null			
numb ed	nothing		
*nun woman in			
convent	nudging		
nut	nugget		
	number ed		
	nutmeg		
	nutty -ier,-iest		
	nuzzle d		*for Scots: ur + ir*
	nuzzling		*are on page 249* ▷

O

*	**	***	****
once	august	august	-obscurity -ies
*one 1			
	-obscure d	obstruction	
	obstruct	obstructive	
	oneself	occurrence	
	onion		
		otherwise	
	other		
◁ *for H . . .*			*for Scots: ur + ir*
see page 123	oven		*are on page 249* ▷

-or **oo** as in woodpecker

In these words you can hear the sound **u** as in duck

127

P

*	**	***	**** *
pluck ed	plover	percussion	presumptuous
plug ged	plugging	percussive	pronunciation
*plum fruit	plumber		
*plumb lead weight	plumbing	-plurally	publication
on a cord / do work	plunder ed		publicity
of plumber	plunging	presumptuous	pulmonary
plumbed	-plural ly	production	punctually
plump ed		productive	punctuation
plunge d	-poorly	propulsion	-purification
plus es			-puritanical
plush	-procure d	publican	-puritanism
		publicly	
-poor	public ly	publisher	
	publish es	-pullover	
pub	published	punctually	
puff ed	-pudding	punctuate	
pug	puddle d	punishment	
-pull ed	puddling	-purify -ies	
pulp ed	puffin	-purified	
pulse d	-pulley	Puritan / puritan	
pump ed	-pulpit	-purity	
pun ned	pulsar		
punch es	pumice		
punched	pumpkin		
punk	punctual ly		
punt	pungent		
pup	puncture d		
-pure	punish es		
*pus liquid from	punished		
poisoned place	punning		
-push es	puppet		
-pushed	puppy -ies		
*-puss es cat	-purely		
*-put place	-pushchair		
-[put]	-pussy -ies		
*putt hit golf ball	putted		
gently / throw weight	putter		
	*-putting placing		
	*putting doing putts		
	putty -ies		
	puttied		
	puzzle d		
	puzzling		

for Scots: ur + ir
are on page 250 ▷

Q

*	**	***	****
	Qur'an / Koran		

-or oo as in woodpecker

In these words you can hear the sound u as in duck

R

*	**	***	**** *
-rook	**refund**	**recover** ed	**recovery** -ies
-room	**result**	**recurrence**	**redundancy** -ies
***rough** uneven /		**recurrent**	**reluctantly**
harsh / crude	**roughage**	**reduction**	**republican**
roughed	**roughen** ed	**redundant**	**resuscitate**
	roughly	**reluctance**	**resuscitation**
rub bed		**reluctant**	
ruck	**rubber**	**republic**	**-Romania / Roumania /**
***ruff** collar	**rubbing**	**repulsive**	**Rumania**
rug	**rubbish**	**resultant**	
rum	**rubble**	**resulted**	
rump	**rucksack**	**resulting**	
run	**rudder**	**revulsion**	
[ran]	**ruddy** -ier, -iest		
[run]	**ruffle** d	**-rookery** -ies	
***rung** step of ladder /	**ruffling**		
sounded	**Rugby**	**ruffian**	
runt	**rugged**		
rush es	**rugger**		
rushed	**rumba**		
rusk	**rumble** d		
rust	**rumbling**		
rut ted	**rummy**		
	rumpus es		
***wrung** twisted	**runner**		
	running		
	runny -ier, -iest		
	runway		
	rupture d		
	rushing		
	Russia		
	Russian		
	rustic		
	rustle d		
	rustling		
	rusty -ier, iest		
	rutted		
	rutting		

*for Scots: ur + ir
are on page 251* ▷

-or oo as in **woodpecker**

S

*	**	***	**** *
scrub bed	scrubbing	scullery -ies	circumference
scruff	scuffle d		
scrum	scuffling	shrubbery -ies	-security -ies
*scull ed row	sculptor	shuttlecock	
sculpt	sculptress es		structurally
scum	sculpture	slovenly	
	scumbling		substitution
-shook	scurry -ies	somebody	subtropical
-should	scurried	somersault	supplementary -ies
shove d	scuttle d		
shrub	scuttling	structural ly	
shrug ged		studying	
shrunk	-secure d		
shunt		subdivide	
shush es	-shouldn't	submarine	
shushed	shovel led	subsequent	
shut	shrugging	subsidise d	
[shut]	shudder ed	ze	
	shuffle d	subsidy -ies	
*skull bone of the head	shuffling	substitute	
skunk	shutter ed	subtitle d	
	shutting	subtlety -ies	
sludge	shuttle d	subtrahend	
slug	shuttling	suddenly	
slum med		suffering	
slump ed	sluggish	suffocate	
slunk	slumber ed	sulphuric	
slush	slumming	sultana	
	slurry	summarise d	
smudge d		ze	
smug	smother ed	*summary -ies brief	
smut	smudging	account	
	smuggle d	summertime	
snuff ed	smuggler	*summery like summer	
snug	smuggling	sumptuous	
		supplement	
*some a certain	snuffing	suppleness	
number or amount	snuffle d		
*son male child	snuffling		
-soot	snuggle d		
	snuggling		
sponge d			
sprung	somehow		
spun	someone		
☞	something		
	sometime		
	sometimes		
	somewhat		
	somewhere		
	southern		
	splutter ed		
	spongy -ier, -iest		
	-sputnik		
	☞		

for Scots: ur + ir are on page 252 ▷

-or oo as in woodpecker

In these words you can hear the sound u as in duck

S

*

**

-stood
struck
strum med
strung
strut ted
stub bed
stuck
stud ded
stuff ed
stump ed
stun ned
stung
stunk
stunt

such
suck ed
suds
sulk ed
*sum med total /
  exercise with numbers
*sun source of sunlight
sung
sunk
sunned
-sure

swung

stomach ed
structure
struggle d
struggling
strumming
strutting
stubbing
stubble
stubborn
stubby -ier, -iest
studding
study -ies
studied
stuffing
stumble d
stumbling
stunning
stutter ed

subject
subset
subsoil
substance
subtle
subtly
suburb
subway
*succour help
*sucker person or
  thing that sucks /
  shoot from stem or
  root / person who
  is easily tricked
suckle d
suckling
suction
sudden
suffer ed
suffix es
suffrage
-sugar ed
sulky -ier, -iest
sullen
sully -ies
sullied
sulphate
sulphur
sultan
summer
summing
summit
summon ed
sumptuous
☞

for Scots: ur + ir
are on page 252 ▷

-or **oo** as in **woodpecker**

In these words you can hear the sound **u** as in **duck**   **131**

* *

sunbathe d
sunburn ed
[sunburnt]
*****sundae** sweet dish
*****Sunday** day
sundry -ies
sunflower
sunken
sunlight
sunlit
sunning
sunny -ier, -iest
sunrise
sunset
sunshade
sunshine
sunstroke
suntan ned
supper
supple
-surely
suspect

*for Scots: ur + ir
are on page 252* ▷

In these words the first letter 'u' is a neutral vowel.   It sounds like the 'u' in 'suspicious'.

S**U**CCESSFUL WORDS

subdue d	subscription	succeed	suggestive	surrender ed
subject	subside	success es	supplied	surround ed
subjection	subsidiary -ies	successful ly	supply -ies	surroundings
subjective	subsist	succession	support ed	susceptible
submerge d	subsistence	successive	supporter	suspect ed
submission	substantial ly	successor	supporting	suspend
submissive	subtend	sufficient ly	suppose d	suspense
submit ted	subtract	suggest ed	supposedly	suspension
submitting	subtract ing	suggestible	suppress es	suspicion
subordinate	subtraction	suggesting	suppressed	suspicious
subscribe d	suburban	suggestion	suppression	sustain ed

-or oo as in woodpecker

In these words you can hear the sound u as in duck

T

*	**	***	****
thrush es	thorough	thoroughbred	thoroughgoing
thrust	thudded	thoroughly	
[thrust]	thudding	thunderbolt	
thud ded	thunder ed	thunderclap	
thug		thundercloud	
thumb ed		thunderous	
thump ed	tongue-tied	thunderstorm	
thus	touchdown	thunderstruck	
	touching		
	touchline		
*ton measure of	touchy -ier, -iest	-tournament	
weight	toughen ed		
tongue d	-tourist	troublesome	
*tonne 1000 kilos		trumpeted	
-took	trouble d	trumpeting	
touch es	troubling	trustworthy	
touched	trudging		
tough	trumpet ed	tunnelling	
-tour ed	truncheon		
	trundle d		
truck	trundling		
trudge d	trussing		
trunk	trustee		
truss			
*trussed tied up	tubby -ier, -iest		
firmly	tugging		
*trust faith	tumble d		
	tumbling		
tub	tummy -ies		
tuck ed	tundra		
tuft	tungsten		
tug ged	tunnel led		
*tun large barrel	turret		
tusk	tussle d		
	tussling		

for Scots: ur + ir
are on page 253 ▷

-or oo as in woodpecker

In these words you can hear the sound u as in duck

133

U

*	**	***	**** **
up ped	onion	otherwise	**ultimately**
us	other	**ugliest**	**ultrasonic** ally
	oven	**ugliness**	**ultraviolet**
	udder	**ultimate**	**unabated**
		umbrella	**unaccountably**
	ugly -ier, -iest		**unaffected**
		unable	**unavoidable**
	ulcer	**unabridged**	**unbearable**
	Ulster	**unafraid**	**unbelievable**
		unaided	**unbreakable**
	umpire d	**unaware**	**uncannier**
		unbeaten	**uncanniest**
		unbroken	**uncertainty** -ies
	unarmed	**unbuckle** d	**uncomfortable**
	unbend	**unbutton** ed	**unconsciously**
	[unbent]	**uncanny** -ier, -iest	**unconventional** ly
	unbind	**uncertain**	**uncooperative**
	[unbound]	**unchallenged**	**undecided**
	unbolt	**uncommon**	**undeniable**
	unborn	**unconcerned**	**undercurrent**
	unchanged	**unconscious**	**underdeveloped**
	uncle	**uncontrolled**	**undergraduate**
	unclean	**uncover** ed	**underlying**
	unclear	**undamaged**	**understanding**
	under	**undaunted**	**understudy** -ies
	undo	**undefined**	understudied
	[undid]	**underclothes**	**undertaken**
	[undone]	**underfoot**	**undertaker**
	undress es	**undergo**	**underwater**
	undressed	[underwent]	**underwritten**
	undue	[undergone]	**undesirable**
	unearth ed	**underground**	**undoubtedly**
	unfair	**undergrowth**	**uneasiness**
	unfit ted	**underlie**	**unemotional** ly
	unfold	**underline** d	**unemployment**
	unharmed	**undermine** d	**unexpected**
	unheard	**underneath**	**unfamiliar**
	unhurt	**underscore** d	**unfavourable**
	unjust	**undersell**	**unforgettable**
	unkind	[undersold]	**unfortunately**
	unknown	**understand**	**ungratefully**
	unlatch es	[understood]	**unhappily**
	unlatched	**undertake**	☛
	unless	[undertook]	
	unlike	[undertaken]	
	unload	**underwear**	
	unlock ed	**underworld**	
	unpack ed	**underwrite**	
	unreal	[underwrote]	
	unroll ed	[underwritten]	
	☛	**undisturbed**	
		undoing	
		unduly	
		☛	

for H . . .
see page 123

for Scots: ur + ir
are on page 254

-or **oo** as in woodpecker

In these words you can hear the sound **u** as in duck

U

SHORT VOWEL **u**   SHORT VOWEL **oo**

* *

unsafe
unscathed
unscrew ed
unseen
unskilled
unsolved
untie d
until
unto
untold
untouched
untrained
untrue
unused
unveil ed
unwell
unwind
[unwound]
unwise
unwrap ped

uphill
upkeep
upland
upper
upright
uproar
uproot
upset
[upset]
upside
upstairs
upstream
upturn ed
upward

usher ed

utmost
utter ed

* * *

uneasy -ier, -iest
unending
unequal led
uneven
unexplored
unfasten ed
unfinished
unfitting
unfriendly -ier, -iest
unfurnished
ungrateful ly
unguarded
unhappy -ier, -iest
unhealthy -ier, -iest
uninjured
unlikely
unlucky -ier, -iest
unnatural
unnoticed
unpainted
unpleasant
unravel led
unravelling
unreal
unscramble d
unscrambling
unselfish
unsettled
unstable
unsteady
untangle d
untangling
untidy -ier, -iest
untying
unusual ly
unwanted
unwelcome
unwilling
unworthy
unwrapping

upbringing
upheaval
upholster ed
uprising
upsetting
upside down

usherette

utterance
utterly

* * * * * *

unidentified
unimportant
uninhabited
unlimited
unmistakable
unnecessarily
unnecessary
unpopular
unpredictable
unprotected
unquestionably
unravelling
unreasonable
unrelated
unreliable
unsanitary
unsociable
unsuccessful ly
unsuitable
unusually

upholstery

> Here the 'u' has a neutral sound.
>
> upon

◁ for H . . .
see page 123

for Scots: ur + ir
are on page 254 ▷

-or **oo** as in woodpecker

In these words you can hear the sound **u** as in duck

V

SHORT VOWEL **u**   SHORT VOWEL **oo**

*

**
vulgar
vulture

***
vulnerable

**** **
vulgarity -ies
vulnerability
vulnerable

*for Scots: ur + ir
are on page 254* ▷

W

*
once
*one 1

-**wolf** wolves
-**wolfed**
***won** gained
*-**wood** timber / area
with many trees
*-**woof!** bark of dog
*-**woof** weft
-**wool**
*-**would** was willing to /
used to / was going to

***wrung** twisted

**
oneself

-**woman** [women]
wonder ed
wondrous
-**wooden**
-**woodland**
-**woodwind**
-**woodwork**
-**woollen**
-**woolly**
worry -ies
worried
-**worsted**
-**wouldn't**

***
-**womanhood**
wonderful ly
wondering
-**woodcutter**
-**woodpecker**

****
wonderfully

*for Scots: ur + ir
are on page 255* ▷

Y

*
young
*-**your** belonging to
you
*-**you're** you are
-**yours**

**
youngster
-**yourself**
-**yourselves**

***

****

-or **oo** as in **woodpecker**

136   In these words you can hear the sound **u** as in **duck**

A

*

ace d
ache d

age d

*aid help
*aide helper
*aids sources of help /
does help
*Aids / AIDS acquired
immune deficiency
syndrome
*ail ed grow weak
aim ed
ain't

*ale beer

ape d

*ate did eat

eh

*eight 8
eighth

for H. . .
see page 144 ▷

**

abate
ablaze
able
ably
abstain

acclaim ed
acorn
acquaint
acre

afraid

again
against
aged
ageing / aging
agent

ailment

amaze d
amen

ancient
angel
anus es

apex
appraise d
April
apron

arrange d
array ed

ashamed
Asia
Asian
assail ed
astray

attain ed

avail ed

await
awake d
[awoke]
[awoken]
away

éclair

eighteen th
eighty -ies

élite

***

abeyance
abrasive

acquaintance
acreage

adjacent

agency -ies

alien

aorta s / -ae

amazement
amazing
amiable

appraisal
apricot

aqueous

arrangement

asexual
assailant

atheist
attainment

awaken ed

eightieth
eisteddfod

**** **

alienation

amiable

Arabia

asymmetric al

atheism

Australia

availability
available
aviation
aviator

for Scots: ae-r ▷
is on page 236

In these words you can hear the vowel sound **ae** as in snail

B

*   ******   *******   ********

*	**	***	****
babe	babied	babysit / baby-sit	babysitter
*bail bar on	baby -ies	bakery -ies	babysitting
cricket stumps /	bacon	basically	basically
payment for release /	bailiff	bayonet ed / ted	bayonet ted
bail out	baker		
bailed	baking	behaviour	
bait	baseball	belated	
*baize cloth	basement	betrayal	
bake d	basic ally		
*bale bundle /	basin	bravery	
bale out	basis	brazier	
baled	bathing	breakable	
*base foot / central		breakwater	
establishment /	became		
worthless	behave d		
*based established	betray ed		
*bass low sound			
*baste cover with	blatant		
melted fat /	blazer		
tack together			
bathe d	bracelet		
bay ed	braces		
*bays more than	brazen		
one bay	brazier		
	breakdown		
beige	breakers		
	breaking		
blade	breakthrough		
blame d	brigade		
blaze d	brocade		

brace d
*braid plait /
edging cloth
braille
brain ed
*braise d gently
cook in liquid
*braise / braize fish
*brake means of
slowing or stopping
brave d
bray
*brayed did bray
*braze d join with
hard solder
*break smash in
pieces / interrupt /
suddenly change
[broke]
[broken]

for Scots: ae-r
is on page 236 ▷

    In these words you can hear the vowel sound **ae** as in **snail**

C

*

cage d
cake d
came
cane d
cape
case d
cave d

chafe
chain ed
change d
chase
*chased did chase
*chaste pure

claim ed
clay

crane d
crate
crave d
craze d
crêche
crêpe / crepe

**

cable d
cabling
canine
casing
cater ed

chamber
changing
chaos
chasing

complain ed
complaint
constrain ed
constraint
contain ed
convey ed

cradle d
cradling
crater ed
crayon ed
crazy -ier, -iest
create
cremate

***

capable

changeable
chaotic ally

complacent
contagious
container
conveyer
courageous

crayoning
craziest
crazily
created
creating
creation
creative
cremation
crustacean

**** *

Canadian
capability -ies

chaotically

complacency

for Qu . . .
see page 148 ▷

for Scots: ae-r
is on page 236 ▷

In these words you can hear the vowel sound **ae** as in **snail**

D

*	**	***	****
dale	dahlia	dahlia	disablement
dame	daily	daintily	disdainfully
Dane	dainty -ier, -iest	dangerous	disgracefully
date	daisy -ies		distastefully
day	danger	deflation	
*days more than	Danish	deism	
one day	data	deity -ies	
*daze state of not	daybreak	derailment	
thinking clearly	daydream ed		
dazed	daylight	dictation	
	daytime	dictator	
deign		disable d	
	debate	disabling	
drain ed	debris	disgraceful ly	
drake	début / debut	displacement	
drape d	*decade ten years		
	decay ed	drapery -ies	
	*decayed did decay		
	décor		
	defame		
	deflate		
	deist		
	delay ed		
	derail ed		
	detain ed		
	détente		
	dictate		
	disdain ed		
	disgrace d		
	dismay ed		
	displace d		
	display ed		
	domain		
	drainage		
	draper		

for Scots: ae-r
is on page 237 ▷

In these words you can hear the vowel sound **ae** as in snail

E

*

eh

eight
eighth

* *

éclair

eighteen th
eighty -ies

elate
élite

embrace d

encase d
engage d
engrave d
enrage d
enslave d
entail ed

equate

erase d

escape d
estate
estrange d

evade

exchange d
exclaim ed
exhale d
explain ed

* * *

eightieth
eisteddfod

elated
elation
élitist

enable d
enabling
endanger ed
engagement
engraving

equation
equator

eraser

evasion
evasive

explaining

* * * *

élitism

for H . . .
see page 144

for I . . .
see page 144

for Scots: ae-r
is on page 237

In these words you can hear the vowel sound ae as in snail

F

*

face d
fade
fail ed
*faint weak
faith
fake d
fame d
*fate destiny

feign ed
*feint mock attack
*fete festival

flake d
flame d

frail
frame d
fray ed
freight

phase d
phrase d

**

fable d
facecloth
facial
faded
failure
faithful ly
famous
fatal ly
favour ed
favourite

flagrant
flavour ed

forgave
forsake
[forsook]
[forsaken]

fragrance
fragrant
framework
freighter
frustrate

***

faithfully
fallacious
fatally
favourable
favourite

filtration

flavouring

formation
forsaken

frustrating
frustration

**** *

favourable
favourably
favouritism

for th . . .
see page 151 ▷

for Scots: ae-r
is on page 238 ▷

In these words you can hear the vowel sound ae as in snail

G

*

gain ed
*gait way of
walking
gala
gale
game
gaol / jail
gaoled / jailed
gape d
*gate entrance
gauge d
gave
gay
gaze d

glaze d

grace d
*grade standard
grain ed
grape
*grate grid / rub
hard
grave
gray / grey
graze d
*great big /
important
grey / gray
*greyed turned
grey

**

gable
gaily
gaoler / jailer
gaseous
gatecrash es
gatecrashed
gateway

glacial

graceful ly
gracious
gradient
grapefruit
grapevine
grateful ly
*grater gadget for
grating
grating
gratis
graveyard
gravy -ies
*greater more great
greatest
greatly
greatness
grenade
greyhound
grimace d

***

gaiety -ies

*glacier mass of
slow-moving ice
*glazier worker
who fits glass
in windows

gracefully
gradation
gradient
gratefully

****

geranium

gymnasium

for Scots: ae-r
is on page 238 ▷

In these words you can hear the vowel sound ae as in snail

H

*

hail hard frozen
rain / call name
or greetings /
come from
hailed
hale very healthy
haste
hate
hay dried grass
haze

hey! ho!

**

halo ed
hasten ed
hasty -ier, -iest
hated
hateful ly
hatred
haven
haystack
hazel
hazy -ier, -iest

hurray!

***

halfpenny -ies
hastily

herbaceous

****

for Scots: ae-r
is on page 238 ▷

I

*

◁ for E . . .
see page 141

**

inflame d
inflate
inhale d
innate
insane
invade

***

impatience
impatient

inflation
inhaler
invaded
invader
invasion

**** *

incapable
inflationary
insatiable

Iranian

for Scots: ae-r
is on page 239 ▷

In these words you can hear the vowel sound **ae** as in snail

J

*
jade
jail / gaol
jailed / gaoled
jay

 for dr . . .
see page 140

* *
jaded
jailer / gaoler

* * *
Jamaica
Jamaican

* * * *
geranium

gymnasium

K

*

*knave rascal

*nave part of church

for C . . .
see page 139

for Qu . . .
see page 148

* *

* * *

* * * *

L

*
lace d
laid
*lain rested
lake
lame d
*lane narrow road
late
lathe
lay
[laid]
*lays poems
*laze take it easy

* *
label led
labour ed
laden
ladies
ladle d
ladling
lady -ies
Laos
*laser apparatus
making light beams
that can cut
lately
later
latest
latex
lay-by
*layer thickness of
laid material /
one that lays
laying
layman [laymen]
layout
lazy -ier, -iest

*-lair den

* * *
labelling
labourer
ladybird
*lazier more lazy
laziest
laziness

lumbago

* * * *

for Scots: ae-r
is on page 239

In these words you can hear the vowel sound ae as in snail

M

*	**	***	****
mace	maiden	maintenance	Malaysia
*made formed	mainframe	majorette	
*maid girl	mainland	Malaya	
*mail post /	mainly	mammalian	
armour	mainsail	mania	
mailed	maintain ed	maniac	
maim ed	major	masonry	
*main chief / strength	maker	mayonnaise	
*maize corn	makeshift		
make	make-up	mistaken	
[made]	making		
*male masculine	manger		
*mane hair, as on	mangy -ier, -iest		
neck of horse or lion	mania		
mate	maple		
may	mason		
*maze puzzle with	matrix -ces		
many paths	matron		
	maybe		
	maypole		
	mislay		
	[mislaid]		
	mistake	*for Scots: ae-r*	
	[mistook]	*is on page 239* ▷	
	[mistaken]		

N

*	**	***	****
*knave rascal	naked	narration	
	naming	narrator	
nail ed	narrate	nasally	
name d	nasal ly	nationwide	
*nave part of	nation		
church	native	negation	
*nay no	nature	neighbourhood	
	*naval concerning	neighbouring	
*née born with	warships	neighbourly	
the name...	*navel tummy-button		
*neigh noise made	navy -ies		
by horses			
neighed	neighbour		

In these words you can hear the vowel sound ae as in snail

O

*

**

obey ed
obtain ed

***

occasion

oration

**** *

Australia

obtainable

occasional ly

P

*

pace
*paced did pace
page d
paid
*pail bucket
*pain suffering
paint
*pale whitish
*pane sheet of
glass
*paste mixture of
powder and liquid
pave d
pay
[paid]

phase d
phrase d

*place d position
plague d
*plaice fish
*plain area of
level land /
simple
*plane aeroplane /
flat surface /
smoothing tool /
tree
plate
play ed

*praise d glorify /
high approval
*pray ask for help
*prays asks for
help
*prey victim

**

pagan
painful ly
painted
painter
painting
papal
paper ed
parade
pastry -ies
patent
*patience ability to
wait for results
patient
*patients people under
medical treatment
patron
pavement
paying
payload
payment
payroll

persuade
pervade

phrasing

placement
placing
*plaintiff person who
takes legal action
*plaintive sad-sounding
player
playful ly
playground
playing
playmate
playtime
playwright

portray ed

prevail ed
proclaim ed
profane

***

pacemaker
painfully
painstaking
palatial ly
paperback
paperclip
patiently
patriot

persuasion
persuasive

playfully

potato es

probation

****
**

palaeontologist /
paleontologist
palatially
papier mâché
patriotic ally
patriotism

phraseology

for Scots: ae-r
is on page 239 ▷

In these words you can hear the vowel sound **ae** as in **snail**

*	**	***	****
quail ed	**Quaker**		
quaint	quasar		
quake d	quaver ed		

R

*	**	***	**** ***
race d	rabies	racially	radially
rage d	racehorse	racism	radiation
raid	racial ly	radial ly	radiator
rail ed	racing	radiant	radioactive
*rain water falling	racist	radiate	radioactivity
from clouds	*radar radio detection	radio s	radiographer
rained	*raider person who	radioed	radiography
*raise d lift up	raids	radium	radiologist
rake d	railing	radius [radii]	radiology
range d	railway	rainforest	
rape d	rainbow	rainier	relationship
rate	raincoat	rainiest	
rave d	raindrop	rapier	Romania / Roumania /
ray	rainfall	rateable	Rumania
*rays beams	raining	ratio s	
	rainy -ier, -iest		
*reign rule	raises	reagent	
*rein strap to control	raisin	related	
an animal	raising	relating	
	raven	relation	
	rayon	remainder	
	razor	remaining	
		Renaissance	
	reclaim ed	replacement	
	refrain ed		
	regain ed	rotation	
	regime / régime		
	reindeer		
	relate		
	remain ed		
	renege d		
	repay		
	[repaid]		
	replace d		
	restrain ed		
	restraint		
	retain ed		

*for Scots: ae-r
is on page 240* ▶

In these words you can hear the vowel sound ae as in snail

S

*

safe
sage
*sail travel by boat /
  sheet fixed to mast
sailed
saint
sake
*sale selling
same
sane
saved
say
[said]

scaled
scraped

shade
*shake move quickly
  in different directions
  [shook]
  [shaken]
shale
shamed
shaped
shaved
*sheikh / sheik Arab
  ruler

skate
skein

slain
slate
slaved
*slay kill
  [slew]
  [slain]
*sleigh sledge

snake
snail

spaced
*spade tool
Spain
*spayed operated
  on to remove ovaries
sprained
sprayed
☛

**

sable
sabre
sacred
safeguard
safely
safer
safety
sago
sailing
sailor
salesman
saline
Satan
*saver person or
  thing that saves
saving
savings
saviour
*savour enjoy a
  taste or smell
saying

scalene
scaly
scapegoat
scraper

seance

shaded
shady -ier, -iest
shaker
shaking
shaky -ier, -iest
shameful ly
shaver
shaving

skateboard
skater
skating

spacecraft
spaceship
spacesuit
spacious
spatial / spacial
☛

***

savoury -ies

shakily
shamefully

slavery

spatially / spacially

stabilised
  ze
stadium
*stationary still
*stationery writing
  materials
straightaway
stratosphere

surveying
surveyor

****

stabiliser
  zer
*stationary still
*stationery writing
  materials

for Scots: ae-r
is on page 240 ▷

In these words you can hear the vowel sound **ae** as in **snail**   **149**

S

*

stage d
***staid** serious and
dull
stain ed
***stake** stick /
bet / prize
staked
stale
state
stave d
[stove]
stay
***stayed** did stay
***steak** meat
***straight** without
curves
strain ed
***strait** channel
straits
strange
stray ed

***suede** soft undressed
leather

sway
***swayed** did sway

* *

stable d
stabling
stagecoach
stainless
stamen
staple d
stapling
stated
statement
statesman
[statesmen]
station ed
status
staying
straighten ed
strangely
stranger
stratus [strati]

survey ed
sustain ed

*for Scots: ae-r
is on page 240*

150   In these words you can hear the vowel sound **ae** as in snail

T

*

tail part at the back
tailed
taint
take
[took]
[taken]
tale story
tame d
tape d
taste

they
they'd
they'll
they've

trace d
trade
trail ed
train ed
trait characteristic
tray board with
raised edges, for
carrying things

* *

table d
tabling
taken
takeoff
taking
takings
tailor ed
taper ed become
thinner towards
one end / waxed
spill or wick
tapir animal
tasted
tasteful ly
tasty -ier, -iest

terrain

today

tracing
traded
trademark
trader
trading
trailer
trainer
trainers
training
traitor

* * *

tablecloth
tablespoon
takeaway
takeover
tastefully

* * * *

titanium

for Scots: ae-r
is on page 241 ▷

V

*

vague
vain conceited
vale valley
vane blade
vaned

veil ed cover
vein blood vessel /
mood / streak

* *

vacant
vacate
vapour

* * *

vacancy -ies
vacation holiday /
process of leaving

vivacious

vocation calling /
occupation

* * * * *

vocational ly

for Scots: ae-r
is on page 241 ▷

In these words you can hear the vowel sound **ae** as in snail

W

*	**	***	****
*wade walk in water	wafer	**wastefully**	
wage d	wager ed		
waif	waistcoat	**weightlessness**	
*wail ed cry	*waited did wait		
*waist narrow part of body	waiter		
*wait stay	waiting		
*waive no longer enforce	waitress es		
wake d	waken ed		
[woke]	wasted		
[woken]	wasteland		
Wales	wavelength		
wane d	waver ed		
*waste rubbish	waving		
*wave hand signal / surge	wavy -ier, -iest		
waved	waylay		
*way path	[waylaid]		
	wayside		
*weigh find the weight of	weighbridge		
*weighed found the weight of	weighing		
*weight heaviness / value	*weighted having added weight		
	weightless		
	weighty -ier, -iest		
*whale sea-mammal	whaler		
*whey watery part of sour milk			

for Scots: ae-r is on page 241

Y

*	**	***	****
yea			

In these words you can hear the vowel sound **ae** as in snail

A

*	**	***	**** *
	achieve d	achievement	abbreviation
	adhere d	adhesive	aesthetically
	agree d	Aegean	agreeable
	anneal ed	aesthetic ally	amenable
	appeal ed	agreement	anaemia / anemia
	appear ed	allegiance	anaesthetist /
	appease d	amino	anesthetist
	asleep	amoeba	appreciable
	austere	anaemic / anemic	appreciate
		appearance	appreciation
		appeasement	appreciative
		arena	

B

*	**	***	****
*be to be / exist	batik	beefeater	believable
*beach es shore			
beached	beacon	bikini	
bead	beagle		
beak ed	beagling		
beam ed	beaker		
*bean vegetable	beanbag		
beard	beanstalk		
beast	beaten		
*beat batter / defeat	*beater person or		
[beat]	thing that beats		
[beaten]	beating		
*bee insect	beaver ed		
*beech tree	beehive		
beef ed	beeswax		
*been from 'to be'	beetle		
*beer drink	beetroot		
*beet plant with	being		
sweet root	belief		
	believe d		
*bier frame to bear	beneath		
coffin	bereave d		
	[bereft]		
bleach es	beseech es		
bleached	beseeched		
bleak	[besought]		
bleat	besiege d		
bleed	*beta Greek letter b		
[bled]	between		
bleep ed			
	breathing		
*breach es gap / act of	briefcase		
breaking	briefly		
breached			
*breaches gaps /			
does breach			
breathe d			
*breech es bottom			
part of gun			
*breeches trousers			
for riding			
breed			
[bred]			
breeze d			
brief ed			

In these words the first letter 'e' is pronounced like the 'i' in 'pig'.

B*E*NEVOLENT WORDS

beatitude	befriend	behold	beside
became	begin	[beheld]	besides
because	[began]	belated	bestow ed
become	[begun]	belong ed	betray ed
[became]	beginner	belonging	betrayal
[become]	beginning	beloved	betwixt
becoming	behalf	below	beware
befall	behave d	benevolent	bewilder ed
[befell]	behaviour	bereft	bewitch es
[befallen]	behead	beset	bewitched
before	beheld	[beset]	beyond
beforehand	behind	besetting	

In these words you can hear the vowel sound *ee* as in *eagle*

C

*	**	***	****
ceased	**career**ed	**cathedral**	**chameleon**
***cede** give up			
	cedar	***cereal** food from	**comedian**
***cheap** at low cost	***ceiling** inner roof	grain / plant	**comedienne**
cheat	of room	producing grain	**congenial**ly
cheeked			**convenience**
***cheep** chirp	**cheaper**	**cheerfully**	**convenient**
cheeped	***cheater** person who		
cheered	cheats	**completely**	
cheesed	**cheeky** -ier, -iest	**completion**	
chief	**cheerful**ly	**conceited**	
	***cheetah** animal		
cleaned	**chiefly**	**creosote**	
cleared	**chieftain**		
cleat		Korea	
cleaved	**cleaner**	Korean	
[cleft]	**cleaning**		
[clove]	**clearance**	*serial parts in order	
[cloven]	**clearing**		
	clearly		
***creak** noise	**cleavage**		
creaked	**cliché**		
creamed			
creased	**compete**		
creed	**complete**		
***creek** inlet / stream	**conceal**ed		
creep	**conceit**		
[crept]	**conceive**d		
keel ed	**creature**		
keen	**creeper**		
keep			
[kept]	keeper		
***key** lever for lock or	keeping		
other mechanism /	Kenya		
important / musical scale	keyhole		
keyed			
	kiosk		
*quay wharf			
	*sealing fastening		
*seed part of a plant			

*seed part of a plant
from which a new one
can grow / selected
player in a tournament
draw

for Qu . . .
see page 167 ▷

Here the first letter 'e' has a short 'i' sound.

CR**E**ATIVE WORDS

celestial	credential
cement	cremate
create d	cremation
creating	crescendo s
creation	crevasse
creative	

In these words you can hear the vowel sound ee as in eagle

D

*	**	***	**** **
deal	**dealer**	**deceitful** ly	**deceitfully**
[dealt]	**decease** d	**decoding**	**decelerate**
***dean** presiding	**deceit**	**decompose** d	**deceleration**
officer	**deceive** d	**defeated**	**decomposer**
***dear** beloved /	**decent**	**deflation**	**decomposition**
expensive	**decode**	**deism**	**decompression**
deed	**decrease** d	**deity** -ies	**deformation**
deem ed	**decree** d	**deletion**	**denitrify** -ies
deep	**deepen** ed	**demeanour**	denitrified
***deer** [deer] animal	**deeper**	**devalue** d	**deodorant**
***dene** small valley	**deeply**	**deviate**	**deposition**
	defeat		**depreciate**
dream ed	**defect**		**depreciation**
[dreamt]	**deflate**		**deteriorate**
	defrost		**deterioration**
	degree		**devaluation**
	deist		**deviation**
	delete		
	demean ed		
	demon		
	detail ed		
	detour		
	diesel		
	***discreet** careful		
	not to embarrass		
	***discrete** separate		
	disease d		
	displease d		
	dreaming		
	dreary -ier, -iest		

In these words the first letter 'e' is pronounced like the short 'i' in 'pig'.

D*E*LIGHTFUL WORDS

debate	defender	demand ed	deposit ed	design ed	deter red
decamp ed	defensive	demobbed	depositing	designer	detergent
decay ed	defer red	democracy -ies	depress es	desirable	determination
December	deferring	demolish es	depressed	desire d	determine d
deception	defiance	demolished	depression	despair ed	determiner
deceptive	defiant	demonstrative	depressive	despatch es	determining
decide	deficiency -ies	denial	deprive d	despatched	deterrence
deciduous	deficient	denomination	derail ed	despise d	deterrent
decipher ed	define d	denominator	derailment	despite	deterring
decision	deflect ion	denote	derivative	despondency	detest
decisive	deform ed	denounce d	derive d	despondent	detract
declare d	defy -ies	deny -ies	derogatory	dessert	develop ed
decline d	defied	denied	descend ed	destroy ed	developer
decry -ies	delay ed	depart ure	descendant	destroyer	developing
decried	deliberate ly	department	descendent	destruction	development
deduce d	delicious	depend ed	descent	destructive	developmental
deduct	delight ed	dependable	describe d	detach es	device
deduction	delightful ly	dependant	describing	detached	devise d
deductive	delirious	dependants	description	detain ed	devote d
defect or	deliver ed	dependence	descriptive	detect ion	devotion
defective	deliverance	dependency -ies	desert ed	detective	devour ed
defence	delivery -ies	dependent	deserter	detector	devout
defend ant	delusion	deport	deserve d	detention	

In these words you can hear the vowel sound **ee** as in **eagle**

E

*

each
ear
ease d
east
eat
[ate]
[eaten]
eaves

eel

eke d

eve

**

eager
eagle
earache
eardrum
earmark ed
earring
earshot
easel
Easter
eastern
eastward
easy -ier, -iest
eaten
eating

*eerie weird

Egypt

either

élite

emu

equal led

era

ether

even
evening
evil ly

exceed
excrete
extreme

*eyrie / eyry -ies nest
of bird of prey

***

aesthetic ally

eagerly
eagerness
easier
easiest
easily

élitist

endearment

equalise d
          ze
equalling
equally

evenly

exceeding
excretion
extremely
extremist

Oedipal
Oedipus
oestrogen

**** ***

aesthetically

easygoing

ecclesiastical ly
ecological ly
economic
economical ly
economics
economy -ies
ecosystem
ecumenical ly

élitism
elongation

equatorial ly
equiangular
equidistant
equilateral
equilibrium

esophagus / oesophagus
[esophagi]

Ethiopia

evangelical
evangelist
evolution
evolutionary

exceedingly
expediency
expedient
experience d
exterior

See also E
on page 65

See also I
on page 72

for H . . .
see page 160

for I . . .
see page 161

First sound = 'i'.

EFFECTIVE WORDS
ecclesiastical ly
eclipse d
ecology
edition
effect
effective ly
effectiveness
efficient
Egyptian
eject ion
ejector
elaborate
elaboration
elastic ally
elasticity
elate d
elation
elect ion
elector
electoral ly
electorate
electrical ly
electrician
electricity
electrocute
electrode
electrolysis
electrolyte
electrolytic ally
electromagnetic ally
electron
electronic ally
eleven th
elicit ed
eliciting
eliminate
elimination
Elizabethan
ellipse
elliptical ly
elope d
elude
elusive
emancipate

emancipation
emerge d
emergence
emergency -ies
emission
emit ted
emitter
emitting
emotional ly
emotive
emulsion ed
enable d
enabling

enact
enamel led
enamelling
enamour ed
enormous
enough
enumerate
equality
equation
equator
equip ped
equipment
equipping

equivalence
equivalent
erase d
eraser
erect
erection
erode
erosion
erotic ally
erratic ally
erroneous ly
erupt ed
eruption

escape d
escarpment
especially
essential ly
establish es
established
establishment
estate
estrange d
eternal ly
eternity
evacuate
evacuation

evacuee
evade
evaluate
evaluation
evaporate
evaporation
evasion
evasive
event
eventual ly
evict
evoke d
evolve d

F

*

fear ed
feast
*feat act
fee
feed
[fed]
feel
[felt]
*feet more than one
foot

field
fiend
fierce
fiord / fjord

*flea insect
*flee run away
[fled]
fleece d
fleet

freak ed
free d
*freeze chill /change
from liquid to solid /
hold steady
[froze]
[frozen]
*frieze decorated
band / type of cloth

for th . . .
see page 172 ▷

* *

faeces
fatigue d

fearful ly
fearless
feature d
feeble
feedback
feeding
feeler
feeling
female
fever ed

fielder
fiercely
fiord / fjord

fleecy -ier, -iest

foresee
[foresaw]
[foreseen]

freedom
freehand
freely
freestyle
freezer
freezing
frequent

* * *

facetious

fearfully
feasible
feverish

fiesta

frequency -ies
frequently

* * * * *

feasibility

Here the first letter 'e' has a short 'i' sound.

ferocious   ferocity   frenetic ally

In these words you can hear the vowel sound **ee** as in **eagle**

G

*	**	***	**** *
gear ed	genie	galena	genealogy -ies
geese	geyser		genially
gene		genial ly	
*genes more than	greasy -ier, -iest	genius es	
one gene	greedy -ier, -iest		
	greengage	graffiti	
gleam ed	greenhouse	greedily	
glee	Greenland	greenery	
	greeted	Greenlander	
*grease oily substance	greeting		
greased	grievance		
*Greece country			
greed	Jesus		
Greek			
green			
greet			
grief			
grieve d			
*jeans trousers			
jeep			
jeer ed			

Here the first letter 'e' has a short 'i' sound.

genetic ally	geology
geographical ly	geometrical ly
geography -ies	geometry -ies
geological ly	geranium

H

*

he
*heal ed   cure /
get better
heap ed
*hear   receive by ear
[heard]
*hears   does hear
heat
heath
heave
[hove]
heaved
*he'd   he had / he
would
*heed   notice / take
seriously
*heel   part of foot /
shoe
heeled
*he'll   he will
*here   in this place
*here's   here is
he's

* *

healer
hearing
hearsay
heated
heater
heathen
heating
heatwave
Hebrew
heedless
hereby
hero es

* * *

haematite / hematite

helium
hereafter
heretofore

* * * *

hysteria

Here the first letter 'e' has a short 'i' sound.

heroic ally

In these words you can hear the vowel sound **ee** as in **eagle**

I

*	**	***	**** **
	impede	illegal ly	illegally
	increase d	immediate	immediate
	indeed	impeachment	immediately
	intrigue d		imperial ly
		increasing	imperialism
		infrequent	imperious
		ingenious	
		intriguing	increasingly
			inferior
			inferiority
			ingenious
			ingredient
			interior

for E . . .
see page 157

See also E
on page 65

See also I
on page 72

In these words you can hear the vowel sound ee as in eagle

J

*	**	***	****
gene	genie	genius es	
*genes more than one gene			
	Jesus		
*jeans trousers			
jeep			
jeer ed			

 for dr . . .
see page 156

K

*	**	***	****
keel ed	keeper	Korea	
keen	keeping	Korean	
keep	Kenya		
[kept]	keyboard		
*key lever for lock	keyhole		
or other mechanism /			
important / musical	kilo		
scale	kiosk		
keyed	kiwi		

*knead press with
hands
knee
kneel ed
[knelt]

*need require

*quay wharf

for C . . .
see page 155

for Qu . . .
see page 167

In these words you can hear the vowel sound ee as in eagle

L

*

*lea meadow
*lead show the way
  by going first / leash
  [led]
leaf leaves
league
*leak unwanted escape
leaked
lean ed
  [leant]
leap ed
  [leapt]
lease
*leased rented
leash es
leashed
*least smallest amount
leave
  [left]
leaves
*lee shelter /
  sheltered side
*leek vegetable
leer ed

*lied German song

**

leaching
*leader leading
  person or thing
leading
leaflet
leaning
leapfrog ged
*leaver person
  who leaves
leaving
leeward
legal ly
legion
lethal ly
*lever tool
levered

*lieder German
  songs
litre

***

leadership
legalise d
    ze
legally
lenient
leotard
leverage

Lima-bean

****

Here the first letter 'e' has a short 'i' sound.

legality -ies   legitimate
legato   lethargic

In these words you can hear the vowel sound **ee** as in **eagle**   **163**

* ****** ******* ****** ******

me	**machine** d	**machinist**	**machinery**
meal	**marine**		**material** ly
*mean intend /		**meaningful** ly	
miserly / poor	**meagre**	**media**	**meaningfully**
[meant]	**mealtime**	**median**	**mediation**
*meat flesh of	**meaning**	**mediate**	**mediator**
animal	**meantime**	**medium**	**meteorite**
meek	**meanwhile**	**meteor**	**meteorological** ly
*meet be in contact /	**measles**	**meteorite**	**meteorology**
encounter	**meeting**		
[met]	**merely**		**mysterious**
mere	***meter** measuring		
	machine		
*mien bearing /	**metered**		
look of person	**methane**		
	*metre unit of		
	length / verse		
	rhythm		
	misdeal		
	[misdealt]		
	mislead		
	[misled]		
	mystique		

Here the first letter 'e' has a short 'i' sound.

meander ed	meniscus es/-i
mechanic ally	meridian
melodic ally	methodical ly
melodious	meticulous
memento es / s	metropolis es
memorial	mnemonic

In these words you can hear the vowel sound **ee** as in **eagle**

N

*

*knead press with
hands
knee
kneel ed
[knelt]

near ed
neat
*need require

niche
niece

**

nearby
nearer
nearest
nearly
neatly
needed
needle d
needling
needy -ier, -iest
negro es
neither
neon

***

**** *

Neapolitan

Here the first letter 'e' has a short 'i' sound.

necessity -ies   neglect   negotiate
negation   neglectful ly negotiation

O

*

**

obscene

***

Oedipal
Oedipus
oestrogen

****

obedience
obedient

oesophagus / esophagus
[oesophagi]

P

*	**	***	**** **
*pea vegetable	peaceful ly	paprika	pediatric
*peace period without war	peacetime		pediatrician
	peacock	peaceable	periodic
peach es	peahen	peacefully	periodical ly
*peak highest point	peanuts	penalise d	
peak ed	peevish	ze	pianoforte
*peal ringing	penis es	period	
*pealed rang	people d		policewoman
peat	perceive d	pianist	[policewomen]
*pee urinate		piano s	
*peel rind / skin	pianist	pierrot	predecessor
*peeled removed the rind or skin	piano s		prefabricate
	pierrot	policeman	prehistoric ally
peen ed		[policemen]	previously
peep ed	pleasing	policewoman	
*peer ed look hard / person of equal rank / lord		[policewomen]	
	police d		
	policeman	preceded	
	[policemen]	preceding	
*piece part		premature	
pieced		premium	
*pier upright support / structure extending into the sea	preacher	premolar	
	precede	previous	
	precinct	procedure	
	prefect	proceeding	
pierce d	prefix es		
*pique hurt pride	prefixed		
	pretext		
plea	preview		
plead	priestess es		
*pleas requests	proceed		
*please used when asking / give pleasure			
pleased			
pleat			
police d			
preach es			
preached			
preen ed			
priest			

In these words the first letter 'e' is pronounced like the 'i' in 'pig'.

PH**E**NOMENAL WORDS

peculiar	precaution	preferring	preside
pedestrian	precipitate	preliminary -ies	presumably
peninsula	precipitation	prepare d	presume d
peninsular	precise ly	preparing	presumptuous
perimeter	precision	prescribe d	pretence
peroxide	precocious	prescription	pretend ed
petition ed	predict	present ed	pretentious
petroleum	prediction	presentable	prevail ed
phenomenal ly	predictable	presenting	prevent
phenomenon	predominant ly	preservative	prevention
[phenomena]	prefer red	preserve d	preventive

In these words you can hear the vowel sound **ee** as in **eagle**

Q

*	**	***	****
*key lever for lock or other mechanism / important / musical scale	**quayside** **queasy** -ier, -iest **query** -ies		
*quay wharf **queen** ed **queer** **quiche**			

R

*	**	***	**** **
reach es **reached** *read look at and understand [read] *real genuine **ream** ed **reap** ed **rear** ed *reed plant / vibrating strip **reef** ed *reek ed stink *reel ed spool / wind / stagger *wreak ed bring about wreath ed	**ravine** **reaches** **reaching** **react** **reader** **reading** **really** **reamer** **rearm** ed **reason** ed **rebate** **rebound** **rebuild** [rebuilt] **receipt** **receive** d *recent not long past **recess** es **recessed** **reclaim** ed **recoil** ed *recount tell a story *recount count again **redo** [redid] [redone] **refill** ed **reflex** es **refuel** led **refund** **regain** ed **regime** / **régime** **region** **regroup** ed **reject** ☛	**reaction** **reactor** **readable** **readjust** **reagent** **realise** d 　　ze **reappear** ed **rearrange** d **reasoning** **reassure** d **recapture** d **receding** **receiver** **receiving** **recently** **reconstruct** **recycle** d **refuel** led / ed **regional** ly **regrouping** **reinforce** d **remodel** led **renaming** **repeated** **repeating** **replacement** **reproduce** d **researcher** **retriever** **reunion** **rewritten** **rheostat**	**reactionary** -ies **realism** **realistic** ally **reality** -ies **reasonable** **reassemble** **reassurance** **rechargeable** **reconstitute** **regionally** **rehabilitation** **reincarnation** **reinforcement** **reiteration** **relaxation** **reproduction** **reunion**

In these words you can hear the vowel sound ee as in *eagle*

* *

***relaid** laid again
relapse
relay
[relaid]
***relayed** sent on as
received
release d
relief
relieve d
remake
[remade]
rename d
repay
[repaid]
repeal ed
repeat
repent
replace d
research es
researched
reset
[reset]
retail ed
retell
[retold]
retread
retreat
retrieve d
reveal ed
rewrite
[rewrote]
[rewritten]

*-resent feel angry at

Here the first letter 'e' has a short 'i' sound.

REFRESHING WORDS

rebel led	regretful ly	repute
rebelling	regretting	request
rebellion	rehearsal	require d
rebellious	rehearse d	requirement
rebound	reject ion	resemblance
rebuke d	rejoice d	resemble d
recall ed	rejoin ed	resembling
receptacle	relate d	resent
reception ist	relating	resentful ly
receptive	relation ship	resentment
recession	relax es	reserve d
recessive	relaxed	reside
reciprocal ly	relent less	resign ed
reciprocate	reliability	resist ance
recital	reliable	resistor
recite	reliance	resolve d
reclaim ed	religion	resort
recline d	religious	resource d
recoil ed	reluctance	resources
record ed	reluctant ly	respect able
recorder	rely -ies	respectful ly
recording	relied	respective ly
recount	remain ed	respire d
recourse	remainder	respond
recover ed	remaining	response
recovery -ies	remark ed	responsibility -ies
recruit	remarkable	responsible
recur red	remember ed	responsive
recurrence	remembering	restore d
recurrent	remembrance	restrain ed
recurring	remind ed	restraint
redemption	reminder	restrict ion
reduce d	remote	result ed
reduction	removable /	resultant
redundancy -ies	removeable	resulting
redundant	removal	resume d
refer red	remove d	resuscitate
referral	removing	resuscitation
referring	Renaissance	retain ed
refine d	renege d	retard ed
refinery -ies	renew ed	retire d
reflect ed	renewal	retirement
reflection	renown ed	retort
reflector	repair ed	return ed
reflexive	repel led	returnable
reform ed	repellent	returning
refract ion	repelling	revenge d
refractive	repentance	reverberate
refrain ed	repetitive	reversal
refresh es	reply -ies	reverse d
refreshed	replied	reversible
refreshment	report ed	review ed
refrigerator	reporter	revise d
refund	repose d	revision
refusal	repress ion	revival
refuse d	repressive	revive d
refute	reprisal	revolt
regain ed	reproach es	revolve d
regard ed	reproached	revolver
regardless	republic an	revue
regatta	repudiate	revulsion
regret ted	repulsive	reward

In these words you can hear the vowel sound ee as in eagle

S

*

cease d
*cede give up

*scene part of play /
display / place / view
scheme d
scream ed
screech es
screeched
screen ed

*sea ocean

seal ed
*seam ed join
*sear burn the surface
with sudden heat
*seas oceans
seat
*see register by eye /
understand
[saw]
[seen]
*seed part of a plant
from which a new
one can grow /
selected player in a
tournament draw
*seek look for
[sought]
*seem ed appear
*seen registered by
eye / understood
seep ed
*seer prophet
*sees does see
seethe d
*seize grab
seize d
☞

* *

cedar
*ceiling inner roof of
room

scenic ally

seafood
seagull
*sealing fastening
sealskin
*seaman sailor
*seamen sailors
seaport
seashore
seasick
seaside
season ed
seated
seaweed
*secret kept hidden
*secrete produce
liquid in body / hide
seedling
seeing
seeking
seesaw
seething
seizure
*semen sperm-carrying
liquid
sepal
sequel
sequence
sequin ned
serene
series
settee
severe

sheepdog
sheepish
sheepskin

*signor Italian for 'Mr.'
sincere

skier
skiing

sleeper
sleeping

speaker
speaking
species
speedy -ier, -iest
☞

* * *

*cereal food from grain /
plant producing grain

scenery
scenically
sclerosis

seafarer
seasickness
seasoning
secrecy
secretion
*senior older / more
important
*serial ly parts in
order
serious
severely

signora
Sikhism
sincerely

sleepily

strategic ally

* * * * *

scenically

seniority -ies
serially
seriously

signorina

speedometer

stereotype
strategically

superior
superiority

In these words you can hear the vowel sound **ee** as in **eagle**   **169**

*

she
sheaf -ves
***shear** ed cut off
wool or hair
[shorn]
shears
sheath ed
she'd
sheen
sheep sheep
***sheer** pure / very
steep / very thin / go
off at an angle
sheered
sheet
she'll
she's
shield
shriek ed

siege
***Sikh** member of
an Indian sect

ski ed

sleek
sleep
[slept]
sleet
sleeve d

smear ed

sneak ed
sneer ed
sneeze d

speak
[spoke]
[spoken]
spear ed
speech es
speed
[sped]
sphere
spree

squeak ed
squeal ed
squeeze d
☞

* *

squeegee

steamer
steeple
steering
streaky -ier, -iest
streamer
streamlined

succeed

sweeper
sweeping
sweetheart
Sweden
Swedish

In these words you can hear the vowel sound **ee** as in **eagle**

S

*

***steal** thieve /
move quietly
[stole]
[stolen]
steam ed
steed
***steel** metal
steeled
steep
steer ed
streak ed
stream ed
street

***suite** pieces that
go together

***Swede** Swedish person
***swede** type of turnip
sweep
[swept]
***sweet** of sugary
taste / nice

Here the first letter 'e' has a short 'i' sound.

SELECTED WORDS

scenario s	selection
secession	selective
seclude d	selector
secure d	sequoia
security -ies	serenity
select ed	severity -ies
selecting	specific ally

T

*

tea drink / meal
teaches
[taught]
teak
team working
group / playing
side
teamed
tear sign of distress
teas drinks / meals
teased mock in fun /
comb
teat
tee support for
golf ball
teem swarm
teemed
teens
teeth

thee
theme
these
thief
three

tier one of a
number of levels
tiered

treat
tree

tweed
tweet

* *

T-shirt / teeshirt

teacher
teaching
teamwork
teapot
teaspoon
tearfully
teeming
teepee / tepee
teeshirt / T-shirt
teething

theatre
theorem
theory -ies
thesis -es

trapeze
treacle
treason
treatment
treaty -ies
treetops
trio

tweezers

* * *

tearfully
teaspoonful
tedious
tedium
teenager

trachea

* * * * * *

theatrically
theodolite
theologian
theologically
theology -ies
theoretically

trapezium

Here the first letter 'e' has a short 'i' sound.

T**E**RRIFIC WORDS
telegraphy
telephonist
terrestrial ly

terrific ally
thesaurus es / -i
tremendous

In these words you can hear the vowel sound **ee** as in **eagle**

V

*	**	***	****
veal	vehicle	vehement	
	veneer ed	vehicle	
via	Venus		
	veto es	viola	
	vetoed		
	via		
	visa		

> **In these words the first 'e' is a neutral vowel.**
> velocity -ies   veranda / verandah

In these words you can hear the vowel sound **ee** as in **eagle**   **173**

W

*	**	***	****

*reek ed stink

weaken ed
weakling
weakness es

wearily
weariness

*we people speaking
*weak feeble
*weal mark left on
skin by whip
*weald open or
wooded country
*weave interlace
threads
[wove]
[woven]
*we'd we had / we
would
*wee small / pass
water
*weed passed water
*weed unwanted
wild plant
*week seven days
weep
[wept]
*weir dam across
river
weird
*we'll we will
*we're we are
*we've we have

wheat
*wheel round rotating
frame or disc
*wheeled did wheel
wheeze d

*wield have and use

*wreak ed bring about
wreath ed

weary -ier, -iest
weasel
weaver
weaving
weekday
weekend
weekly
weevil
 werewolf
[werewolves]

wheelchair
wheelie

wheelbarrow

In these words you can hear the vowel sound ee as in eagle

Y

*

ye
year
yeast

yield

**

yielding

***

****

Z

*

zeal

**

zebra
zero es / s

***

****

In these words you can hear the vowel sound *ee* as in *eagle*

*	**	***	****
*aisle part of church / gangway	abide [abode]	abided	advisable advisory
*aye yes	acquire d	adviser	annihilate
	admire d advice advise d	alignment alliance almighty	
	alight align ed alike alive ally -ies allied	appliance arrival	
	apply -ies applied	assignment asylum	
	arise [arose] [arisen] arrive d		
	ascribe d aside aspire d assign ed		

for H . . .
see page 182 ▷

awhile
awry

In these words you can hear the vowel sound **ie** as in **lion**

B

*

bide d
[bode]
bike d
bile
bind
[bound]
*bite tear with teeth
[bit]
[bitten]

blight
blind

bribe
bride
bright
brine

*buy purchase
[bought]
*buyer purchaser

*by beside / not
after / past /
through / etc.
*byre cow-house
*byte unit of
information

**

behind
beside
besides

bias ed / sed
bible
biceps
binder
binding
biped
biro
bisect
bison

blindfold
blindness

*bridal of the bride
bridegroom
bridesmaid
*bridle headgear for
controlling a horse
bridled
bridling
brighten ed
brighter
brightest
brightly

buying

bye-bye
bygone
bypass ed
byway

***

biasing / biassing
bicycle d
bifocal
bilingual
binary

bribery

by-product

**** **

biennial ly
bifurcated
bilateral ly
binomial
biochemical
biochemist
biochemistry
biographical ly
biography -ies
biological ly
biologist
biology

by-election

C

*

chide d
[chid / chidden]
child
chime d
*choir singing
group / part of
church
Christ

*cite give as
example / quote

climb ed

cried
cries
crime
cry -ies
cried

kind
kite

*quire 24 sheets of
writing paper

*sight vision
*site place

for Qu . . .
see page 189 ▷

**

childhood
china
China
Chinese

cider
cipher ed

client
climate
climax es
climaxed
climber
climbing

collide
combine d
compile d
comprise d
concise
confide
confine d
conspire d

crisis -es
crying

cycle d
cycling
cyclist
cyclone
*cypress es tree
*Cyprus island

kindly
kindness

psychic ally

***

climatic
clitoris

combining
comprising

confinement

psychical ly
psychosis
[psychoses]
psychotic ally

****

criterion
[criteria]

cytoplasm

kaleidoscope

psychiatric ally
psychiatrist
psychiatry
psychically
psychoanalyse d
psychoanalysis
psychoanalyst
psychological ly
psychologist
psychology
psychotherapist
psychotherapy
psychotically

D

*

dial led
dice
☞

**

decide
decline d
decry -ies
decried
☞

***

decipher ed
decisive
defiance
defiant
☞

****

delightfully
desirable
☞

In these words you can hear the vowel sound ie as in lion

D

*

die cease living /
small cube / tool
for stamping or
shaping
died
dike / dyke
dine have dinner
dined
dire desperate
dive d

dried
drive
[drove]
[driven]
dry -ies
dried

dye d stain
dyer person using
dyes
dyke / dike
dyne unit of force

**

define d
defy -ies
defied
delight
deny -ies
denied
deprive d
derive d
describe d
design ed
desire d
despise d
despite
device gadget /
plan
devise d invent /
work out

dial led
dialling
diamond
diary -ies
diecast
diet
digest
dilute
dining
direct
disguise d
dislike d
dissect
diver
diverge d
diverse
divert
divide
divine d
diving

drier more dry
driest
drily / dryly
driver
driveway
driving
dryer / drier person,
substance or
machine that dries
drying
dryly / drily

dyeing using dye
dying ceasing to live

***

delighted
delightful ly
denial
describing
designer

diagnose d
diagram
dialect
dialling
dialogue
diamond
diaphragm
diarrhoea
diatom
digestion
dilemma
diluted
dimension
dinosaur
dioxide
directed
direction
directive
directly
director
disciple
diversion
divided
dividers
dividing
divisor

dynamic ally
dynamite
dynamo s

**** ***

diabetes
diabetic
diabolical ly
diagnosis -es
diagnostic ally
diagonal ly
diagrammatic ally
dialectical ly
diameter
diarrhoea
digestible
dimensional
directory -ies
diversity

dynamically
dynamometer

E

*

*eye visual organ
*eyed looked at
 with interest

*I the person speaking
*I'd I would / I had

**

eider
either

enquire / inquire d
entire

esquire

excite
expire d

eyeball
eyebrow
eyeing / eying
eyelash es
*eyelet small hole
eyelid
eyesight

***

eisteddfod

enlighten ed
enquiry / inquiry -ies
entirely
entitle d

excited
excitement
exciting

eyewitness es

**** **

encyclopedia
environment
environmental ly

excitable
excitedly

for H . . .
see page 182 ▷

for I . . .
see page 183 ▷

In these words you can hear the vowel sound ie as in lion

F

*

fight
[fought]
*file tool / information
system / line of people
filed
*find discover
[found]
fine
*fined made to pay
a fine
fire d
five

flies
flight
fly -ies
[flew]
[flown]

*friar religious man
who lives by begging
fried
*frier / fryer person or
equipment that fries
fright
fry -ies
fried
*fryer / frier person or
equipment that fries

*phial small vessel or
bottle

for th . . .
see page 192 ▷

**

fibre
fibrous
fiery
fighter
fighting
final
finance d
finding
finest
finite
firearm
firefly -ies
firelight
fireman
[firemen]
fireplace
fireproof
fireside
firewood
firework
firing
fiver

flier
flying
flywheel

*friar religious man
who lived by begging
Friday
*frier / fryer person or
equipment that fries
frighten ed
frightening
frightful ly
*fryer / frier person or
equipment that fries

***

fibreglass
finally
financial ly
fire-engine
firefighter
firewoman
[firewomen]

frightening

****

finality
financially
financier

G

*	**	***	**** ***
*gibe/jibe taunt	Geiger	gigantic	gynaecologically
			gynaecologist
glide	giant	Guyana	gynaecology
*gneiss rock	glider	gyroscope	
	gliding		
grime			
grind	goodbye		
[ground]	goodnight		
*guide show the way	grimy -ier, -iest		
*guise appearance	grinder		
guy			
*guyed ridiculed	guidance		
*guys more than one guy / does guy	gyrate		
*gybe/gibe/jibe alter course by swinging sail	jiving		
jive d			

H

*	**	***	**** ***
height	haiku	hibernate	hibernation
		highwayman	hieroglyphics
*hi greeting	heighten ed		
hide		horizon	hydraulically
[hid]	hiding		hydrocarbon
[hidden]	hi-fi	hyacinth	hydrochloric
*high tall / great	higher	hydraulic ally	hydroelectric ally
*higher taller / greater	highest	hydrofoil	hydrometer
hike d	highlands	hydrogen	hygienically
hind	highlight	hydroxide	*hyperbola form of curve
*hire d grant or obtain use if a payment is made/ employ	highly	hygienic ally	*hyperbole exaggeration
hive d	Highness	hyphenate	hyphenated
	highrise		hypotenuse
	highroad		hypothesis -es
	highway		hypothetical ly
	hijack ed		
	hiker		
	hindsight		
	hybrid		
	hygiene		
	hyphen		

In these words you can hear the vowel sound **ie** as in lion

I

*

*aisle part of church / gangway

*aye yes

*eye visual organ
*eyed looked at with interest

*I the person speaking

ice d

*I'd I would / I had

*I'll I will

I'm

*ion charged particle

*iron metal
ironed

*isle island

I've

for E . . .
see page 180

**

eider
either

*eyelet small hole

iceberg
ice-cream
ice-floe
Iceland
icing
icon / ikon
icy -ier, -iest

idea
ideal ly
*idle lazy
*idol image for worship

ignite

ikon / icon

imply -ies
implied

*incite urge
incline d
inquire / enquire d
inscribe d
inside
*insight understanding
inspire d
invite

*ion charged particle

irate
Ireland
iris es
Irish
*iron metal
ironed
ironing

island
*islet small island

item

ivy

***

eisteddfod

icicle

idea
ideal ly
idolise d
    ze

incisive
incisor
inquiry / enquiry -ies
insider
invited

iodine
iota

Irishman
ironic ally
ironmonger

isolate
isotope

itemise d
    ze

ivory -ies

**** ***

idealistic ally
idealise d
    ze
ideally
identical ly
identifiable
identification
identified
identify -ies
identified
identity -ies
ideological ly

ironical ly
ironmonger

isolation
isometric ally
isomorphic
isosceles
isotopic

itinerant
itinerary -ies

In these words you can hear the vowel sound **ie** as in lion

183

J

*
*gybe / gibe / jibe alter
course by swinging sail

*jibe / gibe taunt
jive d

◀ for dr . . .
see page 179

* *
giant

gyrate

jiving

* * *
gigantic

gyroscope

* * * *

K

*
**kind
kite**

knife
[knives]
knifed
*knight Sir — /
chess piece

◀ for C . . .
see page 178

for Qu . . .
see page 189 ▶

* *
kayak

**kindly
kindness**

* * *
kinetic

* * * *
kaleidoscope

In these words you can hear the vowel sound **ie** as in **lion**

L

*

*liar person who
tells lies
lice
*lie d tell untruth
*lie place oneself in a
horizontal position
[lay]
[lain]
life
[lives]
light
[lit]
like d
lime d
line d
lion
lithe

*lyre musical
instrument

**

*liar person who
tells lies
*libel harmful
statement
*licence official
permission
*license d give
official permission
*lichen plant
lido s
lifeboat
lifeless
lifelike
lifestyle
lifetime
lighted
lighter
lightest
lighthouse
lighting
*lightning electric
flash in the sky
lightweight
likely
*liken ed point out
similarities
likewise
lilac
limeade
limelight
limestone
liner
linesman
[linesmen]
lining
lino s

lion
lively -ier, -iest
livestock

lying
*lyre musical
instrument

***

*liable likely /
under obligation
library -ies
*lightening making
lighter
likelihood
livelihood
liveliness

****

librarian

In these words you can hear the vowel sound **ie** as in **lion**

185

M

*

mice
*might would
perhaps / power
mild
mile
mime d
*mind system of
thought and feeling /
look after /
watch / object
mine
*mined did mine
*mite tiny thing

my

**

mica
microbe
mighty
migrant
migrate
mileage
milestone
mindless
*miner worker in
mine
mining
*minor less
important
minus
minute
miser
mitre d

myself

***

Messiah

microchip
microphone
microscope
microwave
mightily
migration
migratory

**** *

microcomputer
micrometer
microprocessor
microscopic
minority -ies
mitochondria

In these words you can hear the vowel sound **ie** as in **lion**

N

*

*gneiss rock

knife
[knives]
knifed
*knight Sir — / chess
piece

***nice** pleasant
nigh
***night** hours of
darkness
nine
ninth

* *

naive

neither

nightclub
nightdress
nightfall
nightie
nightmare
night-time
nineteen th
ninety -ies
nitrate
nitric

nylon

* * *

nightingale
ninetieth
nitrify -ies
nitrified
nitrogen

* * * * *

Nigeria
nitrification
nitrifying

O

*

* *

alright

oblige d

* * *

almighty

* * * *

P

*

*phial small vessel or bottle

*pi 3·142 / Greek letter
*pie meat or fruit baked in pastry
pike
pile d
pine d
pint
pipe d

pliers
plight
ply -ies
plied

price d
*pride high opinion of oneself
*pried did pry
*pries does pry or prise
prime d
prior
*prise / prize lever with a metal bar
*prised did prise
*prize reward / value / prise
*prized did prize
pry -ies
pried

pyre

**

perspire d

phylum
[phyla]

pilot
pious
pipeline
piper
piping
pirate

pliers
plywood

polite

precise
prescribe d
preside
primate
prior
private
provide

psychic ally

pylon
python

***

piety
pineapple
pioneer

politely

precisely
primary -ies
primeval
privacy
provided
providing

psychical ly
psychosis
[psychoses]
psychotic ally

pyrites

**** **

primarily
priority -ies
proprietor

psychiatric ally
psychiatrist
psychiatry
psychically
psychoanalyse d
psychoanalysis
psychoanalyst
psychological ly
psychologist
psychology
psychotherapist
psychotherapy
psychotically

188   In these words you can hear the vowel sound **ie** as in **lion**

Q

*

*choir singing group /
part of church

quiet
*quire 24 sheets of
writing paper
quite

**

quiet

***

quietly

****

R

*

*rhyme / rime to
end with the
same sound
rhymed

rice
ride
[rode]
[ridden]
*right correct /
direction
rile d
*rime hoar-frost
rind
ripe
rise
[rose]
[risen]
*rite ceremony

*rye grain

*write set down on
paper
[wrote]
[written]
writhe d
*wry twisted

**

recite
recline d
refine d
rely -ies
relied
remind
reply -ies
replied
require d
reside
resign ed
respire d
retire d
revise d
revive d
rewrite
[rewrote]
[rewritten]

rider
riding
rifle d
righteous
rightful ly
riot ed
ripen ed
rising
rival led

writer
writing
wryly

***

recital
reliance
reminded
reminder
reprisal
requirement
retirement
revival

rightfully
rioted
rioting
riotous
rivalling

**** **

refinery -ies
reliability
reliable

rhinoceros es / -i

riboflavin

*

*cite quote

scribe
scythe d

shine
[shone]
***shire** county
shrine
shy -ies
shied
***shyer** more shy

***side** edge / surface /
aspect / team
sigh
***sighed** did sigh
***sighs** more than
one sigh
***sight** vision
***sign** ed mark with
a meaning
***sine** function of
an angle
sire d
***site** place
***size** spatial extent /
a weak glue
sized

sky -ies

***sleight** quickness
slice d
slide
[slid]
***slight** small / thin
and delicate / treat
without respect
slime
sly

smile d
smite
[smote]
[smitten]
☞

**

cider
cipher ed

cycle d
cycling
cyclist
***cypress** es tree
***Cyprus** island

psychic ally

science
scientist
scriber
scribing

seismic

shining
shiny -ier, -iest
shyer
shyly / shily

Siam
sideboard
sidelight
sideline
sidetrack ed
sideways
siding
signing
signpost
silage
silence d
silent
silo s
siphon
siren
sisal

skyline

slightly
slimy -ier, -iest
slyly / slily

smiling

spicy -ier, -iest
spider
spinal
spiral led
spiral ly
sprightly -ier, -iest
☞

***

psychically
psychosis
[psychoses]
psychotic ally

saliva

scientist

seismograph

Siamese
silently
sizable / sizeable

skyscraper

society -ies

spiralling
spirally

surprising
survival
survivor

**** **

cytoplasm

psychiatric ally
psychiatrist
psychiatry
psychically
psychoanalyse d
psychoanalysis
psychoanalyst
psychological ly
psychologist
psychology
psychotherapist
psychotherapy
psychotically

salivary

scientific ally

seismology

Siberia

society -ies

In these words you can hear the vowel sound **ie** as in lion

S

*

snide
snipe d

spice d
spike d
spine
spire
spite
splice d
spline d
spy -ies
spied

squire

***stile** barrier
 with steps
stride
[strode]
[stridden]
strife
strike
[struck]
[stricken]
stripe d
strive
[strove]
[striven]
sty -ies
***style** manner
styled

swine
swipe d

* *

stifle d
stifling
stipend
striking
stylist
stylus es / -i

sublime
subscribe d
subside
suffice d
supply -ies
supplied
surprise d
survive d

In these words you can hear the vowel sound ie as in lion   **191**

T

*	**	***	**** *
*thigh upper part of leg	Taiwan	thiamine	titanium
thine	Thailand	timetable d	triangular
thrice	thyroid	tinier	triangulation
thrive d		tiniest	triceratops
[throve]	tidal		triumphally
[thriven]	tidings	trialling	
*thy your	tidy -ier, -iest	triangle	
*thyme herb	tiger	triumphal ly	
	tighten ed	triumphant	
*tide ebb and flow	tightly		
tie	tiling	typewriter	
*tied fastened with knot	timing		
tight	tiny -ier, -iest		
tights	tiresome		
tile d	title d		
*time period			
timed	tonight		
*tire make weary / ring fitted to wheel			
tired	trial led		
	trialling		
trial led	tribesman		
tribe	trifle d		
tripe	tripod		
try -ies	triumph ed		
tried	trying		
twice	twilight		
twine d			
	tying		
type d	typhoon		
*tyre ring fitted to wheel	typist		
	tyrant		

In these words you can hear the vowel sound ie as in lion

V

*
via
*****vial** small vessel
or bottle
vice
vie d
*****vile** disgusting
vine
*****viol** stringed
instrument

* *
via
*****vial** small vessel
or bottle
vibrate
Viking
*****viol** stringed
instrument
violence
violent
violet
viper
virus es
viscount
visor
vital ly

* * *
vagina
vaginal

viaduct
vibrating
vibration
violate
violence
violent
violet
violin
vitally
vitamin

* * * *
variety -ies

vice-versa
violation
vitality
vivarium

W

*
*****right** correct / direction
*****rite** ceremony

*****rye** grain

*****while** time / during
the time that
*****whiled** did while
whilst
*****whine** d complain
white
why

wide
wife -ves
*****wild** untamed
*****wile** trick
*****wind** move by
turning
[wound]
*****wine** drink
*****wined** supplied
with wine
wipe d
wire d
wise

*****write** set down on
paper
[wrote]
[written]
writhe d
*****wry** twisted

* *
whitewash es
whitewashed
whiting
whitish

widely
widen ed
wider
widespread
wildlife
wildly
wily -ier, -iest
winding
wiper
wireless es
wiry -ier, -iest

writer
writing
wryly

* * *

* * * *

In these words you can hear the vowel sound ie as in lion

193

X

*   **   ***   ****

xylophone

Z

*   **   ***   ****

xylophone

     In these words you can hear the vowel sound **ie** as in **lion**

A

*	**	***	**** *
	abode	approaching	ammonia
			ammonium
	afloat	aroma	
			appropriate
	ago	atonement	
		atrocious	associate
	alone		association
		awoken	associative
	approach es		
	approached		
	arose		
	atone d		for Scots: oe-r is on page 256 ▷
	awoke		

B

*	**	***	****
*beau dandy	behold		
	[beheld]		
blow	below		
[blew]	bestow ed		
[blown]			
	blower		
boast	blowing		
boat	blowlamp		
*bode did bide	blowup		
*bold brave			
*bole tree-trunk	boatman		
bolt	bolster ed		
bone d	bonus es		
both	bony -ier, iest		
*bow wood and	boulder		
string / knot /	bouquet		
bend	bowler		
*bowed curved like	bowling		
a bow			
*bowl container /	brocade		
send a ball	brochure		
*bowled rolled /	broken		
bowled out	broker		
bowls			

> In these words the first letter 'o' is a neutral vowel. It sounds like the 'o' in 'policeman'.
>
> Bolivia   bonanza   botanical

*broach es open up
broached
broke
*brooch es ornament

for Scots: oe-r is on page 257 ▷

In these words you can hear the vowel sound **oe** as in **goat**

C

*

choke d
chose
chrome d

cloak ed
clone d
close
closed
*clothe d provide
with clothes
*clothes garments
*clove spice / did
cleave
*cloves spice

coach es
coached
coal
coast
coat
coax es
coaxed
code
coke d
cold
colt
comb ed
cone
cope d
cove

croak ed
crow ed
[crew]
[crown]

for Qu . . .
see page 206 ▷

**

chauffeur ed
-choral
-chorus es
-chorused
chosen

cloakroom
closing
closure
clothesline
clothing
cloven
clover

coastal
coastline
coating
cobalt
cobra
cocoa
colder
coldness
coleslaw
cologne
colon
compose d
console d
control led
corrode
cosine
cosy / cozy -ier, -iest

crochet ed
crocus es / -i
croquet
crowbar

***

chauvinist
chromium
chromosome

cirrhosis

coconut
coincide
commotion
component
*composer writer of
music
*composure calmness
conifer
controller
controlling
corrosion
corrosive
cotangent

kimono s

koala

**** **

chauvinism
chauvinistic

coagulate
coalition
coefficient
coincidence
collinear
colloquial ly
colonial ly
colonialism
coniferous
cooperate
cooperation
cooperative
coordinate
coordinator
coordination

for Scots: oe-r
is on page 258 ▷

**In these words the first letter 'o' is a neutral
vowel. It sounds like the 'o' in 'policeman'.**

COMMUNICATING WORDS

cholesterol	comedienne	committing
chorale	commander	communal ly
cocoon ed	commandment	commune d
collapse d	commemorate	communicate
collapsible	commemoration	communication
collect ing	commence d	communion
collection	commercial ly	community -ies
collective	commission ed	commutative
collector	commissioner	commuter
collide	commit ted	corrupt
collision	commitment	corruption
comedian	committee	

In these words you can hear the vowel sound **oe** as in **goat**

D

*	**	***	**** *
*****doe** female deer	**decode**	**decoding**	**deodorant**
dole d	**denote**	**devoted**	
dome d	**devote**	**devotion**	**diplomacy**
don't			**disposable**
dose d	**disclose** d	**diploma**	
*****dough** flour and	**disown** ed	**disposal**	**domestically**
water	**dispose** d		**domesticate**
doze d		**domestic** ally	
	docile	**donated**	
droll	**domain**	**donation**	
drone d	**donor**		
drove	**doughnut**		*for Scots: oe-r is on page 259* ▷

E

*	**	***	**** *
	elope d	**emotion**	**eau-de-cologne**
		emotive	
	enclose d		**emotional** ly
	encroach es	**enclosure**	
	encroached	**enrolling**	**erroneous** ly
	enfold	**enrolment**	
	engross es		
	engrossed	**erosion**	
	enrol led		
		explosion	
	erode	**explosive**	
		exponent	
	evoke d	**exposure**	
for H . . . see page 200 ▷	**explode** **expose** d		
for I . . . see page 200 ▷			*for Scots: oe-r is on page 259* ▷

In these words you can hear the vowel sound **oe** as in **goat**

F

*

float
*floe floating ice-sheet
*flow ed run

foal
*foaled given birth
to a foal
foam ed
foe
*fold bend double /
crease / sheep
enclosure
folk

fro
froze

phone d

* *

floated
floating
flowchart
flowing

foamy -ier, -iest
focal
focus es / ses / -i
focused / focussed
folded
folder
folding
folklore
foretold
forgo / forego
[forwent / forewent]
[forgone / foregone]

frozen

phobic
phoneme
photo s

* * *

ferocious

focusing / focussing
foliage
folio
fovea
foveal

phobia
photograph ed

* * * * * *

photocopier
photocopy -ies
photocopied
photoelectric
photofinish
photographic ally
photosynthesis

for th . . .
see page 208 ▷

for Scots: oe-r
is on page 260 ▷

In these words you can hear the vowel sound **oe** as in **goat**

G

*	**	***	****
ghost	global ly	globally	
	glowing		
gloat	glow-worm	grocery -ies	
globe			
glow ed	goatskin		
	going		
gnome	golden		
	goldfish		
go	gopher		
[went]			
[gone]	*grocer shopkeeper		
goad	selling food and other		
goal	goods		
goat	*grosser fatter / more		
goes	disgusting		
gold	grotesque		
	grower		
*groan deep moan	growing		
groaned	grownup		
grope d			
gross ed			
grove			
grow			
[grew]			
*[grown] developed			
growth			

*for Scots: oe-r
is on page 261* ▷

H

*

hoax es
hoaxed
hoe d
*hoes more than
one hoe
*hold grip /
support / continue
[held]
*hole opening
*holed hit ball
into hole
home d
hope d
*hose flexible
water-pipe / stockings
hosed
host
hove

*whole total /
complete

**

holding
hold-up
*holey full of holes
holster
*holy -ier, -iest
sacred
homeland
homemade
homesick
homestead
homeward
homework
hopeful ly
hopeless
hoping
hosepipe
hostess es
hotel

wholemeal
wholesale
wholesome
*wholly totally /
completely

***

heroic ally
holiness
hologram
holograph
hopefully
hopelessness
hosiery

hypnosis

**** ***

heroically

homeopathic ally
homogeneous
homosexual ly
homosexuality
hotelier

for Scots: oe-r
is on page 261 ▷

Here the first letter 'o' has a neutral sound.
holography

I

*

◁ for E . . .
see page 197

**

impose d

***

immobile

****

for Scots: oe-r
is on page 262 ▷

In these words you can hear the vowel sound **oe** as in **goat**

J

*   *** ***   *** * ***   *** * * ***

joke d   **joker**   **jovial** ly   **jovially**

◀ for dr . . .
see page 197

K

*   *** ***   *** * ***   *** * * ***

knoll

*know understand
[knew]
[known]

*knows does know

*no not any
*nose part of face

knowing

kosher

kimono s

koala

> **In these words the first letter 'o' is a neutral vowel. It sounds like the 'o' in 'policeman'.**
> Korea   Korean

◀ for C . . .
see page 196

for Qu . . .
see page 206 ▶

L

*   *** ***   *** * ***   *** * * ***

*lo behold
*load amount carried
loaf
[loaves]
loafed
loam
*loan ed lend /
amount lent
loath / loth
loathe d
lobe
*lode vein of metal
ore / ditch
*lone single
lope d
*low not high / moo
*lowed mooed

loaded
local ly
locate
locus [loci]
locust
lodestone
logo s
lonely
lonesome
lotion
lower ed
lowest
lowlands
lowly

locally
located
location
loneliness

locality -ies
locomotion
locomotive
loganberry -ies

for Scots: oe-r
is on page 263 ▶

In these words you can hear the vowel sound **oe** as in **goat**

M

*

mauve

*moan ed complain
moat
*mode way / fashion
mole
mope d
most
mould
moult
mow
*[mowed] cut
*[mown] cut

**

mobile
molar
molten
moment
mostly
motel
*motif / motive theme / figure
motion ed
*motive cause of action
motor ed
mouldy -ier, -iest
mower

***

mobilise d
    ze
Mohammed
molasses
momentary
momentous
momentum
mosaic
motionless
motivate
motorbike
motorist
motorway

**** *

melodious

mobility
molecular
momentarily
momentary
motivation
motorcycle

for Scots: oe-r is on page 263 ▷

> **In these words the first letter 'o' is a neutral vowel. It sounds like the 'o' in 'policeman'.**
> Mohammed   morale

N

*

gnome

knoll
*know understand
[knew]
[known]
*knows does know

*no not any
node
*nose part of face
nosed
note

**

noble
nomad
no-one
nosebleed
nosy -ier, -iest
notebook
noted
notice d
notion
nova
nowhere

***

neurosis -es

nobleman
[noblemen]
nobody
nomadic
notable
notation
noteworthy
notify -ies
notified
November

**** *

negotiate
negotiation

nobility
noticeable
noticeably
notification
notoriety
notorious

In these words you can hear the vowel sound **oe** as in **goat**

O

*

oak
oath
oats

*ode long poem

*oh !

old

*owe must pay
*owed did owe
own ed

**

although

oatmeal

obey ed
oblique
oboe

ocean
ochre

odour

ogre
ogress es

older
oldest

omen
omit ted

only
onus es

opal
opaque
open ed
opening
oppose d
opus es
[opera]

-oral ly

osier

*ova eggs
oval
*over above
ovum [ova]

owing
owner

ozone

***

oasis
[oases]

odious

omission
omitted
omitting

opening
opium
opponent

-orally

osier

ovary -ies
ovation
overalls
overarm
overboard
overcast
[overcast]
overcoat
overcome
[overcame]
[overcome]
overdo
[overdid]
[overdone]
overdraft
overdrive
overeat
[overate]
[overeaten]
overfeed
[overfed]
overflow ed
overgrow
[overgrew]
[overgrown]
overhang
[overhung]
overhauled
overhead
overhear
[overheard]
overjoyed
overlap ped
overlay
[overlaid]
overload
overlook ed
☞

**** *

eau-de-cologne

obedience
obedient
obituary -ies

oceanography

overlapping
overlooking
overwhelming

◁ for H . . .
see page 200

for Scots: oe-r
is on page 264 ▷

In these words you can hear the vowel sound **oe** as in **goat**

O

> In these words the first letter 'o' sounds
> like the neutral 'o' sound in 'policeman'.
>
> *O*BLIGING WORDS
>
> oblige d
> obliterate
> oblivion
> oblivious
> occasion al
> occasionally
> occur red
> occurrence
> occurring
> o'clock
> offence
>
> offend
> offensive
> official ly
> opinion
> opossum
> oppression
> oppressive
> oppressor
> original ly
> originality
> originate

◁ for H . . .
see page 200

***

overnight
overpower ed
override
[overrode]
[overridden]
overrun
[overran]
[overrun]
overseas
oversee
[oversaw]
[overseen]
overshoot
[overshot]
oversize
oversleep
[overslept]
overtake
[overtook]
[overtaken]
overthrow
[overthrew]
[overthrown]
overtime
overtone
overture
overturn ed
overwhelm ed
overwork ed

ownership

for Scots: oe-r
is on page 264 ▷

P

*

phone d

poach es
poached
poke d
***pole** long rod
***poll** number of
voters / head /
cut off top
polled
pope
pose d
post
☞

**

patrol led

phobic
phoneme
photo s
☞

***

pagoda
patrolling

phobia
photograph ed

poetic ally
poetry
polio
postmaster
potency
☞

**** **

petroleum

photocopier
photocopy -ies
photocopied
photographic ally
photosynthesis
☞

for Scots: oe-r
is on page 265 ▷

In these words you can hear the vowel sound **oe** as in **goat**

P

*

probe d
prone
prose

**

poacher
poem
poet
poetry
poker
Poland
polar
pole-vault
Polish
polo
pony -ies
postage
postal
postcard
poster
postman
[postmen]
postpone d
postscript
posy -ies
potent
potion
poultice d
poultry

proceeds
process es
processed
profile d
*program instructions
for computer
*programme plan of
performance /
broadcast
programmed
progress es
progressed
project
prologue
promote
pronoun
propose d
protein
protest
proton
proven
provoke d

***

precocious
programmer
programming
promotion
proposal
prosaic ally
protocol
prototype

**** *

pneumonia

poetically
postgraduate

proletariat
protoplasm
protozoa

In these words the first letter 'o' is a neutral vowel. It sounds like the 'o' in 'policeman'.

PR*O*GRESSIVE WORDS

phonetic ally
photographer
photography
polarity -ies
police
policeman
[policemen]
policewoman
[policewomen]
polite ly
political ly
pollute
pollution
position ed
possess es
possessed
possession
possessive
potato es
potential ly
probation
procedure
proceed ing
proceedings
procession
proclaim ed

prodigious
produce d
producer
producing
production
productive
profane
profess es
professed
professing
professional ly
professor
proficiency
proficient
profound
profuse
profusion
progression
progressive
prohibit ed
prohibiting
prohibitive
projectile
projection
projector
proliferate
proliferation

prolific ally
prolong ed
pronounce d
pronouncement
pronouncing
pronunciation
propel led
propeller
propelling
proportional ly
proprietor
propulsion
prospect ive
prospector
prospectus es
protect ed
protection
protective
protector
protractor
protrude
provide d
providing
provincial
provision s
provisional ly
provocative

for Scots: oe-r
is on page 265 ▷

Q

*	**	***	****
quote	**quota**	**quotation**	
quoth	**quotient**		

R

*	**	***	**** *
roach roach	**remote**	**rodeo**	**rhododendron**
*__road__ track	**repose** d	**rolling-pin**	
*__roam__ ed wander	**reproach** es	**romantic** ally	**romantically**
roan	**reproached**	**rotary**	
roast	**revolt**	**rotation**	
robe d	**rewrote**		
*__rode__ travelled on / by			
*__roe__ fish eggs or sperm / small deer	**roadblock**		
	roadside		
	robot		
rogue	**robust**		
*__role__ actor's part	**rodent**		
*__roll__ ed turn over and over	**roller**		
	rolling		
*__Rome__ city	**Roman**		
rope d	**romance** d		
*__rose__ flower / did rise	**rosebud**		
	rosette		
*__rote__ repetition	**rosewood**		
rove	**rosy** -ier, -iest		
*__row__ line / move with oars	**rotate**		
	rotor		
*__rowed__ moved with oars	**roving**		
*__rows__ lines / moves with oars			

*wrote set down on paper

for Scots: oe-r is on page 266 ▷

In these words you can hear the vowel sound **oe** as in **goat**

S

*

scold
scone
scope
scroll ed

***sew** ed stitch
[sewn]

shoal
show ed
[shown]

***sloe** blackthorn
fruit or bush
slope d
sloth
***slow** at a low speed
slowed

smoke d
smote

snow ed

***so** therefore / to
such a degree /
in that way
soak ed
soap ed
***sold** given for
money
***sole** only / part of
foot and shoe / fish
***soled** fitted with
new sole
***soul** spirit
***sow** ed plant
[sown]

spoke

stoat
stoke d
stole
stone d
stove
stow ed
strobe
strode
stroke d
stroll ed
strove

* *

chauffeur

sauté

scrolling

sewing

shoulder ed

slogan
slower
slowly

smoking
smoky -ier, -iest
smoulder ed

snowball ed
snowdrop
snowfall
snowflake
snowman
[snowmen]
snowshoes
snowstorm
snowy -ier, -iest

sober ed
so-called
social ly
soda
sofa
solar
solder ed
soldier ed
solely
solo s
sonar

spoken
spokeshave
spokesman
[spokesmen]

stolen
stoma [stomata]
stoneware
stony -ier, -iest
***-storey** floor
***-story** -ies tale

suppose d

swollen

* * *

chauvinist

samosa

sclerosis

showjumper
showjumping

sociable
socialist
socially
sodium
soldering
soloist
soviet

spokesperson
spokeswoman
[spokeswomen]

stomata
stowaway

* * * * *

socialism
sociology
Somalia

supposedly

symposium
[symposia]

In these words the first letter 'o' is a neutral
vowel. It sounds like the 'o' in 'policeman'.

society -ies
solicitor
solution

sophisticated
soprano s

---

for Scots: oe-r
is on page 267

T

*

those
though
throat
*throe sharp pain
*throne state chair
throned
throve
*throw hurl
[threw]
*[thrown] hurled

*toad animal
toast
*toe part of foot
*toed placed toes
against / fitted
with a toe
*told did tell
toll
*tolled did toll
tone d
tote
*tow pull behind
*towed pulled
behind

troll

**

throwing

toadstool
toasted
toastie
token
tonal ly
topaz
-Tory -ies
total led
totem

trophy -ies

***

tonally
totalling
totally

In these words the first letter 'o' is a neutral
vowel. It sounds like the 'o' in 'policeman'.

tobacco s   topography
tobacconist   topology
tomato es   torrential ly

****

for Scots: oe-r
is on page 268 ▷

V

*

*-vault gymnastic leap /
underground room /
arched roof

vogue
vole
*volt unit of
electrical force
vote

**

vocal ly
voltage
voted
voter

***

viola

vocalist
vocally
voltmeter

****

In these words the first letter 'o' is a neutral
vowel. It sounds like the 'o' in 'policeman'.

vocabulary -ies   vocation   vocational ly

In these words you can hear the vowel sound oe as in goat

W

*

*hole opening

*rote repetition

***whoa!** stop!
***whole** total /
complete

***woe** distress
woke
won't
wove

***wrote** set down on
paper

* *

*holey full of holes
*holy sacred

wholegrain
wholemeal
wholesale
wholesome
***wholly** totally /
completely

woeful ly
woken
woven

* * *

woefully

* * * *

for Scots: oe-r
is on page 269

Y

*

***yoke** neck-piece
yoked
***yolk** yellow part
of egg

* *

yeoman [yeomen]

yodel led / ed
yoga
yoghourt /
yoghurt / **yogurt**
yogi
yokel

* * *

yodelling / yodeling

* * * *

for Scots: oe-r
is on page 269

Z

*

zone d

* *

* * *

zodiac

* * * * * *

zoological ly
zoology

In these words you can hear the vowel sound **oe** as in **goat**

A

*

****

-about
abuse d

accrue d
accuse d
acute

adieu

-afoot

aloof

amuse d

approve d

for H . . .
see page 215

assume d
assure d

*****

acoustic

*allusion reference

amusement

approval

assurance

*illusion false belief or
appearance

**** *

accumulate
accumulation
accumulator
accusative
acoustical ly

adjudicate
adjudication
adjudicator

alluvial
alluvium

B

*	**	***	****
balloon ed	baboon	bazooka	beautifully
	balloon ed		
*blew puffed		beautiful ly	
bloom ed	*beauty -ies pleasing	Bermuda	
*blue colour	example / loveliness		
		boulevard	
-book ed	bluebell		
boom ed	bluetit	brewery -ies	
-boor		brutally	
boost	booby -ies		
boot	-bookcase	-Buddhism	
booth	-booklet	-bulletin	
booze	-bookshelf	-bulldozer ed	
	-[bookshelves]		
brew	booster		
*brewed fermented	*bootee baby's		
*brews does brew	woollen boot		
*brood offspring	*booty stolen goods		
-brook ed	-bosom		
broom	bouquet		
*bruise injury	boutique		
bruised			
brute	brewer		
	brunette		
-bull	brutal ly		
-bush es			
-bushed	-Buddha		
	-Buddhist		
	bugle		
	-bulldog		
	-bullet		
	-bullfrog		
	-bullock		
	-bully -ies		
	-bullied		
	bureau		
	-bushel		
	-butcher ed		

C

*	**	***	**** *

chew ed
***chews** does chew
***choose** select
[chose]
[chosen]
***chute** slope for
things to slide down

clue d

-**cook** ed
cool ed
***coop** cage
-**could**
***coup** stroke /
successful action
-**course** d
-**court**

crew
***crewed** acted as a
crew member
***crews** more than
one crew
-**crook**
croon ed
***crude** untreated /
done without skill
cruel ly
***cruise** voyage
cruised

cube d
***cue** rod / signal
cued
cure d
cute

***shoot** fire / hit with
bullet / move very fast /
new growth from plant

***queue** waiting line
queued

for Qu . . .
see page 219 ▷

---

canoe d
cashew

chewing
choosing

cocoon ed
commute
compute
conclude
confuse d
consume d
-**cooker**
-**cooking**
coolant
cooler
coolly
-**couldn't**
coupe
coupon

-**crooked**
crucial ly
cruel ly
cruelty -ies
cruet
cruiser
crusade

cubic
cuboid
-**cuckoo**
culottes
curate
-**cushion** ed

Kuwait

---

communal ly
communion
commuter
computer
conclusion
conclusive
conducive
confusion
consumer

crucially
crucible
crucifix es
cruciform
crucify -ies
crucified
cruelly
cruelty -ies

***cubical** cube-shaped
***cubicle** small room
cubism
cucumber
cumulus
curator
curio s
curious

---

communally
communicate
communication
communicative
communion
community -ies
commutative
computerise d
 ze

crucifixion

cumulative
curiosity -ies

In these words you can hear **oo** as in **goose**   or **ue** as in **newt**

D

*

deuce
*dew moisture

do
[did]
[done]
*doer active person
doom ed
*dour unsmiling

drew
droop ed

*due owing
duke
dune

* *

deduce d
dewdrop

diffuse d
disprove d
dispute
disused

doer
doing
doodle d
doodling

*dual double
ducal
*duel led fight
duelling
duet
duly
during
duty -ies
duvet

* * *

delusion

diffusion
disproven

duelling
duplicate
durable
duration
dutiful ly

* * * * *

disunity

durability
dutifully

E

*

*ewe female sheep
*ewes more than
one ewe

*use employ

*yew tree
*yews yew trees

*you person / people

* *

elude

endure d
*ensure d make
certain

Europe

exclude
excuse d
extrude

*insure d protect against
loss

* * *

*elusive hard to find

endurance

eucharist
eureka!

exclusion
exclusive
extrusion
extrusive

*illusive deceptive

* * * * * * *

enthusiasm
enthusiast
enthusiastic ally

eucalyptus es
euphonium
European
Eustachian
euthanasia

exclusively
excruciating
exuberance
exuberant

for H . . .
see page 215 ▷

for I . . .
see page 215 ▷

In these words you can hear **oo** as in **goose**   or **ue** as in **newt**

F

*	* *	* * *	* * * * *
feud	feudal ly	feudally	fluorescence
*few not many	fewer		fluorescent
		flugelhorn	fluoridation
*flew passed in	fluent	fluorescence	
flight	fluid	fluorescent	foolhardiness
*flu influenza	fluoride		
*flue pipe	fluorine	foolhardy	frugality
fluke			
flute	foodstuff	fruiterer	futility
	foolish	fruitfully	
food	foolproof		
fool ed	-football	fuelling	
-foot	-foothill	fugitive	
-fourth	-foothold	-fulfilling	
	-footpath	fumigate	
fruit	-footstep	funeral	
	-forsook	furious	
fuel		fuselage	
fugue	frugal		
-full	fruitful ly		
fume d	fruitless		
fuse d			
	fuel led		
*phew / whew !	fuelling		
	-fulcrum		
	-fulfil led		
for th ...	-fully		
see page 222 ▷	fury -ies		
	fuschia		
	fusion		
	futile		
	future		

G

*	* *	* * *	* * * *
gloom	gloomy -ier, -iest	-gooseberry -ies	
glue d	glucose		
		gruelling	
*gnu animal	-goodbye		
	-goodness		
-good	-goodnight		
-goods	-gooseberry -ies		
goose geese	gourmet		
gourd	grouping		
	gruelling		
grew	gruesome		
groom ed			
groove d	guru		
group ed			
*knew understood			
*new unused			

In these words you can hear oo as in goose   or ue as in newt

H

*

**hew*ed cut down
[hewn]

-**hood**
hoof-ves
hoofed
-**hook**ed
*hoop large ring or
band
hooped
hoot
hooves
-**house**

*hue colour
huge

*who which person or
people
who'd
who'll
whom
**whoop*ed cry out
with joy
*who's who is
*whose belonging to
whom or what

**

hoovered

hula
human
humid
humoured
humus
-**hurrah!**
-**hurray!**

***

hooligan

*humerus bone in
upper arm
humorist
*humorous funny

whoever
whooping-cough

**** **

hallucination

humanitarian
humanities
humanity
humidity
humiliate
humiliation
humility

I

*

for E . . .
see page 213

**

**ensure*d make certain

immune
improved
impure

include
induced
**insure*d   protect
against loss
intrude

***

*allusion reference

*elusive hard to find

*illusion false belief
or appearance

*illusive deceptive

improvement
improving

included
including
inclusion
inclusive
inducement
inhuman
insurance
intruder
intrusion
intrusive

**** *

illuminate
illumination
illusory

immovable
immunity
impunity
impurity-ies

incurable
infuriate
injurious
innumerable
inscrutable
insuperable
intuitive

In these words you can hear **oo** as in **goose**   or **ue** as in **newt**

J

*

*deuce tennis score / devil
*dew moisture

drew

*dual double
*due owing
duke
*dune hill of sand

*Jew
*jewel gem

*joule unit of energy

*juice liquid from fruit,
meat and vegetables
*June month

◀ for dr . . .
see page 213

**

*dual double
ducal
*duelled fight
duelling
duet
duly
during
duty -ies
duvet

*jewelled gem
jeweller
jewellery / jewelry
Jewess es
Jewish

judo
juicy -ier, -iest
jukebox es
July
juror
jury -ies

***

duelling
duplicate
durable
duration
dutiful ly

Jacuzzi

jeweller
jewellery / jewelry

jubilant
jubilee
judicial ly
judicious
juicier
juiciest
jujitsu
junior
Jupiter
juvenile

****

durability
dutifully

jubilation
judicially
judiciary -ies
jurisdiction
jurisprudence

K

*

*knew understood

*queue waiting line
queued

◀ for C . . .
see page 212

**

Kuwait

***

for Qu . . .
see page 219 ▶

****

L

*

*lieu place

*loo toilet
-look ed
loom
loop ed
*loos toilets
loose d
*loot stolen goods
*lose have no longer /
fail to win
[lost]

lure d
*lute musical
instrument

**

lagoon

-lookout
loophole
loosely
loosen ed
loser
losing
louvre

lucid
ludo
lukewarm
lunar
lupin

***

lubricant
lubricate
lucrative
ludicrous
luminous

****

leukaemia / leukemia

lubrication

In these words you can hear oo as in goose   or ue as in newt

M

LONG VOWEL **ue**   LONG VOWEL **oo**

*

mew ed
*mewl ed   mew
*mews houses
converted from
stables

moo
*mood state of
feeling
*mooed went 'moo'
moon ed
moor ed
*moose animal
-mourn ed
*-mouse animal
*mousse sweet dish
move d

*mule animal
*muse think deeply
mute

**

manure d
maroon ed
mature d

-mistook
misuse d

moonlight
moonlit
mooring
-Moslem
-mournful
-mourning
movement
mover
movie
moving

*mucous of / covered
with mucus
*mucus slimy liquid
muesli
mural
music ally
-Muslim
mutual ly

***

manoeuvre d

movable / moveable

museum
musical ly
musician
mutation
mutilate
mutineer
mutiny -ies
mutinied
mutually

**** *

maturity

municipal ly
musically
mutilation

In these words you can hear oo as in goose   or ue as in newt   **217**

N

*

*gnu animal

*knew understood

*new unused
 news
 newt

-nook
 noon
 noose
-now

 nude

* *

neuron
neutral ly
neutron
newly
newscast
newton

nougat

nuance
nuisance

* * *

neurosis -es
neurotic ally
neutralise d
      ze
neutrally
New Zealand
newcomer
newsagent
newspaper

nuclear
nucleus nuclei
nudity
numeral
numerous
nutrient
nutrition
nutritious
nutritive

pneumatic

* * * * * *

neurological ly
neurologist
neurology
neurotically
neutrality

numeration
numerator
numerical ly
nutritionist

pneumonia

O

*

ooze d

-out

* *

obscure d
obtuse

* * *

* * * *

obscurity -ies

for H . . .
see page 215

In these words you can hear oo as in goose   or ue as in newt

P

*	**	***	**** **
*few not many	perfumed Peru	peculiar	peculiar
pew	pewter	plurally	pneumonia
*phew / whew relief!	platoon plumage	pneumatic	presumably
plumed	plurally Pluto	pollution	pugilistic ally purification
pooled *poor badly off *poured flow out	pollute poodle poorly	producer producing profusion	puritanical puritanism
proof proved [proven] pruned	-pouring	puberty pubescent -pullover	
-pulled *pure unmixed -pushes -pushed -pusses -put -[put]	presumed procured produced profuse proofread protrude proven prudence prudent pruning	purify -ies purified puritan / Puritan purity pursuant pursuer putrify -ies putrified	
	-pudding -pulley -pulpit puma puny -ier, -iest pupa [pupae] pupil purée purely pursued pursuit -pushchair -pussy -ies putrid -putting		

Q

*	**	***	**** *
cubed *cue rod / signal cued cured cute	cubic cuboid culottes curate	*cubical cube-shaped *cubicle small room cubism cucumber cumulus curator curio s curious	cumulative curiosity -ies
*queue waiting line queued	Kuwait		
		quintuplet	

R

*

*rood crucifix / an acre
roofed
-rook
roomed
roost
*root part of plant / origin
rouge
*route way

ruched
*rude impolite
rued
*rued regretted
*rues does regret
ruled
*ruse trick

**

raccoon / racoon

rebuked
recouped
recruit
reduced
refused
refute
removed
renewed
repute
-resourced
resumed
*review survey
reviewed
*revue theatrical entertainment

rhubarb

rooftops
roommate
rooster
rouble / ruble
roulette
routine

ruby -ies
ruined
ruler
rumoured
rupee
rurally
ruthless

***

refusal
removal
removing
renewal
-resources
reunion

rheumatic

-rookery -ies

rubella
ruinous
rurally

**** *

removable / removeable
repudiate
reunion

rheumatism

-Romania / Roumania / Rumania

rudimentary -ies

In these words you can hear oo as in goose   or ue as in newt

S

*	**	***	**** **
*chute slope for things to slide down	saloon salute	schoolteacher screwdriver scrutinise d ze	security -ies stupidity -ies
school ed scoop ed scoot screw ed	schoolboy schoolgirl schooner scooter scuba	scrutiny secluded	suicidal ly superannuation superconductor superficial
*shoe footwear [shod] *shoo ed scare away -shook *shoot fire / hit with bullet / move very fast / new growth from plant [shot] -should shrewd	seclude secure d sewage sewer shooting -shouldn't skewer ed	solution souvenir stewardess es studio studious stupefy -ies stupefied stupendous	superfluous superhuman superimpose d superintendent superior superlative supermarket supernatural ly superpower supersonic ally
skew ed	smoothly	Sudanese suicide	superstition superstitious
sleuth ed slew sluice	snooker ed sooner soufflé soupçon	suitable supersede supervise d	supervision supervisor supremacy
smooth ed	spoonful -sputnik		
snoop ed snooze d	steward strudel Stuart student stupid stupor		
soon -soot soothe d *sou coin of little value soup			
spook spool ed spoon ed spruce	subdue d Sudan suet -sugar ed suitcase		
stew ed -stood stool *stoop bend down stooped *stoup basin for holy water strew ed [strewn]	suited suitor super superb supreme surely		
*sue d take legal action / plead suit sure swooped			

T

*

*threw hurled
*through by way
of / because of

*to towards
tomb
*too also
-took
tool ed
toot
tooth ed
tour ed

*troop ed move as
a group
*troupe group of
entertainers
truce
true d
truth

tube d
tune d

*two 2

**

taboo ed
tattoo ed

throughout

today
to-do
tombstone
tonight
toothbrush es
toothcomb
toothpaste
toothpick
toucan
toupee
tourist
toward
towards

trousseau
truly
truthful ly

*tuba wind instrument
*tuber underground
stem or root
tubing
Tuesday
Tudor
tulip
tumour
tumult
*tuna fish
*tuner person who
tunes
tunic
tuning
tutor ed
tutu

twofold

***

together
tomorrow
tourism
tournament

truthfully

tubular
tuition

**** *

tubercular
tuberculin
tuberculosis
tumultuous

In these words you can hear oo as in goose   or ue as in newt

U

*	**	***	**** *
*ewe female sheep	Europe	eucharist	eucalyptus
*ewes more than one		eureka!	euphonium
ewe	**Ukraine**		European
		unicorn	Eustachian
*use employ	**union**	**uniform** ed	euthanasia
used	**unique**	**unify** -ies	
	unit	unified	**ubiquitous**
*yew tree	**unite**	**union**	
*yews yew tree		**unison**	**ukelele**
	urine	**united**	**Ukrainian**
*you person / people		**unity**	
	usage	**universe**	**unanimity**
	useful ly		**unanimous**
	useless	**Uranus**	**unicellular**
	user	**urethane**	**unicycle**
	using	**urinate**	**unification**
	usual ly	**Uruguay**	**uniformity**
	usurp ed		**unilateral** ly
		usable	**universal** ly
		usefully	**university** -ies
		usefulness	
		usually	**uranium**
			urinary
		utensil	
		uterus es / -i	**utilisation**
		utile	zation
		utilise d	**utility** -ies
		ze	**utopia**

◁ *for H . . .*
see page 215

for Y . . . ▷
see page 224

V

*	**	***	****
view ed	**viewer**		
	viewpoint		

W

*	**	***	****
*few not many	-**woman**	**whoever**	
	-**wooden**	**whooping-cough**	
*hew ed cut down	-**woodland**		
	-**woodwork**	-**woodcutter**	
*hoop large ring or band	-**woollen**	-**woodpecker**	
	-**woolly**		
*hue colour	-**wouldn't**		
	wounded		
*whew / phew relief!			
who			
who'd			
who'll			
whom			
☞			

W

*
*whoop ed   cry out
with joy
*who's   who is
*whose   belonging to
whom or what

-wolf [wolves]
-wolfed
*-wood   timber / area
with many trees
*woof   weft
-woof!   bark of dog
-wool
*-would   was willing to /
used to / was going to
wound

Y

*
*ewe   female sheep
*ewes   more than one ewe

*yew   tree
*yews   yew trees

*you   person /
people
you'd
you'll
*your   belonging to you
*you're   you are
yours
youth
you've

yule

 for U . . .
see page 223

* *
Europe

yourself
yourselves
youthful ly

* * *
eureka!

youthfully

* * * * * *
eucalyptus
euphonium
European
euthanasia

Yugoslavia

Z

*
zoo
zoom ed

* *

* * *

* * * * * *
zoological ly
zoology

A

*	**	***	**** **
aft	aardvark	advancement	adagio
		advancing	
ah	advance d	advantage d	arbitrarily
			arbitrary
*alms gifts to the	afar	afternoon	arbitration
poor	after	afterwards	archaeological /
			archeological
*arc curve	aghast	answering	archaeologist /
arch es			archeologist
arched	ajar	apartheid	archaeology /
are		apartment	archeology
*aren't are not	alarm ed		archipelago
*ark (Noah's)	almond	arbitrate	architecture
arm ed		arbutus	Argentina
*arms more than one	amen	archaic	argumentative
arm / weapons of		archery	armadillo s
war	answer ed	architect	arterial
art		argument	artesian
	apart	armada	articulate
ask ed		armament	artificial ly
	*arbor shaft	armature	artillery
*aunt relative	*arbour garden or	armistice	artistically
	part shaded by	armoury -ies	
	trees	arsenal	
	arcade	arsenic	
	archer	artefact / artifact	
	archive	artery -ies	
	arctic	arthritis	
	ardent	arthropod	
	ardour	artichoke	
	argon	article	
	argue d	artifact / artefact	
	armchair	artisan	
	armful	artistic ally	
	armour ed	artistry	
	armpit		
	army -ies		
	artist		
	asking		

for H . . .
see page 230 ▷

Auntie / Aunty

In these words you can hear the vowel sound **ar** as in **shark**

B

*

baa lamb's cry
balm
bar red   prevent /
barrier / rod
barb ed
bard poet
barge d
bark ed   sound like
that of a dog/ outer
covering of a tree
barn
barque boat
barred prevented /
fixed with bars
bask ed
bath ed

blast

bra
branch es
branched
brass es

* *

*balmy -ier, -iest sweet-
smelling / mad
banal
barbel
barber
bargain ed
barking
barley
*barmy / balmy mad
barney
barring
barter ed
basket
basking
bastard
bathroom
*bazaar Eastern
market

behalf

*bizarre peculiar

branches

* * *

Bahamas
banana
Barbados
barbecue d
barnacle
basketball

bravado

* * * *

barbarian

226   In these words you can hear the vowel sound ar as in shark

C

*	**	***	**** *
calf [calves]	carafe	cacao	carbohydrate
calm ed	carbon	carbonate	carburetter /
*calve d produce	carcass es	cardigan	caburettor
a calf	cardboard	cardinal	carnivorous
can't	cargo es	carnation	
car	carmine	carnival	
card	carpet	carnivore	
carp ed	carton	carpenter	
cart	cartoon	carpentry	
*carve d cut	cartridge	cartilage	
cask	cartwheel	cartoonist	
*cast throw / mould /	carving	castaway	
decide parts in a	*caster / castor		
play / squint	powdered sugar /	chancellor	
[cast]	swivelling wheel	chapati	
*caste social class	casting		
	castle	commander	
*chance lucky event /	*castor oil	commandment	
risk	catarrh	compartment	
chanced			
chant	chandler	karate	
*chants does chant /	charade		
more than one chant	charcoal	koala	
char red	charging		
charge d	charming		
charm ed	charring		
chart	charter ed		
	*chorale hymn tune		
clasp ed			
class es	cigar		
classed			
clerk	classmate		
	classroom		
craft			
	command		
czar / tsar	contrast		
	*corral enclosure		
	for cattle and		
	horses		
	craftsman		
	khaki		
	Koran / Qur'an		

D

*

daft
dance d
dark
darn ed
dart

*draft rough plan /
selected group
*draught current of
air / depth of
ship in water /
piece in game
draughts

* *

dancer
dancing
darker
darkness
darling
data

demand
depart

disarm ed
discard
discharge d

drama
drastic ally
draughty -ier,-iest

* * *

demanded
department
departure

disaster
disastrous
dishearten ed

drastically

* * * *

disarmament

drastically

E

*

* *

embark ed

enchant
enlarge d
entrance d

* * *

embargo es
embargoed

enchanting
entrancing

escarpment

example

* * * *

for H . . .
see page 230 ▷

for I . . .
see page 230 ▷

228 In these words you can hear the vowel sound ar as in shark

F

*

far
farce
farm ed
fast

flask

France

* *

far-fetched
farmer
farmhouse
farming
farmyard
*farther greater
 distance
farthest
fasten ed
faster
fastest
*father male parent
fathered

* * *

faraway
farcical
fastener

*fiancé man engaged
to be married
*fiancée woman
 engaged to be married
finale

pharmacist
pharmacy -ies

* * * * *

father-in-law

pharmaceutical

G

*

gasp ed

glance d
glass es

gnarled

gouache

grant
graph ed
grasp ed
grass es
grassed

guard

* *

gala
garage d
garbage
garden ed
gardener
gargle d
gargling
garish
garland
garlic
garment
garnet
garter ed

Ghana
ghastly -ier, -iest

giraffe

glasses
glassy -ier, -iest

gouache

granted
grasping
grassland s
grassy -ier, -iest
gratis

guitar

* * *

gardener

Ghanaian

grasshopper

guardian
Guatemala

gymkhana

* * * *

In these words you can hear the vowel sound **ar** as in **shark**

H

*

half [halves]
halve d
hard
hark ed
harm ed
harp ed
harsh
*hart male deer

*heart organ that
pumps blood /
centre / inmost
feelings
hearth

* *

harbour ed
hardboard
hard-boiled
harden ed
harder
hardest
hardly
hardship
hardware
hardwood
hardy -ier,-iest
harem
harmful ly
harmless
harness es
harnessed
harpoon ed
harvest

heartbeat
heartbreak
heartburn
hearthstone
hearty -ier,-iest

hurrah!

* * *

harlequin
harmfully
harmonic ally
harmonise d
    ze
harmony -ies
harpsichord
harvester
Hawaii
Hawaiian

* * * *   *

harmonica
harmonically
harmonious
harmonium

I

*

* *

impart
impasse

Iran
Iraq

Islam

◁ for E . . .
see page 228

* * *

impartial ly

incarnate

Iraqi

* * * *

impartially
impassable

J

*

jar red

◁ for dr . . .
see page 228

* *

giraffe

jargon
jarring

* * *

gymkhana

* * * *

In these words you can hear the vowel sound **ar** as in **shark**

K

*	**	***	****
	khaki	karate	
	Koran / Qur'an	koala	

◀ *for C . . .*
see page 227

L

*	**	***	****
lance d	lager	lasagne	
larch es	larder		
lard	largely	legato	
large	larger	lethargic	
lark ed	largest		
last	largo		
laugh ed	larkspur		
	*larva [larvae] insect grub		
	lasted		
	lather ed		
	laughter		
	*lava melted rock from volcano		
	llama		

M

*

mar ring
March
march es
marched
mark
marsh es
mask ed
mast

* *

macho
madame
mama
marble d
marching
margin
market ed
marking
marquis
marring
*marshal officer
marshalled
*marten animal
*martial warlike
*martin bird
martyr ed
marvel led
massage d
master ed

mirage

morale
moustache d

* * *

macabre
Mardi Gras
margarine
marginal ly
markedly
marketed
market-place
marmalade
marmoset
marshalling
marshmallow
martini
marvelling
marvellous
masterpiece
mastery

* * * *

marginally
marsupial

N

*

gnarled

* *

nasty -ier, -iest

* * *

narcissus es / -i
narcotic
nastier
nastiest

* * * *

In these words you can hear the vowel sound **ar** as in **shark**

P

*

palm ed
par
parch es
parched
park ed
part
pass es
*passed went by
*past time that has
passed / beyond
path

plant

prance d

psalm

**

papa
parcel led
pardon ed
parka
parking
parlour
parsley
parson
partake
[partook]
[partaken]
partial led
partly
partner ed
partridge
party -ies
passing
passport
password
pasta
pasture d

pianist
piano s

planted
planting
plaster ed
plaza

***

Pakistan
parcelling
parliament
partialling
partially
particle
partisan
partition ed
partnership
passers-by
pasteurise d
   ze
pastoral ly

pharmacist
pharmacy -ies

pianist
piano s
piranha

plantation

ptarmigan

pyjamas

**** *

Pakistani
parliamentary
participant
participate
participation
participle
pastorally

pharmaceutical

pianoforte
pistachio s

> In this word 'ar' is spoken as a neutral vowel.
>
> particular ly

Q

*

**

Qur'an / Koran

***

****

R

*

raft
ranch es
rasp ed

**

rafter
rascal ly
raspberry
rather

***

rascally
raspberry -ies

regarded
regardless
retarded

****

rechargeable
remarkable

S

*

psalm

scar red
scarf -ves
schwa

shaft
shark
sharp

slant

smart

snarl ed

*spa resort with mineral spring
*spar pole / practise boxing
spark ed
sparred
sparse

staff ed
stance
star red
starch es
starched
stark
start
starve d

suave

**

charade

cigar

saga
salmon
sample d
sampler
sampling
sardine
sari

scarlet
scarring

sergeant

sharpen ed
sharpening
sharply

slalom

sparkle d
sparkler
sparkling
sparring
spartan

starboard
starchy -ier / -iest
stardom
starfish
starlight
starling
starring
starry
started
starter
starting
startle d
startling
starving
stratum strata

surpass es
surpassed

***

safari
Sahara
salami
sarcasm
sarcastic ally
sardonic

sharpening
sharpshooter

soprano s

staccato
starvation

sultana
surpassing

**** *

sarcastically
sardonically

scenario s

Somalia

234   In these words you can hear the vowel sound **ar** as in shark

T

*

tar red
tart
task

trance

tsar / czar

* *

target ed
tarmac
tarnish es
tarnished
tarring
tartan

* * *

ptarmigan

targeting
tarpaulin

tiara

tomato es

* * * *

V

*

vase
vast

* *

vantage
varnish es
varnished

* * *

vibrato

* * * *

Y

*

yard
yarn ed

* *

yardage
yardstick

* * *

* * * *

Z

*

czar / tsar

* *

* * *

Zimbabwe

* * * *

In these words you can hear the vowel sound ar as in shark

A

*
****air** atmosphere /
manner / feeling /
tune
aired

****heir** next owner

*for H . . .
see page 238* ▷

* *
affair

aircraft
Airedale
airfield
airline
airmail
airport
airtight
airway

aware

Eire

heiress es
heirloom

* * *
aerial
aerobic
aerobics
aerodrome
aerofoil
aeroplane
aerosol

airliner

area

* * * *
aeronautics

aquarium

B

*
****bare** uncover ed
****bared** uncovered

****bear** animal
****bear** carry
[bore]
[born / borne]

****blare** d sound loudly
****-blur** red go fuzzy

****-bur** bur oak
****-burr / bur** prickly
seedcase / leave a
rough edge
****-burred** murmured

* *
barely

bearer
bearing
beware

* * *
barium

* * * *
Bulgaria

C

*
cairn
****care** attention /
worry / look after
****cared** looked after

chair ed

****-cur** worthless dog
****-curd** soft, fatty
substance

Kurd

* *
careful ly
careless

chairman [chairmen]

compare d

* * *
canary -ies
carefully
carelessly

chairperson
chairwoman
[chairwomen]

comparing
contrary

-Kurdistan

236

In these words you can hear the vowel sound air as in bear

D

*	**	***	****
dare d	**dairy** -ies		
	daring		
	declare d		
	despair ed		

E

*	**	***	****
*air atmosphere /	aircraft	aerial	
manner /	Airedale	aerobic	
feeling / tune	airfield	aerobics	
aired	airline	aerodrome	
	airmail	aerofoil	
*heir next owner	airport	aeroplane	
	airtight	aerosol	
	airway		
		airliner	
	éclair		
		area	
	Eire		

for H . . .
see page 238 ▷

for I . . .
see page 239 ▷

F

*

fair just / funfair / market / fine weather / light in colour
fare charge for ride / food / get on
fared

flair natural skill
flare burst into flame / get wider at the bottom
flared

-fur coat of animal

**

fairground
fairly
fairy -ies magical tiny person
farewell

forbear
[forbore]
[forborne]
forswear
[forswore]
[forsworn]

-furry -ier, -iest feeling like fur

pharoah

***

****

G

*

glare d

**

***

****

H

*

hair thread-like growth
haired having hair
hare animal
hared ran like a hare

heir next owner
-her she / belonging to her
Herr [Herren] German for 'Mr'

**

hairbrush es
haircut
hairdo
hairpin
hairspray
hairstyle
hairy -ier, -iest

heiress es
heirloom
Herren German men

-heron large bird

***

haircutting
hairdresser
hair-drier

****

hilarious

Hungarian

In these words you can hear the vowel sound air as in bear

I

*   **   ***   **** *

         impair ed   **invariably**

◁ *for E . . .*
see page 237

L

*   **   ***   ****

***lair** den

*-**layer** thickness of laid
material / one that lays

M

*   **   ***   ****

***mare** female horse   **mayoress** es   **malaria**
***mayor** head of town
or city

P

*   **   ***   ****

***pair** set of two   **parent**   **preparing**
paired
***pare** d   trim / peel   **pharaoh**

***pear** fruit   **pierrot**
*-**per** for each

                   prairie
prayer   **prepare** d

In these words you can hear the vowel sound air as in bear

R

*	**	***	****
rare	rarely		
	repair ed		

S

*	**	***	****
scarce	scarcely	scarcity	
scare d	scarecrow		
	scary -ier, -iest	shareholder	
share d			
	sharing		
snare d			
	staircase		
*spare extra / give / keep from giving	staring		
*spared did spare			
*-spur projecting part / urge on			
*-spurred urged on			
square d			
*stair step / s			
*stare d look with fixed gaze			
*-stir red move around			
swear [swore] [sworn]			

In these words you can hear the vowel sound air as in bear

T

*	**	***	****
tear [tore] [torn]	**tearing**	**thereafter** **thereupon**	
	thereby **therefore** **thereof** **therewith**		

*****their** belonging
to them
*****theirs** something
belonging to them
*****there** to/in that
place / also used with
'is', 'are', 'was', 'were'
and other forms of
'to be'
there'd
there'll
*****there's** there is /
there has
*****they're** they are

V

*	**	***	****
	vary -ies varied	**variant** **various** **varying**	**variable** **variation**

W

*	**	***	****
*****ware** products for sale / pottery	**warehouse** **wary** -ier,-iest	**whereupon** **wherever**	
*****wear** carry on body / get worse with use [wore] [worn]	**wearing** **werewolf** [werewolves]		
*****-were** form of verb 'to be'	**whereas** **whereby** **wherefore** **wherein**		
*****where** to/in which place			

In these words you can hear the vowel sound **air** as in **bear**

A

LONG VOWEL **er**

*	**	***	**** *
*-**air** atmosphere / manner / feeling / tune	**absurd**	-**aerial**	**adverbial** ly
-**aired**	**adjourn** ed	-**aerobic**	**advertisement**
		-**aerobics**	
*heir next owner	-**affair**	-**aerodrome**	-**aeronautics**
	affirm ed	-**aerofoil**	
		-**aeroplane**	**affirmative** ly
	-**aircraft**	-**aerosol**	
	-**Airedale**		**alternative** ly
	-**airfield**	-**airliner**	
	-**airline**		-**aquarium**
	-**airmail**	**allergic**	
	-**airport**	**alternate**	**assertiveness**
	-**airtight**		
	-**airway**	-**area**	
	alert	**assertion**	
		assertive	
	assert		
	astern	**attorney**	
	avert		
	-**aware**		
	-Eire		

for H . . .
see page 247 ▷

-heiress es
-heirloom

In these words you can hear the vowel sound **er** as in **bird**

B

*	**	***	****
*-**bare** uncover(ed)	-**barely**	-**barium**	-**Bulgaria**
*-**bared** uncovered			
	-**bearer**	**burglary**-ies	
*-**bear** animal	-**bearing**	**burgundy**-ies	
*-**bear** carry	-**beware**	**bursary**-ies	
[bore]			
[born / borne]	**birdseed**		
*-**berth** bunk / place	**birthday**		
for ship at quay	**birthplace**		
berthed			
	blurring		
birches	**blurry**-ier, -iest		
birched			
*-**bird** feathered	**burden**ed		
animal	*-**burger** sandwich		
*-**birth** delivery of	*-**burgher** citizen		
child / origin	**burglar**		
	burlap		
*-**blare**d sound loudly	**burly**-ier, -iest		
*-**blur**red go fuzzy	**Burma**		
blurt	**burner**		
	burning		
*-**bur** bur oak	**burring**		
burned	**bursar**		
[burnt]			
*-**burr** / **bur** prickly			
seedcase / leave			
a rough edge			
*-**burred** murmured			
burst			
[burst]			

> Here 'er' is neutral, like the 'er' in 'perhaps'.
>
> Bermuda

C

*	**	***	**** *
-cairn	-careful ly	-canary -ies	circulation
*-care attention / worry / look after	-careless	-carefully	circulatory
*-cared looked after	certain	-carelessly	circumcision
		certainly	circumference
-chair ed	-chairman	certify -ies	circumstances
chirp ed	-[chairmen]	certified	
church es	churchyard		commercially
churn ed		-chairperson	conservative
	circle d	-chairwoman	convertible
*cur worthless dog	circling	-[chairwomen]	
*curb ed restrain	circuit		
*curd soft, fatty substance	circus	circular	
curl ed	clergy	circulate	
curse d		circumscribe d	
curt	*colonel army officer	circumstance	
curve d	-compare d	clergyman	
	concern ed	[clergymen]	
*kerb edge of pavement	confer red		
	confirm ed	commercial ly	
kirk	conserve d	-comparing	
	converge d	concerning	
*Kurd Kurdish person	converse d	conferring	
	convert	-contrary	
	courteous	convergent	
		conversion	
	curdle d	courteous	
	curdling	courtesy -ies	
	curfew		
	curling		
	curly -ier, -iest	curlier	
	cursor	curliest	
	curtail ed	curvature	
	curtain ed		
	curtsey s / curtsy -ies		
	curtseyed / curtsied		
	curvy -ier, -iest		

for Qu . . .
see page 251 ▷

*kernel seed in nut

Here the 'er' and 'ir' have a neutral sound.

certificate   circumference

In these words you can hear the vowel sound **er** as in **bird**

D

*

-**dare** d

dearth

dirge
dirt

**

-**dairy** -ies
-**daring**

-**declare** d
defer red
deter red
*****desert** leave
deserve d
-**despair** ed
*****dessert** sweet dish
deter red

dirty -ies
dirtied
dirty -ier, -iest
discern ed
disperse d
disturb ed
diverge d
diverse
divert

***

deferring
deserted
deserter
detergent
determine d
deterring

dirtier
dirtiest
dispersion
disservice
disturbance

**** *

determination
determiner
determining

discernible
diversity

E

*

*****-air** atmosphere /
manner / feeling / tune
-**aired**

earl
*****earn** ed get money
by working
earth ed

err ed

*****-heir** next owner

irk ed

urge d
*****urn** vase / vessel

for H . . .
see page 247 ▷

for I . . .
see page 247 ▷

**

-**aircraft**
-**Airedale**
-**airfield**
-**airline**
-**airmail**
-**airport**
-**airtight**
-**airway**

early -ier, -iest
earnest
earnings
earthquake
earthworm
earthy -ier, -iest

-**Eire**

emerge d

exert

-**heiress** es
-**heirloom**

irksome

urban
urchin
urgent

***

-**aerial**
-**aerobics**
-**aerodrome**
-**aerofoil**
-**aeroplane**
-**aerosol**

-**airliner**

-**area**

earlier
earliest
earnestness
earthenware

emergence

encircle d
encircling

eternal ly
eternity

excursion
exertion
external ly

urgency

****

-**aeronautics**

emergency -ies

ergonomics

eternally

exterminate
externally

In these words you can hear the vowel sound **er** as in **bird**

F

*

*-**fair** just / funfair /
market / fine
weather / light
in colour
*-**fairs** more than one
fair
*-**fare** charge for ride /
food / get on
*-**fared** did fare
*-**fares** more than one
fare / gets on

fern

***fir** tree
firm ed
first

*-**flair** natural skill
*-**flare** burst into
flame / get wider at
the bottom
-**flared**

***fur** coat of animal
furl ed
***furred** coated with fur
***furs** coats of animals
***furze** gorse

* *

-**fairground**
-**fairly**
*-**fairy** -ies magical tiny
person
-**farewell**

ferment
fertile
fervour

firmly

-**forbear**
[forbore]
[forborne]
-**forswear**
[forswore]
[forsworn]

furlough
furnace
furnish es
furnished
furring
***furry** -ier, -iest feeling
like fur
further ed
furtive

-**pharaoh**

* * *

fertilise d
ze

fleur-de-lis
flirtation

furniture
furthermore

for th . . .
see page 253 ▷

* * * * *

fermentation
fertilisation
zation
fertiliser
zer
fertility

fraternity -ies

G

*

germ

girl
girth

-**glare** d

jerk ed

* *

gerbil
German

gherkin

girder
girdle d
girdling
girlfriend
girlhood

Guernsey
gurgle d
gurgling

jerkin
*jersey woollen jumper
*Jersey Channel Island

journal
journey ed

* * *

Germany
germicide
germinate

journalist

* * * * * *

germicidal
germination

journalism
journalistic ally

In these words you can hear the vowel sound **er** as in **bird**

H

*

*-**hair** thread-like
  growth
*-**haired** having hair
*-**hare** animal
*-**hared** ran like a hare

 ***heard** did hear
 ***hearse** funeral car
*-**heir** next owner
***her** she / belonging
  to her
 herb
***herd** group of
  animals
*-**Herr** [Herren] German
  for 'Mr'
***hers** her property
***hertz** measure of
  frequency in cycles
  per second

hurl ed
hurt
[hurt]
***hurts** does hurt

**

-**hairbrush** es
-**haircut**
-**hairdo**
-**hairpin**
-**hairspray**
-**hairstyle**
-**hairy** -ier, -iest

-**heiress** es
-**heirloom**
 herdsman [herdsmen]
 hermit
 herpes

 hurdle d
 hurdling
 hurtful ly
 hurtle d
 hurtling

***

-**haircutting**
-**hairdresser**
-**hair-drier**

 herbaceous
 herbivore

 hurtfully

****

-**hilarious**

-**Hungarian**

> Here 'er' is neutral, like the 'er' in 'perhaps'.
>
> herself

I

*

irk ed

**

immerse d
-**impair** ed

incur red
inert
infer red
infirm
insert
inter red
invert

irksome

***

immersion
imperfect

incurring
inertia
inferring
insertion
internal ly
interpret ed
interring
inversion

**** *

impermeable
impersonal
impersonate
impersonation
impertinent
impervious

infirmary -ies
interminable
internally
interpolate
interpretation
interpreted
interpreter
interpreting
-**invariably**

for E . . .
see page 245

In these words you can hear the vowel sound **er** as in **bird**

J

*
germ

jerk ed

**
gerbil
German

jerkin
*jersey woollen
jumper
*Jersey Channel
Island

journal
journey ed

***
Germany
germicide
germinate

journalist

**** **
germicidal
germination

journalism
journalistic ally

K

*
*-cared looked after

*curd soft, fatty
substance

kerb ed

kirk

knurled

*Kurd Kurdish person

**
*colonel army officer

*kernel seed in nut

***

****

◀ for C . . .
see page 244

for Qu . . .
see page 251 ▶

L

*
*-lair den

learn ed
[learnt]

lurch es
lurched
lurk ed

*-layer thickness of laid
material / one that lays

**
learner
learning

***

****

In these words you can hear the vowel sound **er** as in bird

M

*

*-**mare** female horse
*-**mayor** head of town
 or city

merge d

mirth

*-**myrrh** fragrant oil
 or gum

* *

-**mayoress** es

merchant
mercy -ies
merger
merging

murder ed
murky -ier, -iest
murmur ed

* * *

maternal ly

mercenary -ies
merchandise
merciful ly
merciless
*-**mercury** liquid metal
*-**Mercury** planet

murderer
murderess es
murderous
murmuring

* * * *

-**malaria**
maternally
maternity

mercenary -ies
mercifully

N

*

knurl ed

nerve

nurse d

* *

nervous
nervy -ier, -iest

nursing
nurture

* * *

nasturtium

nursery -ies

* * * *

O

*

* *

observe d

occur red

* * *

alternate

observance
observant
observer
observing

occurring

* * * * *

alternative

observatory -ies

P

*	**	***	**** *
*-**pair** set of two / get or put together in twos	-**parent**	**percolate**	**percolator**
-**paired**		**perfectly**	**perforation**
*-**pare** d trim / peel	**perfect**	**perforate**	**permeable**
	perfume d	**permanent**	**perpendicular**
	perky -ier, -iest	**permeable**	**persecution**
*-**pear** fruit	**permit**	**permeate**	**personality** -ies
*-**pearl** jewel	**person**	**perpetrate**	**personally**
*-**per** for each	**perspex**	**persecute**	**perspiration**
perch es	**perverse**	**persevere** d	
perched	**pervert**	**personal** ly	**preservative**
perm ed		**personnel**	**proverbial** ly
pert	-**pharaoh**	**pertinent**	
		perversion	**purposefully**
-**prayer**	-**pierrot**		
		preferring	
purge d	-**prairie**	-**preparing**	
*-**purl** knitting stitch	**prefer** red		
purse	-**prepare** d	**purposeful** ly	
	preserve d		
	purchase d		
	purple		
	purpose		
	purring		

In these words 'er' and 'ur' are pronounced as neutral sounds, like the 'er' in 'perfect'.

P**ER**SISTENT WORDS

perceive d	perform ed	permitting	persistent	persuasive
percentage	performance	peroxide	personification	purport
perception	performer	perpetual ly	personify -ies	pursuant
perceptive	performing	perplex es	personified	pursue d
perceptual ly	perhaps	perplexed	perspective	pursuer
percussion	permissible	perplexing	perspire d	pursuit
percussive	permission	persist	persuade	
perfect ion	permit ted	persistence	persuasion	

for pre . . .
see page 82

In these words you can hear the vowel sound er as in bird

Q

*   **   ***   ****

quirk

R

*	**	***	****
-rare	**-rarely**	**recurring**	**returnable**
		recursion	**reverberate**
	recur red	**referral**	**reversible**
	refer red	**referring**	
	rehearse d	**rehearsal**	
	-repair ed	**researcher**	
	research es	**returning**	
	researched	**reversal**	
	reserve d		
	return ed		
	reverse d		
	revert		

*	**	***	****
-**scarce**	certain	certainly	certificate
-**scare** d		certify -ies	
scourge d	**circle** d	certified	circulation
scurf	**circuit**	circular	circumcision
	circus	circulate	circumstances
search es		circumscribe d	
searched		circumstance	**serviceable**
***serf** slave	-**scarcely**		
***serge** woollen cloth	-**scarecrow**	-**scarcity**	**superfluous**
serve d	-**scary** -ier, -iest		**surgically**
	scurvy	-**shareholder**	
-**share** d			
shirk ed	**searching**	**suburban**	
shirt	**searchlight**	**surgery** -ies	
	sermon	**surgical** ly	
Sir	**serpent**		
	servant		
skirt	**service** d		
	serviette		
	servile		
slur red	**serving**		

smirk ed -**sharing**
  sherbet
-**snare** d **shirty** -ier, -iest

*-**spare** extra / give / **sirloin**
  keep from giving
*-**spared** did spare **skirmish** es
  sperm skirmished
***spur** projecting part /
  urge on **slurring**
  spurn ed
*-**spurred** urged on **spurring**
  spurs
  spurt -**staircase**
  -**staring**
-**square** d **sterling**
  squirm ed **stirring**
  squirt **sturdy** -ier, -iest

*-**stair** step or steps **submerge** d
*-**stare** d look with **surface** d
  fixed gaze **surfboard**
  stern **surfer**
***stir** red move around **surfing**
  surform
***surf** foaming sea **surgeon**
  surfed **surging**
***surge** d rush forward **surly** -ier, -iest
  surname
-**swear** ***surplice** gown worn
  [swore] in church
  [sworn] ***surplus** es excess
  swerve d **survey**
  swirl ed

In these words you can hear the vowel sound **er** as in **bird**

T

*

-tear
[tore]
[torn]
term ed
*tern bird
terse

*-their belonging
to them
*-theirs something
belonging to them
*-there to/in that
place / also used with
'is', 'are', 'was', 'were'
and other forms of
'to be'
-there'd
-there'll
*-there's there is /
there has
therm
*-they're they are
third
thirst

turf ed
Turk
*turn ed change
direction

twirl ed

* *

-tearing

-thereby
-therefore
-thereof
-therewith
thermal ly
thermos
thirsty -ier, -iest
thirteen th
thirty -ies
Thursday

*turban head-covering
*turbine engine
turbot
*Turkey country
*turkey bird
turmoil
turner
turning
turnip
turnout
turnpike
turnstile
turquoise
turtle

* * *

terminal ly
terminate
terminus es / -i
tertiary

-thereafter
-thereupon
thermally
thermostat
thirtieth

turbojet
turbulence
turbulent
turmeric
turnover
turpentine

* * * * *

terminally
termination
terminology -ies

tubercular
tuberculin
tuberculosis

Here 'er' is neutral, like the 'er' in 'perhaps'.

thermometer

U

*	**	***	****
earl	early -ier, -iest	earlier	ergonomics
*earn ed get money	earnest	earliest	
by working	earnings	earnestness	
earth ed	earthquake	earthenware	
	earthworm		
err ed	earthy -ier, -iest	**urgency**	
irk ed	irksome		
urge d	**urban**		
*urn vase / vessel	**urchin**		
	urgent		

V

*	**	***	**** *
verb	-vary -ies	-variant	-variable
verge d	-varied	-various	-variation
verse d		-varying	
verve	**verbal** ly		**versatility**
	verdict	**verbally**	**vertically**
	verger	**vermilion**	
	vermin	**vernier**	**virtually**
	version	**versatile**	**virtuosity**
	versus	**vertebra** s / -ae	**virtuoso** s
	vertex	**vertebral**	
	[vertices]	**vertebrate**	
		vertical ly	
	virgin	**vertices**	
	virtual ly		
	virtue	**virginal**	
		virtually	
		virtuous	

In these words you can hear the vowel sound **er** as in **bird**

W

*

*-ware products for
sale / pottery

*-wear carry on body /
get worse with use
[wore]
[worn]
*were form of verb
'to be'
weren't

*-where to/in which
place
**whirl*ed spin around
*whirr sound
*whirred did whirr
*whorl turn of spiral
*whorled shaped in
a spiral

*word unit of meaning
worked
*world the earth
wormed
worse
worst
worth

**

-warehouse
-wary -ier, -iest

-wearing
werewolf
[werewolves]

-whereas
-whereby
-wherefore
-wherein
whirlpool
whirlwind
whirring
workbench
workbook
worker
workforce
workhouse
working
workload
workman
[workmen]
workout
workplace
workroom
worksheet
workshop
worktop
worldwide
worsen ed
worship ped
worthless
worthwhile
worthy -ies

***

-whereupon
-wherever

workable
workmanlike
workmanship
workstation
workwoman
[workwomen]
worshipper
worshipping

****

workaholic

Y

*

-year
yearn ed

**

yearning

***

****

In these words you can hear the vowel sound **er** as in **bird**

A

*	**	***	**** ****
*all every one	aboard	abortion	accordingly
	abroad	absorber	accordion
*awe fear and wonder	absorb ed	absorption	
awed			adorable
*awl boring tool	accord	accordance	
		according	alternating
*oar rowing blade	adore d		alternative
	adorn ed	adsorption	alternator
*or -marks choice			altogether
*ore mineral	afford	almighty	
		already	auditory
ought	almost	alternate	authentically
	alright		authority -ies
	also		autobiographical ly
	*altar holy table	appalling	autobiography -ies
	*alter ed change	assorted	automatic ally
	although	assortment	automation
	always	assurance	automobile
			autonomic
	appal led	audible	autonomous
	applaud	audience	auxiliary -ies
	applause	audio	
		auditory	orchestration
	ashore	*aurally by the ear	ordinarily
	assault	aurora	ordinary
	assure d	Austria	organically
		authentic ally	organisation
	auburn	authoress es	zation
	auction ed	authorise d	organism
	*auger tool	ze	oriental
	*augur suggest for	autograph ed	orientation
	the future		ornithologist
	*August month	awfully	ornithology
	*august impressive		orthographic ally
	aura s / -ae	*orally by the mouth	orthography -ies
	*aural ly by the ear	oration	
	austere	orbital	
	author	orbited	
	autumn	orbiting	
		orchestra	
	award	orchestral	
	awesome / awsome	orchestrate	
	awful ly	ordeal	
	awkward	ordering	
		orderly -ies	
	*orally by the mouth	ordinal	
	orbit ed	ordinance	
	orchard	ordinary	
	orchid	organic ally	
	ordeal	organise d	
	order ed	ze	
	organ	organist	
	orgy -ies	orgasm	
	orphan ed	orient	
		ornament	
		orthodox	

for H . . .
see page 261 ▷

In these words you can hear the vowel sound **or** as in **horse**

B

*	**	***	****
*****bald** lacking hair	**ballroom**	**befallen**	**borealis**
balk / baulk ed	**balsa**	**beforehand**	
*****ball** round object /	**balsam**		
dance	**Baltic**	**broadcasting**	
*****balled** made into a	**basalt**		
ball	**bauxite**		
baulk / balk ed			
*****bawl** yell	**because**		
*****bawled** did yell	**befall**		
	[befell]		
*****boar** male pig	[befallen]		
*****board** plank / daily	**before**		
meals / committee	**besought**		
*****boor** rough fellow			
*****bore** drill / drilled	*****boarder** person who		
hole / carried / fail to	pays for food and bed		
interest / tide-wave	**borax**		
*****bored** drilled /	*****border** edge / frontier		
lacking an interest	**bordered**		
*****born** delivered at birth	**boredom**		
*****borne** carried	**boring**		
bought			
	brawny -ier, -iest		
brawl ed	**broadcast**		
brawn	[broadcast]		
broad	**broadside**		
brought			

C

*

call ed
***caught** got / trapped
***caulk** ed fill gaps with fibre and tar
***cause** bring about / reason
caused
***caw** harsh bird cry
***cawed** did caw
***caws** does caw

chalk ed
***chord** notes sounded together / string / term in geometry
chore

***clause** words in sentence / part of written agreement
claw ed
***claws** curved nails or limbs

***coarse** rough
***cord** string
***core** central part / take out the core from
***cored** did core
***cork** bark of cork tree
corked
corm
corn ed
corned
***corps** group
corpse
***course** track / direction / part of meal / of course
coursed
***court** enclosed area / friends of sovereign / seek favour

crawl ed

for Qu . . .
see page 266 ▷

**

calling
cauldron
causing
caustic ally
caution ed
cautious

chloride
chlorine
choral
choroid
chortle d
chorus es
chorused

conform ed
cordial ly
corgi
corkscrew ed
corner ed
cornet
cornfield
cornflakes
cornflower
corporal
courting
courtroom
courtship
courtyard

crawling

***

caustically

chloroform ed
chlorophyll
chloroplast

conformist
cordial ly
corduroy
cormorant
cornea
corneal
cornerstone
cornflower
corporal ly
courtier

****

caustically

conformity
cordially
corporally
corporation

In these words you can hear the vowel sound or as in horse

D

*

daub ed
dawn ed

door

*****draw** pull / sketch
[drew]
[drawn]
*****drawer** sliding
container
drawl ed

dwarf ed

* *

daughter
dawdle d
dawdling

deform ed
deport

distort
divorce d

doorbell
doorknob
doorstep
doorway
dormant
dormouse [dormice]
dorsal

drawbridge
drawing

* * *

discordant
disorder ed
distortion
divorcee

dormitory -ies

* * * *

deformity -ies
deplorable

disorganised
                ze

dormitory -ies

E

*

* *

endorse d
enforce d
*****ensure** d make certain

escort

exalt
exhaust
explore d
export

*****insured** protect against
loss

* * *

enforcement
enormous

exalted
exhausted
exhaustion
explorer
exploring

* * * * * * *

extraordinarily
extraordinary

*for I . . .
see page 262* ▷

In these words you can hear the vowel sound **or** as in **horse**

F

*

fall
[fell]
[fallen]
false
fault
*faun goat-god
*fawn young deer /
colour / try to win
favour
fawned

fiord / fjord

flaunt
*flaw ed fault
*floor ed levelled area

*for in place of /
to belong to / because
force d
ford
*fore front / leading
position
forge d
fork ed
form ed
*fort fortress
*forth forward
*fought contested
*four 4
*fourth 4th

fraud

for th . . .
see page 268 ▷

**

falcon
fallen
falling
fallout
falter ed
faulty -ier, -iest

fiord / fjord

flora
floral
fluoride
fluorine

*forbear hold back
[forbore]
[forborne]

forceful ly
forceps
forearm
*forebear s / forbear s
ancestor s
forecast
[forecast]
forefoot
foreground
forehand
foreleg
foreman [foremen]
foremost
forename
foresee
[foresaw]
[foreseen]
foresight
foreskin
forestall ed
foretell
[foretold]
forewarn ed
*foreword preface
forfeit
forgo / forego
[forwent / forewent]
[forgone / foregone]
forlorn
formal ly
format ted
former
forming
formula s / -ae
forswear
[forswore]
[forsworn]
☛

***

fluorescence
fluorescent

forcefully
forecaster
forefather
forefinger
forensic
forever
forgery
formalise d
ze
*formally officially
formation
formatted
formatting
*formerly previously
formula s / -ae
formulate
fortieth
fortify -ies
fortitude
fortunate

**** *

fluorescence
fluorescent

foreseeable
forget-me-not
formality -ies
formidable
forsythia
[forsythii]
fortification
fortunately

Here the 'or' is neutral, like 'or' in 'forget'.
F*OR*GOTTEN WORDS

forbid	forgetful ly
[forbad e]	forgive
[forbidden]	[forgave]
forbidding	[forgiven]
forgave	forgiveness
forget ting	forsake
[forgot]	[forsook]
[forgotten]	[forsaken]

In these words you can hear the vowel sound **or** as in **horse**

F

* *
*forte loud / strength
fortnight
fortress es
fortune
*forty 40
*forward onward
fourteen th

Fräulein

for th . . .
see page 268 ▷

G

*

gaunt
gauze

*gnaw ed keep biting
gore d
gorge d
gorse

jaunt
jawed

*nor and not

* *

gaudy -ier, -iest

glory -ies
gloried

gorgeous

jaunty -ier, -iest

Jordan

* * *

Gibraltar

glorify -ies
glorified
glorious

* * * *

Jordanian

H

*

*hall large room /
passage
halt
*haul drag /
amount gained
hauled
haunt
hawk ed

*hoar white
*hoard store
*hoarse rough and
husky
*horde gang / tribe
horn ed
*horse animal

*whore prostitute
*whored used prostitutes

* *

halter
haughty -ier, -iest
haunches
hawthorn

hoarding
hormone
hornblende
hornet
horseback
horsehair
horseman
[horsemen]
horsepower
horseshoe

whoring

* * *

haughtily

horsemanship
horsepower
horsewoman
[horsewomen]

* * * *

historian

I

*	**	***	**** *
	*ensured make certain	immortally	immortality
		importance	immortally
	ignored	important	
			inaugural
	implored	informally	inauguration
	import	informant	incorporated
		informer	incorporation
	indoors	installing	informally
	indorse / endorsed	instalment /	informative
	informed	installment	
	installed	insurance	
	*insured protect		
	against loss		

◁ for E . . .
see page 259

J

*	**	***	****
jaunt	jaunty -ier, -iest		Jordanian
jawed			
	Jordan		

◁ for dr . . .
see page 259

K

*	**	***	****
	Koran / Qur'an		

> **Here the 'or' is neutral, like 'or' in 'forget'.**
> Korea   Korean

◁ for C . . .
see page 258

for Qu . . .
see page 266 ▷

In these words you can hear the vowel sound **or** as in **horse**

L

*
launch es
launched
*law rules enforced
in a country
lawn

lord
*lore traditions and
facts

**
launcher
launder ed
laundry -ies
laurel
lawyer

lordship

***
launderette
laureate

**** **
laborious ly

M

*
*mall public walk /
walk lined with shops
malt
*maul batter
mauled
mauve

*moor open land /
fasten to land or
to buoy
*more additional /
a larger amount
*morn morning
Morse
*mourn show sadness
at loss or death
mourned

**
Malta

*morning before
midday
morpheme
morphine
morsel
mortal ly
mortar
mortgage d
mortice d /
mortise d
mourner
mournful ly
*mourning showing
sadness at loss or
death

***
Majorca

Minorca
misfortune

moreover
mortally
mournfully

****
memorial

mortality -ies

N

*
*gnaw ed keep biting

naught / nought

*nor and not
norm
north
nought / naught

**
naughty -ier, -iest

normal ly
north-east
Norman
northern
northward
north-west
Norway

***
nautical ly
naughtier
naughtiest
naughtiness

normally
northeaster
northerner
northernmost
northwester
Norwegian

****
nautically

notorious

In these words you can hear the vowel sound or as in horse

O

*   ******   *******   ****** *******

*	**	***	**** *****
*all every one	almost	almighty	alternating
	alright	already	alternative
*awe fear and wonder	also	alternate	alternator
awed	*altar holy table		altogether
*awl boring tool	*altered change	audible	
	although	audience	auditory
*oar rowing blade	always	auditory	authentically
		*aurally by the ear	authority -ies
*or marks choice	auburn	aurora	autobiographical ly
orb	auction ed	Austria	autobiography -ies
*ore mineral	*auger tool	authentic ally	automatic ally
	*augur suggest for the	authoress es	automation
ought	future	authorise d	automobile
	August	ze	autonomic
	august	autograph ed	autonomous
	aura s, -ae		auxiliary -ies
	aural ly by the ear		
	austere	awfully	
	author		
	autumn	*orally by the mouth	orchestration
		oration	ordinarily
		orbital	ordinary
	awesome / awsome	orbited	organically
	awful ly	orbiting	organisation
	awkward	orchestra	zation
		orchestral	organism
	*oral ly by the mouth	orchestrate	oriental
	orbit ed	ordeal	orientation
	orchard	ordering	ornithologist
	orchid	orderly -ies	ornithology
	ordeal	ordinal	orthographic ally
	order ed	ordinance	orthography -ies
	organ	ordinary	
	orgy -ies	organic ally	
	ornate	organise d	
	orphan ed	ze	
		organist	
		orgasm	
		orient	
		ornament	
		orthodox	

◁ for H . . .
see page 261

In these words you can hear the vowel sound **or** as in **horse**

P

*

*pause brief gap /
hesitate
paused
*paw foot of animal
*pawed examined by
paw
pawn ed
*paws feet of animal

*poor badly off
porch es
*pore tiny hole /
study closely
*pored studied
closely
*pores tiny holes
pork
port
*pour flow out
*poured did pour

prawn

* *

palfrey
pawpaw

perform ed

poorly
porous
porpoise
porter
porthole
portion
portrait
portray ed
pouring

purport

* * *

performance
performer
performing

porcelain
porcupine
portable
portcullis
portico
portrayal
Portugal
Portuguese

precaution
proportion

* * * * * *

pornographic ally
pornography
portfolio

proportional ly

In these words you can hear the vowel sound or as in horse

Q

*
quart
*quarts more than
one quart
*quartz mineral

**
quarter
quartet

***

****
quartermaster

R

*
*raw untreated /
sore / chilly

*roar loud noise
roared

wrath
wrought

**
recall ed
record
recourse
reform ed
report
resort
resource d
restore d
retort
reward

roaring

***
recorded
recorder
recording
reported
reporter
resources

****

266   In these words you can hear the vowel sound or as in horse

S

*	**	***	****
salt	salty -ier, -iest	saucily	subordinate
*sauce tasty liquid / rude talk	saucepan		
*saw looked at / cutting tool	saucer	scornfully	
*sawed did saw [sawn]	saucy -ier, -iest	scorpion	
	sauna		
	saunter ed	signora	
	sawdust	signori	
scald			
scorch es	scornful ly	strawberry -ies	
scorched	scorpion		
score d		supported	
scorn ed	shortage	supporter	
scrawl ed	shortening	supporting	
	shorter		
shawl	shortest		
*shore coast	shorthand		
shored	shortly		
shorn			
short	signor [signori]		
shorts			
	slaughter ed		
small			
	smaller		
snore d	smallest		
	smallpox		
*soar fly high			
*soared flew high	snorkel		
*sore painful			
*sort group	stalling		
*sought looked for	stalwart		
*source origin	storage		
	storehouse		
spawn ed	*storey floor		
spore	stormy -ier, -iest		
sport	*story -ies tale		
sprawl ed	strawberry -ies		
squawk ed	support		
	surely		
*stalk stem / hunt / walk stiffly			
stalked	swarthy -ier, -iest		
stall ed			
staunch es			
staunched			
store d			
*stork bird			
storm			
straw			

*sure certain

swarm ed
*sword weapon
swore
sworn

In these words you can hear the vowel sound **or** as in **horse**

T

*	**	***	****
*talk speak	talking	talkative	
talked	taller		
tall	tallest	thesaurus es / -i	
*taught instructed		thoughtfully	
taunt	thorax es / -ces		
*taut tight	thoughtful ly	tornado es	
		torpedo es	
thaw ed	Torah	tortilla	
thorn	torment		
thought	torsion		
thwart	torso s		
	tortoise		
*tor hill	torture d		
torch es	Tory -ies		
*tore did tear	toward		
torn	towards		
*torque turning force / necklace			

V

*	**	***	****
vase			Victorian
*vault gymnastic leap / underground room / arched roof			victorious
*volt unit of electrical force			

268   In these words you can hear the vowel sound **or** as in **horse**

W

*
*hoar white
*hoard store
*horde gang / tribe

walk ed
wall ed
waltz es
waltzed
*war conflict
*ward part of
hospital / person
under legal protection
warm ed
warmth
*warn caution
warned
warp ed
*warred waged war
wart

wharf [wharves]
*whore prostitute
*whored used
prostitutes
*wore was dressed in
*worn carried on the
body / worse for wear

wrath
wrought

**
walking
walnut
walrus
warble d
warbling
warden
wardrobe
warfare
warlike
warmer
warning
warpath
warring
warship
wartime
water ed

whoring

***
wallpaper ed
waterfall
waterfowl
watershed

****
walkie-talkie

Y

*
yawn ed

*yore ancient times
*your belonging to
you
*you're you are
yours

**
Yorkshire
yourself
yourselves

***

****

In these words you can hear the vowel sound or as in horse

269

A

*	**	***	****
	ahoy!	adjoining	
	anoint	annoyance	
	annoy ed		
	appoint	appointment	
	avoid	avoided	

B

*	**	***	****
boil ed	boiler	boisterous	
*boy lad	boiling		
	boycott	buoyancy	
broil ed	boyfriend		
*buoy marker	buoyant		
buoyed			

C

*	**	***	****
choice	cloister ed		
coil ed			
*coin money			
coined			
coy			
*quoin cornerstone			
quoit			

*for Qu . . .
see page 274* ▷

In these words you can hear the vowel sound oi as in oyster

D

*

* *

destroy ed

disloyal ly

doily -ies / doyley s

* * *

destroyer

disloyally
disloyalty

* * * *

disloyally
disloyalty

E

*

* *

embroil ed
employ ed

enjoy ed

exploit

* * *

embroider ed
employee
employer
employment

enjoying
enjoyment

* * * *

embroidery

enjoyable

F

*

foil ed

* *

foyer

Fraülein

* * *

* * * *

G

*　　　　**　　　　***　　　　****

***groin** part where
legs join body
***groyne** low structure
built out into water

H

*
hoist　　　　**　　　　***　　　　****

J

*　　　　**　　　　***　　　　****

join ed　　　**joiner**　　　**joinery**
joint　　　**joining**　　　**joyfully**
joist　　　**joyful** ly
joy　　　**joyous**

　　　In these words you can hear the vowel sound oi as in oyster

L

*
loyal ly

**
loyally
loyalty -ies

***
loyally
loyalty -ies

****

M

*
moist

**
moisture

***

****

N

*
noise

**
noisy -ier, -iest

***
noisier
noisiest
noisily

****

O

*
oil ed

**
oilstone
oily -ier, -iest
ointment

oyster

◀ for H . . .
see page 272

***

****

In these words you can hear the vowel sound oi as in oyster

P

*
point
poise d

**
poignant
pointed
pointer
pointing
poison ed

***
poisoner
poisonous

****

Q

*
*coin money

*quoin cornerstone
quoit

**

***

****

R

*
royal ly

**
recoil ed
rejoice d
rejoin ed

royally
royalty -ies

***
royally
royalty -ies

****

In these words you can hear the vowel sound **oi** as in **oyster**

S

*
soiled

spoiled
[spoilt]

**
soya

***
sequoia

****

T

*
toiled
toyed

**
toilet

***

****

V

*
voiced
void

**
voyaged

***

****

In these words you can hear the vowel sound oi as in oyster

275

A

*	**	***	****
	abound	accountant	accountancy
	about	allowance	
			allowable
	account	announcement	
		announcer	
	*aloud loud enough to be heard		
	allow	astounded	
	*allowed permitted	astounding	
	amount		
	announce d		
	around		
	arouse d		
	astound		

B

*	**	***	****
blouse	boundless	boundary -ies	
	bounty -ies		
*bough branch	bowel		
bounce d	bower		
bound			
bout	brownie		
*bow bend / front of ship			
bowel			
brow			
brown ed			
*brows more than one brow			
*browse d nibble / dip into books			

In these words you can hear the vowel sound ou as in owl

C

*

chow

cloud
clout
clown ed

couch es
couched
count
cow ed
cower ed

crouch es
crouched
crowd
crown ed

**

cacao

chowder

cloudless
cloudy -ier, -iest

confound
*council group for
directing affairs
*counsel advice
counselled
countdown
counted
counter
counting
countless
county -ies
*coward person who
lacks courage
cowboy
cower
*cower ed did cower
cowshed
cowslip

crowded

***

*councillor member of
a council
counselling
*counsellor person
who gives advice
countenance
counteract
counterfeit
counterfoil
counterpart
counterpoint
countersink
cowardice

**** *

counter-attack
counterexample

D

*

doubt
*dour unsmiling
*douse/dowse put into water / put out
doused/dowsed
dowelled
*dower property of bride or widow
downed
*dowse use divining rod

drought
drowned

**

denounced
devoured
devout

discount
dismount

doubtfully
doubtless
dowdy -ier, -iest
dowel led
dowelling
downcast
downfall
downhill
downland
downright
downstairs
downstream
downward
dowry -ies
dowser
dowsing

drowsy -ier, -iest

***

doubtfully
dowelling

****

E

*

**

endow ed

***

encounter ed

****

In these words you can hear the vowel sound ou as in owl

F

*

flounce d
*flour ground grain
*flower blossom
flowered

*foul dirty
fouled
found
*fowl bird

Frau [Frauen]
frown ed

for th . . .
see page 283 ▷

* *

flounder ed

*founded established
founder
*foundered sank /
    collapsed
foundry -ies
fountain

Frauen

* * *

flowerpot

foundation

* * * *

G

*

gouge d
gown

grouch es
grouched
ground
*grouse [grouse] bird
growl ed
*growse grumble

* *

glower ed

grouchy -ier, -iest
groundsel
groundwork

* * *

* * * *

H

*

hound
*hour 60 minutes
house d
how
how'd
howl ed

*our belonging to us

* *

hourglass es
housefly -ies
household
houseman
    [housemen]
housewife
    [housewives]
housework
housing

* * *

houseparent
however

* * * *

In these words you can hear the vowel sound **ou** as in **owl**   **279**

J

*

joust
jowl

◁ for dr . . .
see page 259

L

*

*Laos country

loud
lounge d
*louse insect
lout

**

louder
loudest
loudly
lousy -ier, -iest

***

loudspeaker

****

M

*

mound
mount
mouse [mice]
mouth
mouthed

**

miaow / meow

mountain
mounted
mousy -ier, -iest
mouthful
mouthpiece

***

mountaineer
mountainous
mountainside
mountaintop

****

mountaineering

In these words you can hear the vowel sound ou as in owl

*   **   ***   ****

noun
now

                                 nowadays

O

*   **   ***   ****

*hour 60 minutes	hourglass es	**outbidding**
		outgoing
ounce	**ourselves**	**outlying**
*our belonging to us	**outbid**	**outnumber** ed
	[outbid]	**outrageous**
ours	**outboard**	**outsider**
out	**outbreak**	**outspoken**
	outburst	**outstanding**
owl	**outcome**	**outwitted**
	outcrop	**outwitting**
	outcry -ies	
	outdo	
	[outdid]	
	[outdone]	
	outdoors	
	outer	
	outfit	
	outgrow	
	[outgrew]	
	outing	
	outlaw ed	
	outlet	
	outline d	
	outlook	
	outpost	
	output	
	outrage d	
	outright	
	outrun	
	[outran]	
	outset	
	outshine	
	[outshone]	
	outside	
	outskirts	
	outstretch ed	
	outward	
	outwit ted	

◀ for H . . .
see page 279

P

*

plough ed

pouch es
pouched
pounce d
pound
pout
power ed

proud
prow
prowl ed

**

ploughman
[ploughmen]
ploughshare
powder ed
power ed

profound
pronounce d
proudly
prowess

***

powerful ly

pronouncement
pronouncing

****

powerfully

R

*

round
rouse d
rout

**

rebound
*recount tell a story
*recount count again
renown ed

rounded
rounders
rounding
roundup
router
rowdy -ier, -iest

***

roundabout

****

282   In these words you can hear the vowel sound **ou** as in **owl**

S

*	**	***	****
scour ed	Saudi	showery	
scout	sauerkraut		
scowl ed		south-eastern	
scrounge d	scoundrel	southwester /	
	scourer	sou'wester	
shout	scouring	south-western	
shower ed			
shroud	shower ed	surrounded	
	showery	surroundings	
slouch es			
slouched	sounded		
	sounder		
snout	sounding		
	soundproof ed		
sound	sourdough		
sour ed	south-east		
south	southward		
sow	south-west		
spout	surmount		
sprout	surround		
stout			

T

*	**	***	****
thou	thousand	towelling	
	thousandth	towering	
tout			
towel led	tousle d	trowelling	
tower ed			
town	towel led		
	towelling		
trounce	tower ed		
trout	towering		
trowel led	townhouse		
	township		
	trousers		
	trowel led		
	trowelling		

In these words you can hear the vowel sound ou as in owl

V

*	**	***	****
vouch es	**voucher**		
vouched	*****vouchers** more than		
vow ed	one voucher		
	*****vouches** does vouch		
	vowel		

W

*	**	****	****
wound			
wow			

Y

*	**	***	****
yowl ed	**yowling**		

284

In these words you can hear the vowel sound ou as in owl

SPELLING ACTIVITIES

Dealing with difficult words

There are a number of words that many people find it difficult to spell. It is particularly important to pay special attention to difficult words that occur very commonly.

In the final section of the *ACE Spelling Dictionary* there are some strategies to help with spelling words that frequently cause problems. The techniques used in the activities can also be applied to other words that may be difficult for individuals.

The activities are suitable for use either by students working on their own – with a helper – or by a teacher in class work. They have in general been presented for individual use; a little adaptation will fit them to class use.

WORDS YOU NEED
TO KNOW

Some of the words you come across every day are not easy to spell. Once you can cope with those you will feel much more confident about spelling. On page 288 there is a Master List of suspect words.

What to do

1   Put a tick next to each word on the list which you know very well. These words are innocent and may even be friendly. The others will make up your own list of suspects. You will find that some of the suspects have split personalities and may seem to be two or more separate words, but they are really only one.

2   Get a piece of card which will fit into your *ACE Spelling Dictionary* if folded down the middle.

3   Copy your list of suspects, with further particulars if provided on page 289, in two columns. You can add some words of your own if you want to. Then use a highlighter pen to mark any special features of the suspect words which will help you to remember them.

4   Make a second copy of your list of suspects on the back of your card, but this time do not add any further particulars. Leave a space or draw a box beside each word so that you can put tally marks to show how many times you have recognised a suspect.

5   Ask a helper who is good at spelling to check your card when it is ready for use.

6   Get to know your suspects better. Take four words at a time and make up some sentences using these words. Write out your sentences. When you get to a suspect word, find it on your card so you can copy it. Try to copy it after looking at it once only, and as you write it take note of any special features. When you have finished, ask your helper to double-check what you have written, using your card and the *ACE Spelling Dictionary* if necessary.

How to use your card

Get your card out every time you do some writing.

Whenever a suspect word comes along, check it on your card before you write it down. Every time you do this, turn your card over and put a tally mark next to the word. You can cross off suspect words when you no longer need to check them on your card, but you should not do that until you have at least ten tally marks against a word.

MASTER LIST
OF SUSPECT WORDS

again		right	(✓ or →)
always	(all _ _ _ _)	running	
an	(a .. e .. i .. o .. u ..)	sometimes	
another		still	
bought		stopped	
caught	(did catch)	suddenly	
decided		their	(ownership)
friend		there	(there is …
heard	(_ ear _)		there are …
hour	(60 minutes)		there was …
inside			there were …
into			there will be …
it's	(it is)		there would be …
kept			there could be … etc.
knew	(silent k)	⟶	to or in that place)
know	(silent k)	thought	
lot	(a lot)	through	(by way of)
might	(?igh?)	too	(too much/as well)
myself		tried	
off	(not on)	turned	
opened		until	(_ _ till)
outside		want	
police		were	(in the past)
		where	(place)

It is a good idea to make a new card about every three months until you have narrowed down your list of suspects to one or two. Eventually you will have no words at all on your list. If you are working in school, you could make out a new card once a term.

SPECIAL FEATURES
OF SOME OF THE SUSPECTS

always	This is **always** one word with one **l**, all the time.
an	An egg, **an** anything beginning with **a e i o u.**
caught	Her naughty daughter **caught** a cold.
heard	Did hear, by **ear.**
hour	60 minutes.
it's	**It's** short for 'it is' and the ' stands for the letter i.
knew	(silent **k**) – understood.
know	(silent **k**) – understand?
lot	'**A lot**' is NOT one word.
might	I **might** get it right!
off	On and off, '**off**' is confused with 'of'.
right	Did you write it on the **right** and get it **right**?
their	Our dog is ours, not yours – **their** dog is theirs.
there	Here and **there there** are some rare bears.
through	Although it was rough, he thought we would get **through**.
too	Not TOO many **o**'s to count in twos!
until	One 'l' as in **1-nil**: unlike fill, hill, kill, pill, till, will.
were	Why **were** we waiting when the light was green?
where	**Where** were you when the fire broke out in that place?

SOME REALLY
USEFUL WORDS

Learn to spell these words so that you get them right when you write!

Three lists, each containing 220 useful words, have been prepared from samples of children's speech and writing. The lists do not include the forty common words which are most often misspelt. Those words are the ones in the Master List and are best learned by using your card in the course of writing. Simple words which present no spelling problems have not been included in the three lists. Taken together, the three lists plus the words in the Master List account for between 40% and 60% of the words found in children's writing at ages 9–11.

Using the lists at home

If you are using the lists to work on your spelling at home, the first thing to do is set your own programme. Consult your helper about this. You will need to have a realistic target, one that enables you to make steady progress without having too much to do. A lot will depend on how quickly you need to achieve results, and you should bear in mind any other activities you are committed to on a regular basis.

You will also need to find out which words you should concentrate on. It is not intended that you should simply work your way through the lists. Use the tests that follow to decide which list should be used.

Using the lists in school

If these lists are used in school, one could be covered in one term, at the rate of twenty words a week. That allows for some repeated learning of words misspelt in weekly tests. Lists 1, 2 and 3 are suitable for NC Levels 2, 3 and 4–5 respectively, and for Scottish Levels A, B and C. Those who need an accelerated spelling programme can work on the lists for a whole year.

Note that it is not intended that the same list should be given to all members of a class. The following tests can be used to decide which list should be used by which students.

Spelling test

Your helper says each word, repeats it in a phrase or sentence, pauses briefly and then says the word again. You should not write it down until you hear it for the third time.

1   SHIP ... The passengers boarded the SHIP ... SHIP
2   FOOTBALL ... My FOOTBALL strip ... FOOTBALL
3   READING ... What are you READING? ... READING
4   TELL ... TELL me a story ... TELL
5   SEVEN ... SEVEN puppies in a basket ... SEVEN
6   SPOKE ... I SPOKE slowly to Gran on the phone ... SPOKE
7   SLOWLY ... We walked very SLOWLY ... SLOWLY
8   NEAR ... We live NEAR the park ... NEAR
9   PERSON ... Who is that PERSON crossing the road? ... PERSON
10 ANYTHING ... Have you ANYTHING to report? ... ANYTHING
11 PRETTY ... The garden was looking very PRETTY ... PRETTY
12 BEFORE ... Tidy your room BEFORE you go out ... BEFORE
13 OWNER ... Who is the OWNER of this car? ... OWNER
14 MUSIC ... I listen to MUSIC on my Walkman ... MUSIC
15 HAPPENED ... What HAPPENED in the playground? ... HAPPENED
16 FOLLOWED ... The stray dog FOLLOWED me ... FOLLOWED
17 SUGAR ... SUGAR in your tea ... SUGAR
18 MOUNTAIN ... The top of the MOUNTAIN ... MOUNTAIN
19 USUAL ... I woke up at seven, as USUAL ... USUAL
20 INTERESTING ... An INTERESTING story ... INTERESTING

When you have written down all the words, your helper should check them. From your score, find out which list of words is right for you.

Score 0–4:   Work with List 1
Score 5–14:   Work with List 2
Score 15–20: Work with List 3

The 220 words in each list have been grouped into sets of four words, on the basis of a topic or language pattern. There are five word sets across the page; five sets are normally enough for a week's work. Nouns, verbs, adjectives and adverbs have been grouped together, with some miscellaneous sets at the end. This has been done to help you to think of meaningful links between words and to use the words in sentences.

Note that words with an asterisk (*) against them may need special attention. These are ones for which it is hard or impossible to find a rhyming word with the same spelling pattern. You may be able to think of a non-rhyming word with the same letter string (e.g. watch/match) or find some other way of remembering the letters.

The word sets are not arranged in order of difficulty.

Individual lists

You should follow your own individual path, so that you do not study words that you can already spell.

As already explained, you will need to set your own target of how many words to learn. Here are some examples of how a programme of learning could be drawn up. Adapt them to suit your situation. Remember to ask your helper for advice about this.

Every fortnight choose 20, 40 or 60 words to learn from one of the lists. These are words which you would like to be able to spell. Underline the words and then write them down in sets of 4. If possible, there should be some meaningful link between the words in a set, as this makes the words and their spellings easier to remember. You can choose words that will fit into the same sentence, that are linked by topic or that have the same spelling pattern. If you cannot find enough words you need to learn in the list, words may be taken from other sources.

With individual lists, individual daily tests are needed. This is best organised with a helper. In class, students may test each other in pairs.

Another kind of individual list, for use in correcting drafts (NC Level 3, Scottish level C and above) is described on pages 294–295.

How to learn

If you look at words in a list and get your helper to test you, you may find you do not remember the spellings very well. A more active approach will lead to better results. You should STUDY – COPY – CHECK – HIGHLIGHT and then LEARN.

STUDY	– look at the word and count the syllables
COPY	– you are only allowed one glance per syllable
CHECK	– letter by letter or in strings of up to four letters
HIGHLIGHT	– mark the parts you need to remember
LEARN	– by one or more of the methods below.

Try the different methods of learning suggested below and decide which works best for you.

a) Pronounce the words in a different way, according to the spelling.
b) Trace over or write the word, saying the letter names before you write each letter string.
c) Shut your eyes and say or spell the word as you 'write' it in large letters with your finger.
d) With eyes shut see the word in your mind, count the letters in groups and then check.
e) Study the word, say a tongue-twister or count to 10, then spell the word.
f) Think of a memory link or mnemonic for the whole word or just for the tricky part (e.g. On **Fri**day and at the week**end** I'll see my friends. Find **Real**ly **Interest**ing **Fri**ends.).

g) Use the *ACE Spelling Dictionary* to find a word that rhymes with the one you are learning and is spelt in the same way; think of a rhyme and then check the spelling, or simply look through the 1- and 2-syllable columns in a single vowel section. Remember that words in the lists that are marked * do not have suitable rhymes.

h) Find another word you already know that has the same spelling pattern (e.g. tongue, argue).

i) Learn the tricky part (or parts) first, before trying the whole word.

REPEAT	– say, write and spell really rapidly, like a R–A–PP–E–R
TEST	– look, cover, write, check.

At the end of a learning session, write down a sentence containing the words you have studied. This should help you to spell those words correctly later on when you are writing.

The daily routine

Every day you will study two, four or six words from your list (or a different number, depending on your own programme). It is helpful if the words are related in some way. Enter the date and the words to be learned in a jotter.

Steps to success

1st word	– learn (using chosen method)
self-test	– look – cover – write – check
2nd word	– learn
self-test	– look – cover – write – check
double-check	– look at both words – cover – write – check Continue if both words are correct; otherwise practise and try the test again.
3rd word	– learn
self-test	– look – cover – write – check
4th word	– learn
self-test	– look – cover – write – check
double-check	– look at both words – cover – write – check Continue if both words are correct; otherwise practise and try the test again.
final test	– all four words should be written correctly when dictated in a random order

If you do not pass the final test, you must try to learn the words again, perhaps by a different method. On the other hand it may be better to reduce the number of words.

When you succeed in the final test, your helper should initial the list in your jotter and record the learning method(s) you used (from the a) to i) list).

If you find it easy to learn the number of words you studied each day, you might like to increase the number by one or two.

Note that if you are trying to learn six words you can double-check with groups of two or three words.

The weekly test

Once a week a test session should be held. In class, this can be set up in pairs, so that each learner both gives and receives a test on the words chosen for that week. Words spelt correctly should be given a tick in the jotter and on the Master List. Those not spelt correctly should be studied again the following week. They should be spaced out over the week, not tackled on a single day along with the new words for that day.

Spelling correctly and correcting mistakes

If you use the STUDY – COPY – CHECK – HIGHLIGHT – LEARN approach, you will probably make fewer mistakes with words you have recently studied. You cannot expect that you will never again have to think about those words. Indeed, every time you realise that you have used a word that is on your list or seems to fit a familiar pattern, you score a success. All you then have to do is to check the spelling. If it is correct, that is excellent.

Good spellers are aware of common paterns between 'families' of words. The more often you look up words in the *ACE Spelling Dictionary*, the more you will notice these patterns. Looking for word families based on Lists 1–3 can introduce you to thousands of words. Learning method g) (looking up rhyming words) is one of the best ways of 'getting to know' more word families. This method also encourages you to use a wider vocabulary when you write.

Most people miss spelling mistakes when they read through a piece of work. You can improve at doing this if you make a personal alphabetical list of the words you want to learn from Lists 1, 2 and 3. It is sensible to include some interesting words from the same 'families' and any hard-to-spell words you have previously attempted. If you arrange the list in syllable columns, as in the *ACE Spelling Dictionary*, it wil be easier to scan. Read through the list before you check your draft; this will make it much more likely that you will recognise the words in the piece you have written.

Your list might look like this:

*	**	***(+)
aren't	against	ambulance
board	allow	arrival
break	answer	beautiful
brought	answered	disappeared
clothes	believe	February
course	buried	hospital
guard	curtain	idea
it's	harbour	investigate
knocked	haunted	parliament
let's	later	remembered
passed	people	suitable
past	present	unfortunately
piece	quickly	vegetables
race	really	
spare	swimming	
they're	themselves	
threw	without	
you're		

It is a good idea to check your draft at least three times, each time concentrating on a limited range of words. First, look for any words of three or more syllables which need to be checked. Then go through the passage again, looking for 2-syllable words which might present problems. Finally, concentrate on 1-syllable words, taking care not to skim over words such as 'its', 'they' and 'was'. These are so common that it is easy for your eye to pass over them without really noticing them.

The more often you correct your own spelling mistakes, the better your spelling will become. When you know how to put things right, you can concentrate on what you are writing.

LIST 1

father	* baby	dog	bus	money
dad	babies	hair	car	gold
mother	boy	way	road	bank
mum	girl	park	street	shop
look	ask	come	be	* are
looked	asked	* coming	been	will
find	call	came	being	could
found	called	went	stay	couldn't
one	some	bad	* front	* his
* two	left	good	ready	* her
three	all	better	nice	our
four	more	best	happy	your
garden	door	tea	book	king
farm	room	water	story	queen
wood	window	time	bed	lady
sea	fire	things	night	man
go	* was	woke	see	catch
goes	* wasn't	help	saw	make
* going	would	told	* put	made
gone	wouldn't	sleep	seen	eat
black	big	next	my	away
blue	little	last	* this	around
red	new	long	that	back
white	old	round	other	home
* children	* morning	* Christmas	* woman	* people
sister	* afternoon	tree	teacher	name
brother	week	day	school	hand
* aunt	year	dinner	work	* eyes
do	* has	give	dance	* watch
don't	* have	gave	walk	* watching
did	* having	take	walking	start
* didn't	had	took	walked	started
when	how	first	no	by
just	so	* once	yes	for
now	down	out	* very	with
then	here	over	well	without
giant	he	him	* who	please
* castle	she	himself	* someone	me
ghost	we	you	which	* that's
house	they	them	* something	much
play	named	like	upon	or
playing	think	married	about	but
played	say	live	* from	* because
fell	* said	* lived	after	while

296

LIST 2

* aeroplane	* animals	present	* clothes	prince
air	bird	balloon	* body	princess
plane	snake	* colour	* shoes	life
* world	* horse	* music	foot	love
tell	listen	read	point	hold
spoke	listened	reading	write	* build
shouted	* answer	mean	writing	built
hear	* answered	meant	written	* covered
* these	high	* every	wide	* usual
those	* higher	its	* straight	* different
any	smaller	sure	near	* interesting
many	short	true	real	* coloured
wife	* family	* sugar	boat	* football
* husband	table	* breakfast	ship	field
* person	chair	meat	shape	line
* group	* kitchen	* course	* owner	* corner
hope	pick	drop	try	* finish
hoped	picked	dropped	trying	* finished
hoping	pull	break	cry	leave
getting	* pulled	* breaking	cried	fly
* young	whole	tired	dead	* nearby
* beautiful	closed	* lonely	broken	* maybe
* pretty	past	dark	dry	quite
dear	seven	* careful	strange	alright
* machine	dragon	ears	* word	* radio
wheel	head	nose	* idea	station
hole	* heart	mouth	* notice	* minutes
light	blood	* voice	* language	* sentence
seemed	die	sitting	meet	should
* imagine	died	waiting	brought	* does
guess	jumped	* happen	passed	* doesn't
* understand	killed	* happened	followed	done
quickly	already	* even	nearly	onto
slowly	behind	* also	* usually	across
early	ever	* really	* finally	along
later	o'clock	enough	together	against
mountain	piece	* numbers	few	* no one
side	* picture	* nothing	half	* everyone
ice	place	* thousands	* anyone	* everything
winter	* village	* difference	* anything	whose
buy	before	* I'd	* you'd	* what
wear	why	* I'll	* you'll	* what's
used	whether	* I'm	* you're	* let's
grown	* whenever	* I've	* you've	* themselves

297

LIST 3

mouse	* squirrel	creatures	fish	chocolate
mice	goat	* butterfly	* rabbit	coffee
* puppy	* wolf	* dinosaur	* potato	flour
* puppies	* elephant	* monster	* potatoes	* apron
wash	* allow	swim	* arrived	threw
washing	* allowed	swimming	* offered	throw
washed	wished	rain	received	blew
dressed	* cannot	raining	grabbed	blow
* basket	lawn	shirt	* drawer	crash
* bowl	flowers	skirt	shelf	surprise
* board	patch	sheet	shelves	fright
brush	* vegetables	* curtain	stairs	* skeleton
fishing	believe	approach	lie	drag
float	* wondering	* recognised	lying	dragged
floated	* realised	remember	lay	* bury
drowned	* investigate	* remembered	laid	* buried
shock	* uncle	* February	* harbour	pony
* ambulance	* cousin	* months	beach	* ponies
* hospital	* grandfather	* holiday	* island	saddle
* oxygen	* neighbours	* Saturday	cave	stables
* climb	push	hopped	* whisper	* burst
tied	* pushed	hopping	* whispered	guard
falling	knocked	pretended	* whistle	* chase
slipped	smashed	hurt	screamed	* disappeared
pencil	* alphabet	* camera	* parliament	noise
* rubber	* calendar	* film	* palace	* policeman
* ruler	fractions	* submarine	* television	* uniform
* scissors	* graph	* magazine	* programme	* court
* dangerous	frightening	* favourite	* curious	lazy
* terrible	* poisonous	* orange	spare	dirty
massive	frightened	* purple	* quiet	* impossible
* enormous	scared	* visible	haunted	funny
* telephone	* visitor	* system	switch	flame
* message	* Germany	defence	* contact	volcano
rhyme	* London	* exhibition	* explosion	thunder
* tongue	* countries	* manager	bridge	* lightning
* motor	* excellent	* British	dining	* downstairs
racing	* wonderful	* Chinese	* hungry	* upstairs
tight	* fantastic	* Japanese	fried	* somewhere
* physical	* exciting	* Egyptian	frozen	* everywhere
* bicycle	* hello	he'd	* aren't	* anyway
bike	* everybody	he'll	we'd	* somehow
race	* quietly	* he's	we'll	* anybody
track	* sixth	* they're	* we're	* somebody

298

SEARCHING FOR PATTERNS

Here are some further ideas to help you recognise some of the many spelling patterns and the exceptions.

1   When you add -**ing** to words ending with 'e', you knock off the 'e'. This does not apply if the ending is a double vowel (**ee, ie, ue**). See how many words that fit this pattern you can find in 10 minutes.

2   See how many 3-syllable words you can find where a final 'y' changes to 'ie'. Group these under the headings: **ies, ied** and **ier/iest**. Spend 10 minutes on this.

3   With words like **wit** (with a single-letter vowel and a single final consonant) you double the final consonant when you add endings such as -**ed**, -**ing**, -**er**, -**est**, -**y**, -**ier** and -**iest**. So you get: slow-**witted**, out**witting**, **witty**, **wittier**, **wittiest**. See how many 1-syllable words that fit this pattern you can find in 10 minutes.

Are there any exceptions?

4   Find ten words like **itch** (one syllable, with a single-letter short vowel and the (**tch**) sound right after the vowel).

Find ten more 1-syllable words with a letter between the short vowel and the (**ch**) sound, such as: **belch, inch, lunch**.

Find twenty words ending in (**ch**) from any of the long vowel sections.

What pattern do you notice? Are there any exceptions? Can you explain in a simple way when to use **tch**?

Carry out similar searches in order to establish when to use **edge** rather than **ge** and when to use **ck** rather than **k**.

5   'I' before 'e' except after 'c'. What is the ratio of hits to misses if this rule is applied to words in the long vowel (**ee**) section?

6   How many words of four or more syllables in which the last syllable contains a neutral vowel sound can you find in 5 minutes?

7   Make a list of homonym pairs from the (**or**) section where spelling confusion is likely.

8   truthful – truthfully   helpful – helpfully   grateful – gratefully

Full of …? Find five more words listed in the *ACE Spelling Dictionary* that fit this pattern.